PEAT

I can think of no other piece of New Zealand writing that is really like Jenner's seemingly casual, but carefully constructed engagement of one life with another, with its play of enduring values against the grain of immediate contemporary experience.

– Vincent O'Sullivan

… intriguing and thought provoking; a cornucopia of literary history, biography, memoir, politics, community activism and stimulating ideas. Such an unlikely juxtaposition of subjects shouldn't work but it does!

– Mandy Hager

PEAT

Lynn Jenner

OTAGO UNIVERSITY PRESS

Published by Otago University Press
Level 1, 398 Cumberland Street
Dunedin, New Zealand
university.press@otago.ac.nz
www.otago.ac.nz/press

First published 2019

ISBN 978-1-98-853169-4

Published with the assistance of Creative New Zealand

ARTS COUNCIL OF NEW ZEALAND *TOI AOTEAROA*

Editor: Anna Hodge
Index: Barbara Frame
Design/layout: Fiona Moffat
Author photo: Simon Neale

Cover and maps: Charlotte McCrae

Printed in China through Asia Pacific Offset

Peat is an archive. The black soil, the tea-coloured water, the sticks and the great trees. Whole ecosystems from the past are safely stored down there.

Contents

Author's Note

The essays in the first part of *Peat* are accompanied by two glossaries titled 'One Starless Night' and 'The Prettiest Road in New Zealand'.

When I began *Peat*, both Charles Brasch and the building of the Kāpiti Expressway were new subjects to me. 'One Starless Night' is a glossary of my developing acquaintance with the work of Charles Brasch; 'The Prettiest Road in New Zealand' is a glossary of my acquaintance with the building of the Kāpiti Expressway. The framework of a glossary allowed me to explore the language of these two subjects and to record questions and reflections as I spoke to people, read books, newspapers and poems and formed my own ideas. The glossaries run parallel to the essays, as research often runs parallel to or underneath other writing. They can also be read as stand-alone pieces.

A small proportion of glossed theme-words are highlighted in the essays. Those linked to 'One Starless Night' are marked with the symbol *, and those linked to 'The Prettiest Road in New Zealand' are marked with the symbol †.

Together, these twenty-seven theme-words tell the story of *Peat*.

A Necessary Protection

How can you ever explain the reasons why you like someone or why you are drawn to explore a certain way of living or a way of thinking? There must have been a day that I started looking out for places **Charles Brasch*** mentioned or books he had written but I didn't mark the first 'Charles Brasch day' on the calendar. I can say that I noticed Brasch's presence, and formally decided to make his acquaintance, in 2013, the year they started to build the Kāpiti Expressway. The Expressway was on the mind of everyone in Kāpiti then. It was everywhere. The signs, the flags, the trucks, the newsletters, the radio interviews, the maps, the job ads – it was an Occupation. And then Brasch arrived. Or, more correctly, I went looking for him. That was the order.

As the Expressway showed itself, arriving like an army in each new location along the route, I knew I needed the close company of a writer as a bulwark against all its enacted power and concrete. I needed to gather up pages and pages of words and take them inside with me, to a place where machines could not follow. I needed to make a word-nest, to read beauty as a form of psychic acceleration. Some world of my own should be prepared, somewhere meditative, cryptic or sublime. I was very surprised to find in myself this vestige of the idea that lyricism can be an actor in the material world, but I have learned to follow any literary or artistic suggestions that the universe provides, at least as far as an initial investigation.

I was attracted to Brasch by the 'c' in his name (a hint of Jewishness which he decided to retain), by his decision that *Landfall* would contain non-fiction commentaries on contemporary issues, and by what another writer described as his off-putting tone of 'high seriousness'. I suspected I might like this tone because I like people who are serious about their activities, and because I am serious myself, although in a low way. Of course I was intimidated by the whole notion of 'Charles Brasch' because he was such a famous person. I knew almost nothing about him except that he was a poet whose work I couldn't relate to when I was young, that he was often uncomfortable here in New Zealand but wrote poems about the land, and that he had founded the literary journal *Landfall*, which itself intimidated me. But once you have decided to begin, it is just a matter of choosing a doorway.

I wanted a back-door beginning, something that allowed me to be in Brasch's presence without being in any sense accountable, so I started by asking the Special Collections librarian for permission to visit the books from Charles Brasch's library, now housed in the University of Otago Library. I wanted to look at books that had been Brasch's books and touch them, which I did. Those books were the tools of his trade. They are personal and yet public objects. The collection ends when Brasch's life ends. There is something intimate about that.

Dear Mr Brasch

On Monday last I visited your library at the Special Collections section of the University of Otago Library. I may not be telling you anything you don't know already, but I thought I should say that those footsteps, those probing fingers and that scratching pencil noise were all me.

When the librarian asked why I wanted to come and visit these books as if they were people, or this collection as if it were you, and told me that the books in your library are just books and most – or perhaps all of them – are available in other places, I produced only a sort of mumble about 'instinct'. I am glad that I didn't have to explain my visit to you in person, because we don't know each other and it would have been awkward. I would probably have done more mumbling about 'the land and the people' or our shared Dunedin heritage and that wouldn't have helped. After all, your Dunedin and mine were very different.

All I could say to the librarian, in answer to his very reasonable question, was 'I just want to see these books in the physical context of the collection. Not 100% rational.' In reply he sent me this long thin message, which I read as a signal flag that the channel was clear for me to proceed, and a bright fluttering ensign of the miracle and wonder of libraries.

L

Ok

D

I would like to say right away, Mr Brasch, that I will not put words in your mouth as I once did with Harry Houdini. I am older now, and sometimes I would rather listen than speak. And you, if you will forgive my saying, do not have the sweaty East European warmth that Houdini has, either. I have a feeling in my water that no matter how often I read your poems, we will remain strangers. However, just this once, I will presume to say that I think you might have been happy with D's considered and, at the same time, welcoming approach to your books.

With the way opened, I headed into your library about 9 o'clock with my little notebook and my pencil. I wasn't nervous exactly, but nor was I relaxed. I reminded myself to be polite and careful and listen to all the instructions, as I would have reminded a child about her manners before visiting an elderly relative.

I didn't have a plan in mind so I decided I would browse. I wouldn't read yet; I would just try to take in the 'feeling' of the collection. I started at the front, near where the librarians work. Straight away I noticed that this library of yours looks quite modest and manageable in a university library but is a huge number of books to have in a house. No house I have ever lived in could contain this many books.

Then I noticed that your collection goes everywhere. It goes to Asia, the Middle East, Russia, Eastern Europe, Australia, England, France, Italy and Germany. It interests itself in the recent and distant past. It also goes everywhere in terms of topics. You have books to answer questions on politics, aesthetics, philosophy, sexuality and all the great religions of the world. The first book to catch my eye was small, had a soft cover and was published in 1960. It is about 110,000 refugees, mostly from the Eastern Bloc, who have been in camps in Austria, Italy and Greece for 15 years, dying slowly of starvation and tuberculosis and despair. Some of them are children. Some were probably Nazi supporters, and some are mad, but no one cares about any of that. These people have been denied entry to every country except the one in which they are stuck. No reasons are given for the rulings and nothing changes except that the people get older. This book, with its pencil and ink drawings of the camps, could be written again today.

Homer's *Odyssey* and *Iliad* are in your library too. Proust is here. Tolstoy is here. The **Baal Shem Tov*** is here. The *Kama Sutra* is here. *Seven Pillars of Wisdom*, *The Wealth of Nations*, *Bullshit and Jellybeans* and *Station Life in New Zealand* are here. Reuel Anson Lochore's *From Europe to New Zealand* is here. *Nga Moteatea, Parts I* and *II*, collected by A.T. Ngata, is here. And everywhere there are families of books. That tells me that if you decided to read the Russians, you could read the novels themselves and read about the novels, in whichever order pleased you. You could make circles from one to the other and back again. I like to read like this, but, living in Kāpiti, it is hard to get the necessary books.

By the time I was browsing the second shelf I was feeling my time in the library moving very quickly even though, objectively, only half an hour had gone by. If I saw a book that particularly interested me, I would slide the book out, prop it up for a minute and take its picture as if we were on holiday together. Sometimes it was a book I was surprised to see, or a book with a particularly nervy shade of green on the cover, or a title that called out to me in some way. Surrounded by so much knowledge, I felt a bit frantic and also very rich and happy. Much later in the day, once I was back at Carey's Bay looking down at the dredge working in the channel as it has done for 150 years, I realised that on the second shelf I had seen Martin Buber's translation of the stories of the Baal Shem Tov. I had tried unsuccessfully to buy this book in 2010. An encounter with that one book would be worth a Jetstar fare to Dunedin and several days away from my usual occupations.

And then, at 9.45am, in the movement from the second shelf to the third, I was washed over by a feeling of shame. I felt I was fossicking, with unbridled enthusiasm, in your private … *something*. I wasn't in your underwear drawer, because what I was seeing was books, and books are inherently public. I wasn't in a wardrobe with a secret door leading to a different country, because the doors led to every country; and it wasn't a room full of your outer clothes, because there was no smell of you, or of mothballs. Nor was I in your journal, where your hopes or fears might be written in small neat letters. I was, I decided, in your brain, the structure within which your thoughts and feelings were made possible. A brain is an object with functions. It doesn't feel pain. This idea helped with the shame.

I would have liked, then, to ask you whether you imagined such uses as mine when you left your library of books to the university library. But, in the absence of your reply, all I can do is apologise if my probing caused you pain.

At 10.15 I moved, without any conscious decision, from browsing the library to receiving psychic suggestions from the library about poems I might write. The most fevered scratchings of the pencil happened then as I made notes of words or phrases or forms for later use. Salt water, blue sky, shining, flow, evening breeze, mist, hollow sound, whirlwind, butterfly, abundance, running south, empty cockle shells, going now, foam, bubbles, bitter, stingray and dream, for example.

I would like to visit your library for two days, then spend two weeks writing in response to what I found. I would like to do this 10 times, 10 being the largest possible number I can imagine, given that I live an expensive distance from Dunedin. On some of these visits, your books of poetry – and your books about poetry – will be my focus.

Thank you for having me. That's what I really want to say.

Yours sincerely

Lynn Jenner

P.S. Did you ever go to Hoffman's Pharmacy in Princes Street? Maybe if you had a cough? If you did, you might have seen my grandfather. I'm thinking hard here, but I can't think of any place in his house where there were books.

The Information Booth

BEFORE CONSTRUCTION of the Expressway† started in Kāpiti, the Alliance formed to build the road installed an information booth at Coastlands Mall, containing, among other things, five very tasteful light-stained wooden boxes, each just larger than a shoe box, and with a clear plastic lid. The first box contained peat. The second box contained Holocene sand, the third Pleistocene sand, the fourth Pleistocene gravel and the fifth Rakaia Terrane greywacke. I think you were supposed to read the five boxes from left to right like a book. As you moved towards the right, you headed down towards the centre of the earth and also backwards in time.

Peat:

The peat† sample, in its little wooden box, doesn't look attractive. It is dark brown and full of sticks, lumps of preserved vegetation and water. In engineers' language, peat has high compressibility and low stability. In layman's terms, it is squishy. In the café this morning I overheard two locals discussing whether it is better to live in a house built on peat or a house built on sand. It all hinged on what happens when a train goes past which, I agree, is a stern test of any house. When a train goes past the 'peat' house, the whole house rises and falls, vases fall down, and objects the size of a flowerpot jump across the room, the owner said. She keeps her planter pots on the ground and heavily weighted. The 'sand' house, on the other hand, rolls lazily from side to side; ornaments rattle a bit but nothing falls over, its owner said with a hint of smugness. With the confidence of small-business women, and in response to a successful demarcation of pecking order, they nodded gently at each other and agreed that the woman who owns the 'sand' house is better off. Much later, after the boxes had been taken away, I found out that if peat is disturbed it gives off CO_2, but left to itself it is the most efficient carbon sink on earth.

Holocene dune sand:

The Holocene dune sand box was my initial favourite because each time I visited the information booth there were droplets of water on the underside of the plastic lid of the box. This made me think the sand in the box was alive, that it breathed *in* 11,700 years ago, and was breathing *out* this week. Apart from being alive, the Holocene dune sand in the wooden box is completely unremarkable; grey, with a hint of black, just like the sand I wash off my salad leaves all summer. The pattern of the warm exhaled droplets is not always the same. Yesterday there was a messy elongated circle of small droplets, a bit like the tail of a comet, with an inner circle of larger fuller droplets, all shining in the white mall light like big round diamonds. So, if droplets of water like big round diamonds condense on the lid of the box, is that water old too or are these droplets rain water from earlier this winter, just before someone dug up the sand and put it in the box?

Pleistocene sand:

Unless it is disturbed, Pleistocene sand lies cool and still, between 10 and 30 metres under the grass. The Pleistocene sand in this box must be alive too, because there is always a little scatter of tiny droplets of water on the lid of its box, but it is not as warmly alive as the Holocene dune sand because it breathes out a smaller quantity of water in finer drops. Maybe the deeper you go, the colder it is down there – like the sea? Maybe what changes as we go down is the quantity and residual presence of other life, the sticks and leaves and light bones of birds? This is my second-favourite box because of its still discernible life, but other visitors have their own preferences. Some go straight to the maps. I notice that the loop of film showing the minister and the Alliance bosses in their high-vis vests being interviewed about the road catches the attention of first-time visitors. The warm friendly manner of the interview and the size of the machines in the background are the main impressions I take away.

Pleistocene gravel:

I am, as far as I know, the only information booth stalker, fiddling with my camera and exchanging soliciting glances with more normal visitors to the booth. I am the one who phones the named spokesperson for the project to tell her that the touch-screen display is not working and, instead of showing photographs of the road, today it offers a doorway to internet shopping. I would like to photograph the Pleistocene gravel so that I can remember exactly what it looks like in case I meet it somewhere else, but my camera is full of hundreds of pictures of the road being built and it refuses to add even one more image. I have to content myself with a promise to the Pleistocene gravel that I will come back when I have emptied my mind of other images. No one talks to me in the information booth.

Rakaia Terrane greywacke:

To all intents and purposes Rakaia Terrane greywacke looks like rock. You could continue to think that it was rock if it stayed 60 metres down, under the grassy surface, the peat and two types of sand. But a couple of weeks ago, while walking down a steep track in Whareroa Farm, I reached out to grab a clump of rock to keep me steady and it immediately came away in my hand. That is Rakaia Terrane greywacke. It may be some way along the way to becoming rock, but right now it is compacted sand and cannot be trusted at all.

The [Taniwha] of Poplar Avenue

In September 2014 I met a young Māori man working on the Mackays to Peka Peka Expressway. At some point in my conversation with him I became certain that he had a taniwha CLIMBING UP HIS NECK. From now on this [taniwha] will appear in my text in brackets to make it crystal clear that if there was a [taniwha] of the waterways between the hills and the sea, a being who had lain hidden in the shade of the trees beside these watery passageways, and if he has been disturbed, or has come back after a long time, he would not reveal himself to me, a Pākehā woman of Jewish and Celtic origin. Nevertheless, in September 2014, at the corner of Poplar Avenue and the new Expressway, a provisional space opened in which a [taniwha] appeared on a man's neck, and in my mind. That felt like an important thing.

Immediately before I became aware of the [taniwha], I had been photographing signs at the gate of the Poplar Avenue construction site. I focused my camera on a list of hazards, a needle pointing to the need for visitors to go to the office and the full names and cellphone numbers for Dave and Mike, the men in charge of the site. Delivery of yellow rock, for example, was an ongoing hazard, and had been since late July, when the sign had last been updated.

And then a white sedan pulled up beside me. The driver, a young man of perhaps 20 or 25, asked me very politely what I was doing there.

Just having a look, I said. Don't worry. I'm just looking at how fast things are changing. I'll stay on my side of the fence.

Are you from the street over there? the young man asked, pointing to Leinster Avenue.

Leinster Avenue was, at this time, a place of anger and stress. Several houses had been compulsorily purchased and then moved away on trucks or demolished. Several others were on the market and had been for months, because who would buy a house right next to an Expressway?

No, I said. I'm from further down, near the sea.

I waved my arm airily towards the west. He continued to look at me. I had that feeling of authority being asserted, of a rope being fed out. I stood my ground. So there we were. Him, leaning on the car. Me, standing there, beside the signs.

I looked back at him. Track pants. High-vis vest. An old Nokia phone in his hand. A tattoo rising in curls up one side of his neck. In this moment the idea arrived that a [taniwha] might be connected to this man and to this place. And further, that it was made of or lives in water, had been disturbed by the attempts to drain the swamp, and would, in the end, be stronger than the road. To say this surprised me is an understatement. The man had not, at this point, mentioned water, or the swamp or how they were building the road.

It's such a big thing, I said [the taniwha]. And it changes so fast [the Expressway].

Yeah, he said. It's an **Alliance†** – Fletchers, Higgins and Beca.

What's it like to work for? I asked.

It's all right, I suppose. Good in some ways and not good in others. We work 10-hour days. People come along all the time and some of them come onto the site yelling that it's wrong and we shouldn't be building it. And cursing, he said, as if swear words offended him. I don't argue, he said. We have to keep good relations with the public.

And anyway, if one of them made a complaint over there at the office, they'd soon work out who it was …

I made a motherly noise.

I understand how they feel, anyway, the ones that are against it. I'd feel the same if it was me, he continued. I feel like telling them it's nothing to do with me. It's coming from way up high. The other day we had the big boss here and he was telling us that he has a boss and his boss has a boss, and we just have to do our job.

I made a bread-on-the-table noise.

I'm just a very unimportant man, the young man said. I support myself and my partner and our baby. We moved down from Hawke's Bay for this job. The other day, he said, a dude here said that this road had been in the pipeline for 30 years. They should have known it was coming.

I offered the idea that in my time there had been a local road marked on council maps but not an Expressway.

Anyway, they started on Transmission Gully last week, he said. There needs to be another way out of Wellington. It only takes one slip and the coastal highway is closed. My partner and I moved here last year just when we had those earthquakes and we thought there *definitely* needs to be another way to get out of Wellington.

I nodded. Anyone who lives here would nod at this.

The conversation turned then to yellow rock because the Expressway on the south of Poplar Avenue was currently just a couple of kilometres of yellow rock raised two or three metres above the surface of what used to be a swamp. See those two hills there? The man pointed. That's where the Transmission Gully road will go. They're using yellow rock over there to push down and force out water, he said, pointing to the south side of Poplar Avenue. It used to be a swamp, he said. All marshy.

Yes, I said. In pre-European times people could paddle from here to the sea. I had read this on a sign up high on the ridge above this site.

I don't know anything about that, he said, but I worked over there for months and I asked what they are doing. They told me they take all the peat away and then they put the yellow rock down and the theory is that the rock presses down and any water left down there is squished out the sides. And then these surveyor guys come and they put pipes underneath and they can see if the water is being squished down and out to the side like it is supposed to.

And is it? I asked.

I don't know, he said.

* * *

At this time construction of the Expressway had been under way for about nine months. The contractors had dug out thousands, or perhaps hundreds of thousands, of cubic metres of dark and boggy peat, made piles of it, and separate piles of the logs they had found submerged in the peat. They gave some of the peat away. We have a few sacks of peat from Poplar Avenue now in the garden, under the broad beans. There was so much peat that even with the whole neighbourhood there, taking the peat away in trailers, only a symbolic amount was moved.

* * *

Back in the 1990s I used to walk along the banks of the Manawatū River. After a lot of rain, the water level between the banks would rise, as everyone expects with rivers. But water also travelled through and across flat land and appeared, a kilometre or two away, in our back yard. From that great dirty river I learned that water has power and cunning and reach.

In the months before I met the young man in the white sedan, I had found myself with a recurrent awareness of the road as an exoskeleton, expanding across the sand and the wetlands, ready to join up. The word 'awareness' is a pale version of the experience I am trying to describe here. I am talking about feeling the rigidity of the road spreading over the land as if it was steel spreading across my own skin. Something about the rigidity of all this concrete, compared with the soggy peat full of twigs and water-logged tōtara and kohekohe tree trunks, made me understand on that September day in 2014 that the road and the water in the peat are enemies. First, I heard from the young man that the road-builders saw the watery peat as an enemy. Then suddenly it seemed possible that the water and the peat might also see the concrete as an enemy. The enmity of water felt like an important thing.

Mackays to Peka Peka Expressway Route

Kāpiti Coast, NZ

RB

RS

Poplar Ave

Raumati Rd

Kāpiti Rd

Rata Rd

Leinster Ave

Coastlands Mall

OLD HIGHWAY 1

 Paekākāriki
Wellington

N
W · E
S

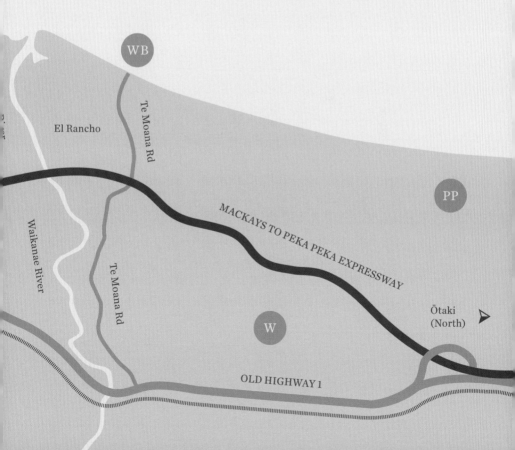

K

RS   Raumati South

RB   Raumati Beach

W   Waikanae

WB   Waikanae Beach

PP   Peka Peka

K   Kāpiti Island

WB

El Rancho

Te Moana Rd

PP

Waikanae River

Te Moana Rd

MACKAYS TO PEKA PEKA EXPRESSWAY

W

Ōtaki
(North)

OLD HIGHWAY 1

Brasch Comes Over the Hill

In November 1950 Charles Brasch visited the Kāpiti coast. Those few days are recorded in his journal.

We drove to Palmerston yesterday to see Mrs Bertram … Took a road which led us to the top of Paekakariki Hill & that magnificent view of the coast & Kapiti, but the South Island was lost in cloud. Called on Douglas Lilburn in Paekakariki both going & returning; he has bought a small house (44 Ames St) & goes in to Victoria a few times a week. The house is admirable for one person, compact, simple in design, with large windows looking onto a small lawn of buffalo grass & a low parapet beyond which is the sea, Kapiti to the right & the South Island in the distance to the left – the beach, narrow & at the foot of a steep bank, is invisible from the house. His section too is narrow & rises up behind the house over a ridge which hides it from the road. It is an ideal quiet home for him.

[…] [material removed by journal editor]

The corridor country from Paekakariki to the Manawatu, backed by the rough Tararuas, has always seemed to me an extension of the South Island, yet it is very different in character – richly green, & with an exotic sub-tropical flavour in the nikaus & the garden plants, the Maoris and their tumbledown bungalows, the low swampland, the scattered remnants of bush. It was very beautiful as we drove south into the late sunlight through the soft green glow. Visited the Maori church at Otaki: the interior has great dignity, even nobility, in its fine simple lines & restrained decoration; only the shiny varnish on the carved woodwork of pulpit & altar-rail is offensive.

Douglas gave us a meal (with cress and lettuce from the garden &
Earl Grey china tea which I have only drunk at the de Beers before)
& we drove back to Belmont in the dark.[1]

In Wellington the next day, Brasch called on a dizzying number of
people, ending the day with a walk down from Messines Road to the
railway station in a strong southerly wind and pouring rain.

… I reached the train very wet & at the station found that I had
to wait an hour for a train to Paekakariki to stay with Douglas
Lilburn – it was nearly eleven when I got there & after I had had a
hot shower we drank tea & talked late.

His house is wood outside & pinex within, with glass doors to help
light the living room which has windows only in front. The living
room is carpeted from wall to wall – plain buff carpet: he took over
everything in the house; the furniture is sober but very ordinary.

Douglas has a few small paintings by Rita Angus, Leo Bensemann
(a renaissance style portrait of Lawrence Baigent in profile, making
him look swollenly red & angry), Lee-Johnson and Douglas
MacDiarmid, & 2 small bookcases of books, and his piano; yet the
pinex walls, the glass doors, the carpet & furniture are depressingly
lacking in character. The noise of the sea encloses one, shuts out the
human world – particularly at night. The whole house, the whole
sand hill on which it stands, shakes when trains pass. Planes out at
sea all day to or from Paraparaumu.

We got up late & walked along the beach to Raumati South in
the middle of the day; sunny with a fresh southerly blowing. Peter
Munz & his wife Anne (they got married recently) & Bill Oliver are
staying there in a small bach with a minimum of water – & it has
to be boiled before they can drink it – for which they pay 3 guineas
a week. The bach is sheltered from the southerly & we sat in our
shorts in the hot sun & talked desultorily for an hour.

[…]

It seemed a very long walk back along the beach to Paekakariki in the mild still afternoon – we'd had no lunch, which I am not used to, & I was quite tired. But we sat & talked quietly after dinner by the sea window till half past ten – slow talk with silences, much of it about people – Bill Oliver & Pat Wilson & especially Alistair Campbell, who is alone in the world without relations & whom Douglas feels anxious about: he does not want a stock dull job, yet he has no university degree, & he would like to get married. Insoluble problem, witness Cresswell, Toss, Colin McCahon, & others.

Everywhere the scent of lupin, not sweet, but like clear water with a special flavour.[2]

This Place

When Brasch says 'Kapiti' he means only the island. I think he would have said the word as 'capitee', with the emphasis on the first syllable. When I say Kāpiti, the 'a' sound is different and I mean the Kāpiti coast from which you see the island, rather than the island itself. My part of this territory starts in Paekākāriki where there are many poets, and has its centre in Raumati South, where I live and where Charles Brasch was given no lunch. Moving north from there, I am connected by commerce to Paraparaumu, and by water to Waikanae. I have only a faint connection with Ōtaki.

By nature my head is usually in the clouds, but in the 11 years since I came to Kāpiti I have been more present on the ground than ever before in my life. These have been years when the sea took metres of land, and if the land in question happened to be concrete or asphalt-covered, the sea just went underneath that surface and lifted pieces of concrete off like scabs. These have also been the Expressway years and the hottest years on record. I have watched all this from the beach, the street, the path beside the river, and from articles in the local media. At the same time, for reasons previously mentioned, I have visited Charles Brasch's 1940s, '50s and '60s. The day I read of Brasch's visit to the Kāpiti coast in 1950 was an early high point, a moment when this place and that time joined and I saw this place through his eyes.

As Brasch says, the explosion of beauty you see when travelling north by road or train from Wellington is everything a sweep of coast should be and more. It is certainly worthy of a journal note. But the conventional front-facing approach is not the only path to appreciation. A friend showed me a slow-building form of pleasure available only to those who travel by train. When travelling south, she said, sit with your back to the engine. That way, the view unfolds progressively. The tiniest peek of the island grows to be the whole island, the long bay of Paekākāriki and Queen Elizabeth Park stretches to include the houses of Raumati South and, in the distance, the Norfolk pines at Paraparaumu Beach appear. The Links, a glass tower block of apartments, built when someone thought Paraparaumu Beach might become the Gold Coast, is also visible, but my friend didn't mention that.

The small house suited to artistic endeavour and an irregular income, the place to live quietly? Yes, I have one of those. It had Pinex ceilings but they are gone now, along with concrete water tanks sunk into the ground outside the back door. Like Douglas Lilburn I have a table to eat at, chairs to sit on, beds to sleep in and a few chests of drawers. It seems on reflection that all these very ordinary items arrived almost by chance. The weekly rental price of three guineas paid for the Raumati South bach by the Munzes and Bill Oliver clearly caught Brasch's attention. Perhaps Brasch was just paying attention to the financial realities of life, as he usually did, or perhaps he thought this rent was high, given the water restrictions and the scale and construction of the house. I would love to know which bach the Munzes were renting that spring, and where it was. Mostly the old baches are either gone or built into a newer house and obscured from public view. These days Raumati has piped water from the Waikanae River. It is chlorinated, high-intensity-UV treated, pH corrected and fluoridated. More and more, the towns of Kāpiti are suburbs of Greater Wellington, rather than places where people might have a holiday house.

I commute to Wellington as Lilburn did. At least once a year, walking around the city, I get caught in a southerly storm as Brasch did. After about 10 minutes in the wind and rain, no raincoat in the world keeps you dry, no shoes are waterproof, water runs down your nose and the further you go, the colder you feel. At night, you still wait an hour for a train to Paekākāriki, as Brasch did. The train is well heated, though, so you ride home in a steamy fug.

A pūriri and two pōhutukawa of great size live with me on a sand dune across the road from the beach. Probably they have yet to notice me, but I have noticed them. I have more domesticated companion trees too: apples, a bay, olives, lemons, orange and kaffir lime, and a tamarillo tree which has grown from the compost. This summer, which has been so hot, the tamarillo has ripe fruit. In November I would probably give visitors a meal of lettuce from the garden, as Lilburn did. I would wash every leaf and dry it as if it was a delicate piece of silk. I would place each leaf in a Japanese blue bowl, add a few mint leaves, some Italian parsley and dress it all with a capful of peppery olive oil from Waiheke Island. In November each soft green leaf is a treat, after all the months of winter.

Over the road, yes, a narrow beach and the sea. The abundance of it all! Cockles, pipi, mud whelks, mudflat topshells and horse mussels. Hundreds and hundreds of shells, empty and full, on the surface of every metre of beach sand, and more buried, waiting for the next wave. These shellfish are part of the reason that the archaeologist employed by the Expressway Alliance called Kāpiti 'the fish and meat aisle' for Māori in pre-European times. Gulls open cockles and pipi by dropping them from the height of a house. Waves are made by yesterday's wind; some locals like to walk by the sea straight after a storm when waves crash over the path; they like the excitement of that, but I like the shining metallic days when the sky is blue and the air is still enough for copper butterflies and daydreams.

Down at the Jeep Road boat ramp, someone has written 'welcome to the dirty south' on the concrete. Some days the whole beach is a metre deep in chips of wood and no one knows where the chips come from. Some days baby-shit-coloured foam floats in the shallows and coats the sand. It has bubbles that do not pop and I would not let it touch my skin. On a smaller scale of pollution, most people, especially women, pick up their dog's shit on the beach, but some people don't. Some days a dead fish with just a head and a skeleton washes up, the flesh taken with a knife out on someone's boat. Once or twice in my time a seal has died slowly on the sand, surrounded by people, and once a young woman's body washed up, or so I heard. An old Greek man told his son never to swim at our beach because there are stingrays lying in the shallows. His son passed on the old man's warning to me, and since then I wear shoes to swim, although I know that in a stingray encounter shoes will not help because it is the flick of the tail that puts you in hospital.

At first when I came here I wasn't sure whether I heard the sea from my bedroom or not. I thought the low hiss I heard might be a goods train passing in the night. But now I know the night noises better. Mostly there is the sea, in ordinary mood, which makes you fall asleep like a child on holiday. But there is also the sea in stormy mood, which tells you to get up and check for damage to the house. At night, after days of wind, the sea sounds like a train arriving, except that the train never arrives. Other times each wave falls with a bang like gunshot. A long goods train passes through Kāpiti in the wee small hours, and, on a clear night, you can hear it in the distance. These days there is also a barely audible whine made by trucks on the Expressway. I know these noises as a mother knows her baby's cry.

Some days, from the beach, the fingers of the Marlborough Sounds look as close as the island. Other days, no sight of land, just a line of cloud on the horizon. On fine winter days, between Mana Island and Pukerua Bay, to the south, a few sharp white peaks of the Southern Alps. To the north, rarely, and therefore a wonder, the perfect shape of Taranaki.

And, yes, in November, lupins. If we made perfumes from the Kāpiti coast, a business my friend and I once considered while walking in Queen Elizabeth Park, lupin would be one of the range. Lupins, the label would say, are an introduced species but we love them anyway. Lupins are old-fashioned girls, sweet vanilla and cinnamon on their breath, soap and sweat rising from the armpits of their starched dresses and the tiniest hint of salt in their hair.

We coasters are encouraged to replant dunes with pīngao, instead of lupin and marram grass. Unfortunately, pīngao cannot flourish where there are rabbits, and Kāpiti has a lot of rabbits and feral cats living in scrub and dunes. We also have a rat plague, and an ant plague which might have been caused by the construction of the Expressway. The ant exterminator and a woman I initially thought was a bit crazy both told me that the excavation of the Expressway had broken up layers of sand where ants had been nesting, and that for every nest destroyed, the ants had gone out and established thousands of new nests.

I spend quite a bit of time in Waikanae, the next town north after Paraparaumu. On the way to Waikanae there is a reserve of nīkau palms on a hill, tucked away in regrown bush. When they were building the Expressway, I used to climb up that hill sometimes to get a view of the road as it grew. The town of Waikanae, named after the river that flows past it, used to be called Parata, but as the land around it was 'opened up' for purchase, the town changed its name. The main trunk railway runs through Waikanae, effectively cutting the town in half.

Over the railway line, to the east, is St Luke's Anglican church. A woman who told me the Waikanae River was shown in the veins of her arm showed me inside the church. Light pours through a round window. In the centre of the window are stained-glass images of three men. In the left-hand window is Wiremu Parata Te Kākākura, who had the church built at Tuku Rākau, near Waikanae Beach, in

1877. These days **El Rancho†**, a Christian camp, is near the Tuku Rākau site. Bones of a woman were found near El Rancho during the construction of the Expressway.

In the right-hand window is Octavius Hadfield, a missionary. In the centre window is St Luke, who is a little taller than Parata or Hadfield. There is something extraordinary about seeing Wi Parata and Octavius Hadfield, two real men who walked the earth not long ago, in coloured glass. Strange, too, from my perspective, seeing St Luke, the local chief and the missionary together, their interests apparently in harmony.

Inside, the church is dark and light at the same time. Light from the east blasts through these windows, the dark burnished wooden walls glow, the dark wooden pews glow, and perhaps the varnish is shiny and therefore offensive. I did not notice if it was. Wi Parata's grave is next to the church. A white marble bust of him stands out against the blue of a Kāpiti sky.

In the township of Waikanae itself, right next to the railway line and the shopping centre, is Te Ātiawa's Whakarongotai Marae. I have never been inside the marae. Its meeting house, now named Whakarongotai, was also built in Tuku Rākau, and was moved to its present site in the 1880s. In those days Wi Parata's grand house was next to the marae. When I came to Kāpiti, Parata's house was long gone and there was a pub on the site. In 2016 the pub was demolished and now that piece of land is a park-and-ride carpark for commuters.

Whenever I return from Dunedin, where I go to think about Charles Brasch, I feel Kāpiti to be a very temporary place. There are so few old buildings, nothing is made of stone, and many of the houses show their bachy beginnings in ugly add-ons that no architect ever saw. In Dunedin, the yellow light, all that granite, and a photograph in Toitū of my great-great-grandparents, anchor me. My life here, where the washing blows and the vegetables from the garden taste of salt, has a slightly improvised feeling, but that is my own contribution. There are older stories here, too. Stories in trees and bones and water.

Places of Personal Interest

Poplar Ave

Leinster Ave

Raumati Rd

Rata Rd

Kāpiti Rd

OLD HIGHWAY 1

Paekākāriki
Wellington

N
W E
S

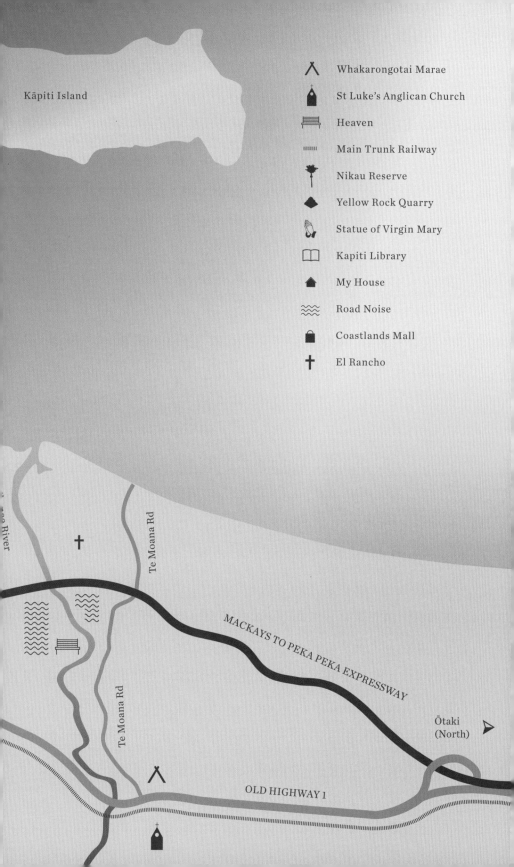

Kāpiti Island

Whakarongotai Marae

St Luke's Anglican Church

Heaven

Main Trunk Railway

Nikau Reserve

Yellow Rock Quarry

Statue of Virgin Mary

Kapiti Library

My House

Road Noise

Coastlands Mall

El Rancho

River

Te Moana Rd

Te Moana Rd

MACKAYS TO PEKA PEKA EXPRESSWAY

Ōtaki
(North)

OLD HIGHWAY 1

The Mackays to Peka Peka Expressway: *It's here now and it's part of our lives*

24 February 2017

> *The Expressway is open. Cars and trucks are whizzing up and down on it. State Highway 1 is deserted.*

A friend texted me this news about 7.15 in the morning. He saw this new world from the train, where thousands of public transport commuters were waking up as gently as possible by looking out the window, playing games, reading books and not talking to each other, on their 48-kilometre journey from the Kāpiti coast to Wellington.

Although the news reached me in this rather low-key way, and with no media fanfare, it was not altogether a surprise that the Mackays to Peka Peka Expressway 'opened for traffic', as they say, on that day. There had already been two other openings. On 16 February there was an official opening by the Minister of Transport. That event was reported in the media but the public was not invited. On Saturday 18 February there was an open day, named ExpressDay, where members of the public could walk a five-kilometre section of the Expressway between Paraparaumu and the Te Moana Road exit. If you were less energetic you could ride on a bus, with a guide. ExpressDay was extremely popular with locals. Thousands turned out to walk, scoot, be cajoled, led or pushed in prams, along this bit of road. There was even a set of four-wheeled vehicles, a bit like giant ride-on mowers, shuttling up and down, bringing people who had over-estimated their mobility back to their cars. Kāpiti had a cool and wet summer in 2016–17 and the morning of ExpressDay was windy and grey with a few spots of rain. But later the sun came out, and it was hot walking on the smooth black surface of the road.

ExpressDay was careful, engineered exposure for the Expressway. Originally, I described the day as 'engineered fun', but the more I thought about the day, the more I realised that it was never light-hearted enough to be fun in the normal sense of the word. Before ExpressDay Kāpiti residents had seen the road but not been allowed to touch it, like prospective spouses in an arranged marriage. The road would never look better than it did on 18 February 2017 and the Alliance wanted us to like it, so they put their best foot forward.

There was plenty of parking and friendly people on hand to show you where to go. At either end of the five-kilometre open section of the Expressway there were food stalls, bottled water supplies and activities for kids. Five of the Alliance's experts gave talks about their area of expertise. You could find out how the road surface was constructed, how the bridges and paths were built, how the flow of traffic is monitored, which plants were used along the route or how the project archaeologist worked. There was music and face painting. Along the Expressway, toilets and rubbish bins had been placed at regular intervals. The disposition of the toilets, exactly a kilometre apart, demonstrated both the thoroughness of the planning and the significance the Alliance placed on this day.

I walked from Kāpiti Road to the Te Moana Road exit and caught the bus back because I was curious to hear the commentary provided on the buses. Hundreds of people wanted to catch the buses and sometimes the queue got quite long, but there was no chance that an unsafe number of people would crowd onto the buses because someone stood at the front with a clicker, counting us as we climbed into the bus. The young Irish engineer who was our guide pointed proudly to the bridge over the Waikanae River. He told us he had designed this bridge. 'If there's an earthquake,' he said, 'stand under that bridge. It's the strongest thing for miles.' I looked at his bridge. It was in two parts. The north-bound section was separated from the south-bound section by perhaps a metre. I had never seen a bridge with a cleft before. The whole thing sat on heavy heavy concrete legs and on top of the legs were panels of concrete with the sealed road on top of that. Standing under that bridge in an earthquake would be one of the most terrifying things I could imagine. While I was occupied with these thoughts a man on the bus asked the engineer how many bridges he had built before. This was his first, he said. I imagined him sending pictures of the bridge to his mother in Ireland. Oddly, the only thing the engineer was not confident about was whether we would be able to understand him. He kept asking us if we could.

Near the end of the tour, our engineer/guide told us that there were only four or five days of sealing left to do, and that if the weather cooperated, the road would be open to traffic by the end of the next week. The weather after the 18th was hot and dry. A certain open-hearted confidence which I caught from the Irish engineer enabled me to understand that conditions during that next week were perfect for sealing.

While the date of the third and final opening was not a surprise, the slightly occult manner of the 'opening for traffic' felt out of character. The Expressway had always seemed to like talking about itself. From the moment the project had received consent, the Expressway began to speak with its own voice, and for more than three years, it had not stopped. The Expressway exhibited its machines, showed us its experts and explained construction techniques. It described the noises we would hear, vibrations we would feel and it gave running commentaries on its progress. I had expected it to shout its opening from the roof-tops.

Later I was told that the reason for allowing users to find the new road in their own time was to prevent a traffic jam of confused rubber-neckers on its first day. I would have been there, rubber-necking, if I had known when the barriers would come down, so the secrecy was probably a prudent decision. But still, the third and final opening was a bit of an anti-climax and a bit out of character.

In 2017 I still believed that the Expressway had a character and that I could discern that character from its behaviour, as you might with a person. Back in 2009, when the Expressway was announced, other people had known immediately what they thought of it. Some thought it was a fine fellow and pinned great hopes on its arrival. These people licked their lips at the predicted growth the Expressway would bring. They were confident there would be new jobs for locals and an end to the 10- or 15-kilometre traffic jams on State Highway 1 that we had endured for years. Others thought the Expressway itself was evil and a symbol of other evils. They resented the way it had been imposed on Kāpiti, when we had an alternative local road all ready to start being built. They objected to the encouragement big new roads give to petrol-driven transport. They were angry that the Expressway would destroy wetland habitat for fish and birds, especially near the Waikanae River, and they grieved for the river which would soon have a giant bridge, built by the young Irish engineer as it turned out, blocking out light and making noise. Right from the beginning, in 2009, I had been unable to arrive at a simple 'love it or hate it' view of the Expressway. My natural sympathy was more with the opponents of the Expressway, because, for environmental reasons, I wanted to see less emphasis on roads rather than more, but I saw, every day, that the version of Highway 1 that ran through Kāpiti was grossly unsafe and completely inadequate for its job.

I pursued this notion of character for the three years of its construction, expecting to find out there was good and bad in the Expressway, as there is with the rest of us. I visited the places where you could see the work. I took hundreds of photographs. I watched the drainage of swamps and the construction of the concrete bridges, I chatted to other locals standing at the fence gawping like me, and to construction workers if I could. I met a number of Alliance specialists who gave me background on their roles and I kept a clippings file of news items about the Expressway. All the time, I was listening for hints and watching for signs of the road's character.

Obviously, I thought, an 18-kilometre, high-spec road, with 18 bridges, would not have a simple character. With all that concrete and rock, there would be a hard, domineering side to it. And, as I have said, it has always had a slightly show-offy side. It also had a prudent side. All that emphasis on health and safety during the construction was evidence of that. But I was sure there was more to its character than a desire to be the centre of attention and a desire to avoid liability. Did it want to be liked, for example? I thought it did. Did it want to be virtuous? I wasn't sure. I thought perhaps it did, by its own lights. Could it respond, reflect on its actions or show fellow feeling? I thought not. Was it as neat and clean on the inside as it looked? No doubt it had its secrets as we all do. For a while one of those was the date it would open to traffic.

In the week after the third opening people didn't talk about the new road itself. They talked about how wonderfully quiet the old Highway 1 had become now that the heavy trucks had moved to the Expressway, and how that had happened right from the first day the Expressway opened. They talked about driving from Paraparaumu north to Waikanae without those traffic jams that used to happen every afternoon and every holiday. They talked about turning right from Raumati South towards Wellington without having to look out for trucks and all the other fast traffic of Highway 1. It was as if people had suddenly noticed how frightening those turns had been.

People noticed the planting along the sides. They said they found the Expressway attractive. They said the Expressway passes through beautiful country and they were seeing parts of the district that they had never seen before. I had this experience myself on ExpressDay. As I walked the part near the Te Moana Road turn-off to Waikanae Beach I saw a cemetery up on the hill to the west of the Expressway. What looked like a Victorian angel caught my eye. I had never seen that before.

In a café, a woman told me how much nicer our Expressway looked than older motorways. That made me look harder at older motorways and I found she was right. Ours looked fresh and clean. No old Coca-Cola bottles and plastic bags in the gardens and the plants all young and full of promise. People immediately loved the shared pathways along the sides where you can cycle safely for 32 kilometres from one end of the Expressway to the other and back again. Right from 24 February, when the barrier fences came down, those paths have been crowded. John, who has a lawn-mowing business and drives up and down from Paekākāriki to Ōtaki and everywhere in between, said that when he used the new Expressway his trips up and down from Paraparaumu to the beach side of Waikanae reduced from 15 minutes to 10. It didn't sound like much to me, but the way he said it I could tell it counts for him. Local people started using the Expressway as a way to get around the Kāpiti towns and, judging by the changed volume and nature of traffic on the old Highway 1, trucks started using the Expressway to travel city to city, too.

'Alliancing'. It's a Thing.

IN 2007 when I moved to Kāpiti, transport between Wellington and Kāpiti and within Kāpiti itself was a dangerous, time-consuming shambles. There was no road linking Paraparaumu and Waikanae except for State Highway 1, so local Kāpiti people had to use Highway 1 to get about the district. State Highway 1 between Kāpiti and Wellington was narrow, prone to slips and would close every time there was a storm. North of Paraparaumu, Highway 1, a two-lane road with no median divide, gave people no second chances. The passenger rail system was unreliable. It was common for trains to break down, especially if there was heavy rain or high winds. We used to notice a month of daily train commuting with no break-downs and speak of it as a wonder. The tracks and electric power systems were old and fragile and the trains themselves were old, dirty and cold. The only forward-looking part of the transport system was the local bus service which connected well with the commuter trains.

We had no choice but to use these creaky systems as best we could. Local people would avoid travelling at certain times and on certain days. New residents like me learned pretty darned quickly. Ten or 20 kilometres of crawling congestion was a regular daily experience for commuters travelling into, or home from, Wellington. At holiday time the situation was 10 times worse. In the summer of 2016–17, just before the Mackays to Peka Peka Expressway opened, I was working at Beach FM radio, based at Lindale, just north of Paraparaumu. Over the Christmas and New Year period it took me nearly an hour to travel about five kilometres to work. At the radio station, we did traffic reports by going outside and looking south towards Paraparaumu at a line of cars that had no end.

Before the Expressway there was only one bridge over the Waikanae River and that was on State Highway 1, so if you wanted to travel from Paraparaumu to Waikanae, you had to drive around three sides of a square. You would drive east to Highway 1, turn left onto Highway 1, join the throng of traffic on its way to Auckland, make your way seven kilometres north, cross the bridge and then turn off to the west to get to the township of Waikanae Beach.

I remember hesitating slightly about buying a house at Raumati South, not because rising sea levels are taking parts of the coast away in alarming chunks and Raumati South is severely affected, but because the turn-off from Raumati South onto Highway 1 to get to Wellington involved turning right from a give way, across north-bound traffic travelling at 100 kilometres an hour, to join fast-moving south-bound traffic. For the first few months I used to drive an extra few kilometres north along a local road, so that I could make the right turn onto Highway 1 with the help of traffic lights. Then I would drive south again past the turn-off I was too scared to use. These transport problems were not unique to Kāpiti and I do not list them out of any sense of outrage. I am just saying that there was a problem and it had more than one dimension.

The Kāpiti Coast District Council (KCDC) had a plan for improving things. The council wanted to build a two-lane local road, called the Western Link Road (WLR), which involved building a second bridge over the Waikanae River near its mouth. The Western Link Road would remove the need for local traffic on Highway 1 and increase connection between Kāpiti's communities. However, there were two obstacles to building it. The first was opposition from locals concerned about the environmental damage that would be caused by building a road across sand dunes, wetlands and over the river. The second was that the council did not have the money for the road and needed government assistance. Local opposition to the Western Link Road was serious and sustained. When I moved to Kāpiti in 2007, the topic of the Western Link Road was rumbling and growling in an apparently endless loop.

By 2008 though, things were moving forward. KCDC had consent for the WLR and the Labour-led government had committed to provide 90 per cent of the money to build the road. But in November 2008 things changed dramatically when the three-term Labour government was voted out and a National government took office. By March of 2009 Steven Joyce, the Minister of Transport, had announced the new government's plan to build seven Roads of National Significance (RoNS), one of which was described as the Wellington Northern Corridor between Levin and Wellington. In his press release Joyce described the rationale for Roads of National Significance.

The purpose of listing roads as 'nationally significant' is to allow the government to have input into the development of the land transport programme and the National Infrastructure Plan from a nationwide perspective.

These roads are already very important in their respective regions. We want to signal to the NZ Transport Agency through the Government Policy Statement their significance to the country as a whole.[1]

The name 'Roads of National Significance' made my skin crawl. I wondered how anyone could come up with a name of such grandiosity. I understood the semiotic communication of the capital letters clearly. The word 'input' was probably going to be an understatement of the government's influence. When a 'nationwide perspective' is used to decide what should happen in a local situation, local knowledge, views and needs are unlikely to carry much weight.

Between August and December 2009 the NZ Transport Agency (NZTA) 'undertook its assessment of and consultation on options for locating an Expressway between MacKays Crossing and Peka Peka.[2]

Despite the weight of the RoNS policy announcement, and while NZTA was carrying out 'assessment and consultation' for an Expressway, KCDC held on to its plan for the Western Link Road.

In October 2009, right in the middle of NZTA's 'assessment and consultation' for an Expressway, KCDC made a submission to NZTA arguing for the Western Link Road plus cycleways, improvements to the current State Highway 1 as far as Palmerston North and continued development of the rail network for freight and passengers.[3] Not surprisingly, given the direction and brio of government policy, KCDC's arguments were not accepted.

On 11 December 2009, NZTA's board indicated its preference for the Expressway to follow the 'sandhills option', which was essentially the Western Link Road route. Several major elements of the current situation were then in place. There *would* be a Road of National Significance through Kāpiti, it would likely follow the Western Link route rather than the existing State Highway 1 route, and there would *not* be government funding for the Western Link Road or a push towards rail rather than road for freight transport or passenger transport.

In 2017 when I discussed those turbulent times with Jenny Rowan, who was mayor of Kāpiti in December 2009, she explained that at this point the council had nowhere to go. They had no money to build the Western Link Road themselves and this other road, the Mackays to Peka Peka Expressway, 'was going to happen anyway'.[4] Her 16 years of experience as a commissioner for the Environment Court prior to her role on KCDC had taught Rowan that 'you never win against government on matters of infrastructure'. Rowan felt very strongly that KCDC should not oppose NZTA over the

Expressway in the Environment Court. 'I didn't want to spend tens of thousands of ratepayers' money fighting NZTA because they would win anyway,' she said.

In February 2010, in a move which was never publicly explained, NZTA wrote to KCDC inviting the council to join the board of the Alliance which was to construct the Mackays to Peka Peka Expressway (M2PP). NZTA had never worked so closely with a local territorial authority before. Exactly one week after NZTA invited KCDC to join the Alliance board, KCDC accepted, suggesting that it was not a difficult decision.

Rowan says that the council made the decision 'with my strong comment that we go in with the Alliance and see what we can get for the community'.[5] In 2009, Rowan says, NZTA was 'in the business of building roads and not much more' so KCDC would be there, inside the Alliance, to advocate for added value for the community. I remember meeting Rowan at a poetry reading in the summer of 2009–10. She said almost exactly what she told me in 2017, except that in 2010 I did not understand what 'see what we can get for the community' meant. I remember her mentioning interchanges and cycleways and footbridges, but I had no picture in my mind of what an expressway would be like if there weren't enough interchanges and footbridges. Rowan, on the other hand, knew exactly what a no-frills expressway would be like. She identified the Taupō bypass, completed in 2010, as an example of what a road looks like without the community input Kāpiti had by joining the Alliance. She is right. The Taupō bypass looks plainer, with no planting obvious. Things are different now, she says in 2017, meaning that the roads built by NZTA are not just concrete monoliths.

In 2009–10 continuing community opposition to the Expressway was clearly seen by NZTA as a direct threat to the whole project. I see the invitation for KCDC to join the Alliance as a strategy by NZTA to neutralise future opposition to the Expressway from KCDC at the Environment Court. In addition to preventing direct opposition from the council, this strategy cut off any capacity for opposition to the Expressway from the Kāpiti community to be supported by the council.

In 2015, with the project consented and well under way, Darren Utting, the stakeholder manager for M2PP, said that back in 2010 the Expressway had been described as 'unconsentable'.

Critical community, environmental and cultural issues led to Crown lawyers dubbing the proposal for the MacKay's to Peka Peka Expressway on the Kāpiti Coast 'the unconsentable project'.[6]

This comment forms part of an entry in a competition, and is intended to highlight the scale of the achievement, but even so, I was shocked to read the word 'unconsentable'. From the front – the face of the Alliance the community saw – the communications exuded confidence and inviolability. This word seemed like a momentary glimpse of the Expressway project from the back. In 2010, when the council made the decision to join the Alliance, perhaps the capacity of NZTA to build the Expressway was more in doubt than Rowan thought?

The word 'alliance' in this context is more than just the name of a group of companies. 'Alliancing' is a form of collaborative working found in infrastructure projects. An alliance-style contracting model is used for projects where there are significant and perhaps unquantifiable risks. NZTA made the decision that the Mackays to Peka Peka Expressway would be built by an alliance. Several factors made M2PP a project with significant risks, including ongoing community opposition and complex terrain. In an alliance-style contract a team is brought together to deliver a project. This team includes the funder and the construction contractors. Everybody talks about creating teams, but in an alliance, the team function is much more than a nice idea. It is connected to the financial contingencies of the project. The parties are not adversaries as they are in a conventional contract, where the construction company would be penalised for delays or cost overruns. Solving problems along the way is the joint responsibility of the team members and any extra costs or surplus are shared. (For example, the cost of repairs to the pavement which turned out to have a short **design life†**, and started failing almost immediately after the Expressway was opened in 2017, will be shared between all parties in the Alliance.)

From early 2010, with KCDC now on the Alliance board, the M2PP Alliance became a super-Alliance. The super-Alliance board was made up of two representatives from each of the Alliance's commercial participants – Fletcher, Beca and Higgins – and one each from the Kāpiti Coast District Council and the NZ Transport Agency. KCDC was represented on the board by the chief executive. The board operated according to the process called 'alliancing'. Utting describes this in action.

> *The authentic collaboration from the outset between the Council, the Transport Agency and the planning and construction teams fits well with the 'one team' philosophy of alliancing. This built trust that has been strengthened by the construction team consistently delivering on the promises made during the consultation and consenting stages.*[7]

According to Rowan it was a pleasant surprise to find that there were people on the board who were very skilled at collaborative work. Right from the start, she says, the two fundamental premises of the board were 'asking us what we wanted to see' and 'wanting to build a road people would be proud of'. Those two things changed the whole dynamic, she says. Discussions in the board were 'pretty tough', she says, but over time 'they agreed to what is sitting there now'. According to Rowan, the driver for the process was knowing that the road 'is going to be built'. Once that was no longer in contention, KCDC could and did focus on reducing potential harm and maximising potential benefits from the new road. Results of this process include the cycleway from Paekākāriki to Peka Peka, the largest roading landscape plan in the southern hemisphere and the agreement to maintain the planting for three years.

From the vantage point of 2017, Rowan said she was very pleased with the results from joining the Alliance. She is not alone in this. Current deputy mayor Janet Holborow also believes KCDC's close involvement with the Mackays to Peka Peka Alliance has been well worthwhile. At the ceremony held on the new Waikanae River bridge on Thursday 16 February 2017 to mark the completion of the Expressway, Holborow explained the decision that the council made to join the Alliance:

> After some initial resistance for the project in favour of the long planned Western Link Rd, the council and in particular the mayor at the time, Jenny Rowan, and chief executive Pat Dougherty, realised it was critical to work with the Transport Agency and its partners to achieve the best possible outcome for the district, realising potential benefits as well as minimising the impacts. They made the decision to work to bring the community alongside the project to ensure local aspirations were at the heart of decision making. Joining the Mackays to Peka Peka Alliance enabled us to influence design decisions that would have a long last[ing] impact on our community.[8]

On that February day in 2017, when the road was sleek and black because the seal had not broken down, traffic hadn't started making noise on the Expressway yet, and everyone was a bit ecstatic, Holborow was even grateful to the people who had objected to the Expressway. Their 'strong passionate initial resistance' had led to this project 'setting new standards in community engagement and collaboration', she said. She acknowledged NZTA and the Mackays to Peka Peka Alliance for their 'commitment to consultation

throughout the project', thanked those who had attended meetings
and hui along the way, and acknowledged 'the great sacrifice of
those who have lost their homes, businesses, wāhi tapu, special
places and lifestyles to make way for this expressway'.

In an opinion piece at around the same time, Pat Dougherty, chief
executive of KCDC, said he was very sure that the council did the
right thing by joining the Alliance and that the council has 'looked
after the community's interests'. 'This has been an example of central
and local government collaboration at its best,' he said.[9]

Just a few days later, Dr Viola Palmer, a supporter of the 'Save Kāpiti'
campaign against the Expressway and therefore less likely to be
delighted with the outcome, expressed a reasonably positive view of
the council's role. 'The Kapiti Coast District Council had no choice
but to co-operate. It collaborated very effectively,' she said,
'... making the best of a bad job for residents.'[10]

I noticed what Dr Palmer said about a lack of choice. Eight years
after KCDC made this decision, I am still unable to decide whether
the council had 'real' choices or not. On the surface, there were
at least two choices. KCDC could have continued its opposition
to the Expressway in the Environment Court. It could also have
given up its opposition to the Expressway but remained outside
of the Alliance. From this position it might have been more
straightforwardly an advocate for affected residents.

At an individual level, when there are disagreements between two
people, one person will often exert pressure to demonstrate that the
other has no choice, even if that is not true. In this case, where the
two parties were central and local government, might other choices
have become apparent if the council had continued its opposition
to the Expressway? The writer **Patricia Grace†**, for example, faced a
situation where her land was in the proposed Expressway route and
it seemed as if that land would be subject to compulsory purchase by

NZTA. But because of her skilful opposition, NZTA found another route for the road.

Palmer certainly believes that residents benefitted from the council's decision. Despite this, and despite assurances from Jenny Rowan and Pat Dougherty, I remain sceptical about the council's decision. I am particularly sceptical about the potential for subtle, perhaps unspoken influence from NZTA at every stage in the project. In 2015, about half way through construction, Utting said:

> The Council worked as part of the alliance throughout the planning and consenting for the new expressway. While it has stepped back to some extent to fulfil its regulatory role during construction, its Chief Executive remains a valued member of the Project Alliance Board. And collaboration occurs on a daily basis between Council staff and project teams.[11]

If you are part of something, and do not stop being part of it, can you really 'step back to some extent' for tasks where critical scrutiny is required? Maybe I should just trust that different parts of the local council can act without pressure from each other? Apparently, it is normal for a council to have multiple roles. For example, if KCDC had proceeded with the Western Link Road, it would have had to scrutinise and consent its own project. Despite being told that multiple roles are 'normal' for a council, I am left wondering whether KCDC's joining the Alliance had any constraining effect on the council's ability to use the full range of options to influence planning decisions regarding the Expressway. I also wonder how, as a ratepayer, I would ever know if there was significant influence. And what about *now*, in 2018, when the Alliance is winding down but the noise problem for some residents near the new road is *not* winding down? Would either the elected members of council or paid staff have been less likely to voice opinions which are in opposition to NZTA, because KCDC, from the chief executive down, has been in alliance with NZTA for so long?

Utting's competition entry report says that up to June 2015, 202 Kāpiti coast businesses had received payments totalling $63.1 million from M2PP. Would a local authority really stand up and challenge an organisation that brought this much money into the district in just under two years?

These questions are my doubts and worries about how this alliancing process, which everyone praises, worked, once the degree of separation between the local council and the government's project had been so much reduced. KCDC *might* have been outflanked by NZTA and realpolitik *might* have stripped the council of some of its capacity to act independently of NZTA and central government's policy. How would we ever know?

Alliancing happened here. It is an extremely powerful process. That is my summary.

I decided to give Rowan the last *last* word. I asked her what transport would have looked like in the Kāpiti coast if Labour had won the 2008 election. There probably wouldn't have been an Alliance and there probably would have been a Western Link Road, she said. The main criticism of the Expressway before it was built, she says, was that it would split the communities on the west of it from those on the east, but in fact, she says, there *is* an internal flow now and the communities from Paekākāriki to Ōtaki are better connected than they were in 2010. Businesses on the old Highway 1 have suffered because much of the traffic has moved onto the Expressway, but that same shift has freed up traffic movement inside the Kāpiti community.

The Fight Against Muddle and Sham

THERE ARE SO MANY Charles Brasches. As a writer – and that is only part of the man – there is the poet, the editor of *Landfall*, the diarist and journal writer and the memoirist. In each of these forms Brasch has a range of recognisable voices. The 36 letters Charles Brasch wrote to the editor of the *Otago Daily Times* (*ODT*) between October 1950 and November 1972 are yet another type of written communication with its own content, style and purposes. I think of *this* Brasch as a tūī, the big one that sits highest in the kōwhai tree, looking out over his territory, ready to defend or attack. It isn't easy to find a single phrase to describe the territory Brasch guards in these letters, but it includes Dunedin city's heritage buildings, the University of Otago's architecture, role and standards, everything to do with Dunedin Public Art Gallery, noteworthy trees and the shape of hills, contemporary theatre in Dunedin, censorship in public broadcasting, funding for artists and the landscape of Queenstown and Aramoana.

The values of this territory are both explicit and implicit in the letters: it is a privilege to have this landscape, these buildings, these cultural institutions and activities; there is beauty in this legacy, and this beauty is vulnerable to haphazard development; if cared for now, and that means active and strategic care, this beauty and cultural activity will enrich our lives, both now and in the future, so let's start building now as if this rich future will happen. The treasures of the natural world and of the arts are for everyone, not just for the wealthy. The power of painting and sculpture and music and theatre will help us grow into people who understand ourselves better as New Zealanders.

Expedience and parochial complacency are the enemy here. Brasch swoops on them and tries to drive them away. But he is not just a shiny black attack force. He also puts forward his ideas about how situations could be managed right now, to get started on this future that he can clearly see. These letters from Charles Brasch, ostensibly to the editor of a provincial paper but spoken as if everyone in New Zealand might be listening, are a form of political intervention, outside of the formal structures of politics. In the letters Brasch puts pressure on the relevant authorities to influence their actions in particular directions and he tries to persuade others towards his view.

The letters are Brasch in the daytime, Brasch in major chords. The tone is confident and generally constructive. It makes sense that a person like Brasch would understand the genre 'letters to the editor' and do the best possible job of these pieces of communication to advance his **causes***. But even when you know this from a rational point of view, the letters are a surprising contrast with the punishing self-criticism and occasional deathly melancholy of Brasch's memoir *Indirections* and his journals.

These letters feel as if they come from a 'man of affairs' who knows the ways of the world and knows how to harness power to a specific end. But this 'man of affairs' who speaks authoritatively about money and planning departs every now and then, just for a moment, leaving in his place a highly emotional poet. I enjoy both moods.

The 1962 letter in defence of poplar trees at Logan Park is probably the least controlled. It starts out in facetious vein.

> *Sir, – Your issue of December 14 reports that the line of poplar trees at Logan Park is to be removed because they interfere with the high-tension power lines. Has it not occurred to the City Council that it is the power lines which ought to be removed because they interfere with the growth of these most lovely trees?*[1]

The second paragraph starts off calmly as he points out that visitors will not be drawn to Dunedin if it is an ugly mess of overhead wires. Then there is a moment of despair that citizens of Dunedin might have to 'live in such a wilderness for all time'. Reason returns and he points out that overseas cities are sometimes admired because of the 'fine trees in their streets', but then emotion takes over again.

> The poplar trees at Logan Park are one of the most beautiful sights in Dunedin. The City Council that destroys them will be my enemy and, I suspect, the enemy of many other citizens, too.

This is Brasch the chivalrous knight, declared foe of tree-cutters and overhead wires.

In 1968, complaining about the quality of cultural offerings at New Zealand House in London, he writes three long, rational paragraphs on the lessons that could be learned from the United States Embassy's cultural programme, the necessity to appoint a permanent cultural affairs officer and the links that could be made between such a role and the Queen Elizabeth II Arts Council. Then he seems to lose his patience.

> At present, New Zealand House is a big head with nothing inside it, suggesting to hundreds of passers-by every day that New Zealand is an empty and boring country, more dead than alive.[2]

I do not know exactly why Brasch wrote his first letter to the editor of the *ODT* in 1950 and not before, but it makes sense to guess that the late 1940s would have been a stressful and busy time for him. He returned to New Zealand in 1946. Shortly after that his grandfather Willi Fels became ill and Brasch, together with other family members, sat with Fels day and night and read to him as he slowly faded. After Fels died in June 1946 there was his house, Manono, to empty and sell and a collection of classical objects to be purchased and given to Otago Museum in Fels' memory. The first issue of *Landfall* appeared in March 1947, less than a year after Fels' death, and from then on, for the time of Brasch's editorship, there were four issues per year. The journals make it clear how much work and stress that involved. Brasch's second book of poetry, *Disputed Ground*, was published in 1948. For these first few years, Dunedin civic affairs may have been well down his list of priorities.

The immediate impetus for the first letter to the editor was a report in the *ODT* on 13 October 1950 that the Dunedin City Council had approved plans for the addition of a new wing to the art gallery, located at that time at Logan Park. Brasch was one of six authors of the letter, published on 26 October 1950. Their names appear in alphabetical order, so his is first. The authors of the letter opposed the new wing on several grounds. First, the gallery on its current site was too far away and difficult for the public to get to, secondly, art galleries ought to be somewhere central so that 'both young and old could drop in frequently and get to know the pictures well', thirdly, the Logan Park gallery was originally a temporary building and should not be added to and, finally, the Logan Park gallery would not need to be expanded if it abandoned its practice of showing all its pictures at once.[3]

For Brasch, the location of a public art gallery, as well as its contents and how it operated, was no trivial matter. The centrality of the arts in understanding life was part of the rationale for starting *Landfall*. One part of this idea, the significance of the arts, appears in the editor's notes in the first issue.

> *Their present isolation is disastrous. They [the arts] have been made to appear unreal, a decoration on the surface of life, which may be of use in whiling away a few leisure hours, but is scarcely worth the attention of those engaged in the serious business of mankind. It is the contrary which is true ... Without them, society would in the long run be intolerable, because meaningless – its meaning (if any) could not be communicated.*[4]

The role of the arts in showing us our own world remained a key idea for Brasch and appeared, many years later, in the report of a talk he gave to students on 26 March 1969, when he said that New Zealanders need to see 'reflections and embodiments of themselves in works of art'. In this context, it does not seem surprising that Brasch would have been drawn into the topic of the Dunedin art gallery.

The arguments in that 1950 letter are clearly expressed. The tone of the letter is reasonable.

> *If a new wing is built as contemplated, the Gallery will probably be committed to remain permanently at Logan Park. But this site has proved most inaccessible; it can only be reached by an infrequent bus service which stops about a quarter of a mile away, and the time taken in getting there and back means that very few except retired people and owners of motor cars are able to visit except at weekends.*

Brasch says in his memoir *Indirections* that when he first stayed in London, on his way to Oxford, he formed the habit of going to the National Gallery almost every day and that this was 'the beginning of my absorption in pictures',[5] so we know that this way of learning about art had been his own first method and his London experience had convinced him that art galleries need to be where people are. But there is a statement at the end of the 1950 letter that makes me think 'Brasch' more than any of the rest of the letter. It is this:

> *But in any case, do all the Gallery's pictures have to be shown all the time? They are far from being of equal value as works of art.*

These two sentences are written by someone who believes some works of art have more value than others, and that he or she knows which are which. I think I detect a hint of exasperation too. This cocktail is, in my view, as distinctive as a fingerprint.

Something about the process of marshalling your opinions and sharing them with the readership of the *ODT* through the person of the editor must have appealed to Brasch, because there were letters in 1956, 1958 and two in 1959. None of the letters after the first one was signed by a group. Three of the 1950s letters related to art. In another, Brasch defended the local productions of plays by Samuel Beckett and Eugène Ionesco put on by Patric and Rosalie Carey, arguing that he wanted to be able to see, in Dunedin, the plays the rest of the world was talking about. After the five 1950s letters there was a big increase in the 1960s, to 23 letters.

Typically, in his letters, Brasch joins in discussion about a topic that has appeared in the news pages of the paper or he writes on a topic that is being discussed in the community at the time. Many of his letters are about very specific Dunedin city concerns, like the council plan to remove the clock tower of the Town Hall (1963), or the effect of continued quarrying of Saddle Hill on the shape of the hill (1964). Brasch always looks forward to a city that would be planned and not haphazard, and planned with beauty in mind.

In 1961 Brasch noticed that new University of Otago buildings and those being planned did not seem to be linked by any architectural aesthetic. He wrote to the editor of the *ODT* about the subject, at some length.

> *Has the University of Otago considered planning as an architectural unity the whole area over which it is building? Without giving the matter much thought, I had taken it for granted that it must be following so obvious and necessary a course, but as one building after another appears, each in an entirely different style … it becomes apparent that no general architectural plan is being followed.*
>
> *If this piecemeal process continues, the university quarter of the city will soon become an architectural babel, a free-for-all in which*

a dozen styles meet and clash stridently … Certainly it is not easy to relate old buildings to new ones, but that is no reason for not having any plan at all.[6]

He goes on to propose an international competition or an invitation to a renowned architect to submit plans. This letter must have hit a nerve because the editor sought and published a response:

Commenting on this letter, Dr F.G. Soper, vice-chancellor of the University of Otago, said: 'There is much to commend Mr Brasch's view, but to harmonise buildings erected over a period of almost 90 years is almost impossible. Where buildings are contiguous, as in the Home Science School and new wing in Union Street, efforts have been made to match the new with the old' – Ed., O.D.T.

Clearly Dr Soper's response did not satisfy Brasch. Eight days later, on 10 May 1961, Brasch's second letter to the editor on this subject was published.

Sir, – In his comment on my letter, the vice-chancellor well illustrated the architectural possibilities open to an expanding university, as set out by Dr Margaret Dalziel. He said that where buildings are contiguous, like the Home Science School and its new wing, efforts have been made to match the new with the old. This is an example of what Dr Dalziel calls timid uniformity of style, which she rightly says is much worse even than muddle. The new wing in question is concrete pretending to be stone – in other words, a sham. Is the University of Otago really going to be content for all time with a combination of muddle and sham – sham posing as uniformity? If it has not enough spirit to take pride in its appearance, can it continue to take pride in its standards of teaching and scholarship?[7]

Timid uniformity of style, muddle and sham. Of these, muddle is the least evil, timid uniformity is much worse, and sham is the most evil of all. If Brasch describes something as a sham, there is a literal meaning and a moral criticism. Concrete made to look like stone, for example, is a pretentious fake and also cheap and expedient. Advertising, banal photography and bad painting are shams, with good painting an antidote.

> *... we do not live in the world that advertisers and most photographers and bad painters try to foist upon us: that is a sham world of make-believe, a lie. The work of good painters will help to expose that lie: it will refresh and purify our seeing for us.*[8]

***

A side note on sham and false notes:

In May 2017, while I was reading Brasch's letters, the University of Otago clock tower was under repair and covered in scaffolding. The university had decided to drape the clock tower with a huge piece of fabric painted with an image of the clock tower so that graduates could take photographs of themselves in front of the 'clock tower' even though the real tower was under repair. Apparently, this was a cheaper solution than removing the scaffolding for the duration of graduation ceremonies and then replacing it. It was a week or two of sham, and trivial compared with the complaints Brasch made about the campus, but all the same, I don't think he would have been amused by the sheet painted to look like the clock tower.

I think the concept of sham or falseness, and by implication its opposite, might also have had a place in Brasch's theory of personal relationships. In his journal entry for 2 December 1946, he says of his growing friendship with Douglas Lilburn, 'I am at ease with him; he takes no liberties, strikes no false notes.'[9]

***

There are more letters about painting than writing. In 1962, Brasch wrote to the *Otago Daily Times* to put forward his ideas on how an art gallery should operate.

Two main points were made by your [previous] correspondents: that special exhibitions in the Art Gallery are not well attended; and that the Art Gallery is too far from the middle of Dunedin. Neither point is true without qualification, nor are the two points necessarily connected.

Special exhibitions in the Art Gallery are well attended when good publicity persuades people of their interest. The Henry Moore exhibition drew large crowds. This need not be an exception – it is only necessary to persuade people that the Art Gallery is always a lively and interesting place to visit.[10]

The idea that the gallery must be active in the community to draw crowds seems thoroughly contemporary. Although, as Brasch says, there is more to a successful gallery than its location, Dunedin's art gallery *did* move to a new site in the Octagon in 1996, 46 years after Brasch's first letter. The new Dunedin Public Art Gallery took over a site previously occupied by the DIC, one of the Hallenstein businesses. This strikes me as thoroughly appropriate since Brasch was a descendant of Bendix Hallenstein, a founder of the 'Hallenstein Brothers' factory and stores, and used his share of this legacy to fund his own activities, including his art collection. This episode led me to consider the possibility that Brasch was precisely 46 years ahead of the rest of New Zealand in his opinions about the relationship between arts and the community.

In 1967 Brasch wrote a letter of protest that the New Zealand government was committing the country to more support for the American forces in Vietnam. He begins by suggesting that the war should be called 'the American war against Vietnam'.[11] He then attacks the subservience of the New Zealand government to the United States.

It has long been clear that the New Zealand Government sees only what it wishes to see, ignores all sources of information about the war except American Government ones, and tries to get New Zealanders to take a purely American (that is, official American) view of the war.

He goes on to discuss terror as a weapon and calls out America for its atrocities against the Vietnamese people.

If burning people alive with napalm is not effective enough, what further horror must we expect? No doubt the Viet Cong use terror too; both sides usually do, in war; but the Americans have vastly greater resources, and they are terrorising not their own country and people, but Vietnam and the Vietnamese.

The New Zealand Government is committing us to support these atrocities more fully at the very moment when the above evidence of them has been made public.

In this letter, Brasch widens his territory to include everyone who is a victim of war and its concomitant terror. This letter is something of an outlier in its scale and geography but arguably the most human of them all. It reminded me that Brasch had lived in Britain through World War II and knew, in a way I do not, the suffering war causes for ordinary people.

One of the longer letters is a response in 1969 to a man called Mr Esplin who had seen the work of M.T. Woollaston and Colin McCahon showing at the time at the art gallery and thought they failed to demonstrate 'a complete understanding of colour and tone'.[12] Brasch does not leap to the defence of these paintings. Instead he defends the serious intent of the artists and the role of critics in weighing individual pieces of an artist's work against others.

It is clear enough that Woollaston and McCahon are (like Nolan and many others) uneven painters: they are attempting something

new, they take risks, they are not content merely to follow Mr
Esplin's rules. So their successes and failures must be distinguished,
and this is not always easy. Hence the need for criticism: it is part
of the critic's business to analyse and make distinctions. But Mr
Esplin abandons the difficult task of criticism, throws in his hand
as a critic, and simply dismisses their work altogether.

In September 1969 Brasch writes in astonishment that there has
been so little reaction to the news that the Bank of New South
Wales was to be demolished and replaced with a new building.
With the demolition of the Dunedin Stock Exchange building in
the same year, it must have felt like an epidemic of destruction was
afoot. Sitting on the bus in my school uniform in 1969, watching
a bulldozer drive in through the main door of the Exchange
and up a set of stairs, I was shocked. When I saw that machine
inside the human place I felt something new. I didn't know what
the destruction of the Stock Exchange meant, but Brasch saw
the destruction of buildings which had been soundly built as
'conspicuous waste',[13] as well as a loss of spirit and beauty.

In his letter about the NSW bank Brasch says that 'a good building
of this kind is of far more than private concern'. He asked the city
planning department to draw up a schedule of older buildings and
give them prominence in its publicity to raise public awareness of
these buildings, so that the ownership of one would confer prestige
and owners would be more likely to try to keep the old buildings
alive as long as possible. If steps like this were not taken, it would be
Dunedin city's loss.

If further good older buildings are destroyed, Dunedin in a very
few years will have lost much of the strong character and dignity
which make it so unusual in New Zealand and so interesting
and enjoyable to live in, and which is also its chief attraction for
visitors.

In a 1971 letter J.G. Blackman, a noted photographer of Dunedin's built environment, and Brasch plead for the preservation of the ANZ Bank building, quoting the role of the Historic Places Trust as 'an authoritative and informed local conscience in the matter of historic building and sites'.[14] I wondered if either man noticed that this is a perfect description of what their letter to the editor aims to do.

> We can sympathise with owners of fine old buildings who now need more space than their premises provide. It is not unnatural that they think of pulling down the old building and putting up a new one on the same site. But a building as important as the ANZ Bank is to Dunedin becomes a civic possession, part of our pride in the city. It is then the duty of the city and its citizens to cooperate with the owners in finding means of saving the building. Some new economic use for it must of course be devised; but this should not be beyond our wit.

Brasch's letters are not anti-business. Quite the reverse. It is accepted that buildings must have some 'economic use'. The letters point out that if we, as citizens, want these buildings, we will have to join a collaborative process by which an economic use can be found. The ANZ Bank building survived that destructive purge. It stopped being used as a bank in 1992, and is now listed as an attraction for visitors to Dunedin.

In the years after I saw the demolition of the Stock Exchange from the window of the St Clair bus in 1969, Dunedin's old synagogue, the railway station, the old university building, the banks and other less august old buildings slowly rose through the murk of my late adolescence, its pressures and its preoccupations, and imprinted themselves on consciousness as something beautiful. For years after I left Dunedin I would dream of their granite, their old-wood smell, their stained-glass windows and mosaic floors and always, in these dreams, I would feel pleasure as vivid as a drug.

Brasch's final letter to the editor, published in November 1972, six months before his death, concerned a 'proposed' aluminium smelter to be built at Aramoana, at the entrance to Otago Harbour. Brasch does what he always does: he thinks carefully around the project, considers its implications and poses questions that have not been raised, let alone answered.

> *The effect of similar industries elsewhere is relevant. For example, are wastes from the Bluff Smelter poisoning the oyster beds in Foveaux Strait, as has been stated? If so, what will be the effect of a smelter at Aramoana on fishing off the Otago coast? How has the oil refinery at Marsden Point affected Whangarei and district? Will the north-east wind blow fumes from Aramoana over Dunedin? Other questions have already been raised in your pages. They are of vital concern to Dunedin. They must be asked now, while there is yet time, and the answers be made public in full, before the project is begun.*[15]

Brasch looks around at groups who might have information or perspectives to offer and he calls for much wider consultation before the final decision is made. The letter has, for the most part, a typical Brasch tone of reasonableness and logic. But it also has an intensity around the question of time. *This* is the time to ask these questions, he says.

> *Too much damage has been done to the country because the effect of ambitious, attractive-sounding schemes has not been made clear before it was too late.*

On the same day, on the same page, in the same paper, this letter was printed next to Brasch's.

> *Sir, – It does seem that conservation and environment, including raising and lowering of lakes, etc., is getting a bit out of hand. Every county appears to have the most beautiful lake in New Zealand, if not in the world. There is a saying that 'there is only*

*one perfect baby, and every mother has it.' So with the lakes etc.,
but it is a rather wonderful thing that Nature soon beautifies
changes in the environment, even if dams are built, until it is hard
to visualise how it looked before.*

*Often the alterations make the environment more attractive to
tourists, and even the locals find the change quite attractive after a
time …*

*If, however, through not being allowed to alter the environment we
had power cuts as we had last winter, or worse, if more power was
needed and could not be supplied, causing hardship to young and
old alike, need would supercede environment etc., I think.*[16]

According to this person, who wrote under the name 'Be
Reasonable', the immediate needs of the people should take priority
over protection of the environment. New Zealand has been built on
this principle. The shallowness of this dichotomy exercised Brasch
and it exercises me. Yes, people need to keep warm, and yes, freight
needs to move around the country. But couldn't we think of ways
that the need can be met and the future left with many resources? As
Brasch says, this should not be beyond our wit.

On 25 August 1948, Brasch recorded in his journal that he had
heard his own physical voice on the radio. The voice he heard was
'of some cool cultivated remote Englishman au-dessus de la mêlée'.[17]
But when the Charles Brasch of these letters and articles defends
his territory, he does not hover. He either flies right into a mêlée or
makes a mêlée where there was none. In his journal, on 17 July 1946,
Brasch said this of himself:

*… I stand for something so strange & no doubt offensive to the
community, outside it & therefore endangering it …*[18]

For someone who had thought he was outside the community and
offensive to it, even if this was only the thought of one day, the

decades of letters are a very public pinning of one's colours to the mast.

A few final words in respect of the tūī: The highest place in the pūriri or the kōwhai tree is reserved for the biggest, sleekest, blackest male tūī. He sits up there alone, always watchful. It was this sense of territory and the weight of responsibility for protecting it that made me pair Charles Brasch with the tūī on the highest branch. The sense of that bird's dominance over other birds was something I dragged in as collateral and only noticed much later.

Sixteen Chapters of the Kāpiti Expressway Noise Story

ONE

Early morning A

Walking along Tennis Court Road at dawn, I listen to the breathy voice of Swami Madhuram's flute which circles, loops and dives like a hawk in an updraft. In the up of it, the top peep of it, pink camellias, purple hebe, white daisies, pink tī kōuka strings, smudgy buddleia and scrappy yellow weeds are colours and lights and musk in the gloom. In the low of it, the drone of it, grey eucalypts, shiny coprosma, pōhutukawa shaved by the wind and a few old macrocarpa reach up to find light. I understand the stretching and the waving of branches as a matter of life or death.

Mist as fine as perfume falls in folds from the hills. Dawn sky with streaks of wind. Dawn sky with a washed-out moon. Morning sea a gentle hush. Far away to the south, white peaks. The world hums like a harmonium. Tūī sing the same phrase over and over. This is Dayspring, alive as an animal is, but for just a moment, still. The whole day afterwards belongs to thinking, to argument and contention, to the economy, to taking the good with the bad, but this part of the day belongs to itself.

Early morning B

Two kilometres north, in Rata Road, in a house less than 100 metres from the road, everyone wakes at three. The westerly wind carries the low rumble of trucks and the high-pitched hiss of engine brakes across the sand, through boarded-up windows and into the house. Nothing stops it coming in. The couple with the boarded-up windows know that they are not the only ones. Knowing there are others doesn't help. *Da-dum, da-dum* is the sound of one truck driving over one rubber strip joining two concrete panels of a nearby bridge. Every day, on average, 2000 trucks and 20,000 cars cross that bridge. The couple with the boarded-up bedroom say the bridge noise is like sharing the house with someone learning to play the drums. Except that they never stop practising and they never get any better.

Two

What are the sources of road-traffic noise?

Many people notice road-traffic noise after a new road is constructed or after an existing road is modified. Because the noise is new or different it is potentially more annoying *[my emphasis].*

Sounds you may hear include:
- *Tyre noise (or road-surface noise) – noise created when the tyre meets the road surface – over the course of a day this will be the dominant source of noise from the Mackays to Peka Peka Expressway*
- *Vehicle noise – engine/exhaust noise, rattling of vehicle bodies, noise of engine braking*
- *Bridge joints – can make a distinctive sound as vehicles pass over them.[1]*

Three

This is what the locals said

On 17 July 2017 Raumati residents met about Expressway noise. The meeting was called by Labour MP Kris Faafoi, the electorate MP for Mana, which includes Raumati Beach. Faafoi had been told about the noise problem at a neighbourhood party meeting. The general election was eight weeks away.

Seated at the top table at the front of the hall were Janet Holborow, Kāpiti Coast District Council's deputy mayor, and Jonny Best, chair of both the Paraparaumu/Raumati Community Board and the **Community Liaison Group†** (set up to liaise with the Alliance via the smaller, local **Neighbourhood Information Forum†**). Best, as I found out later, lives in a street near the Expressway where noise is significant. The meeting was opened and chaired by Roger Booth, also an affected resident and a former Kāpiti Coast District Council deputy mayor.

Booth began by saying that we were not there to relitigate the question of whether there should be an Expressway. 'It's here now,' he said, 'and it's part of our lives.' At the time, I thought this sounded defensive, as if he was worried that he would lose control of the meeting if people started saying why they thought the Expressway should not have been built. But since that meeting I have realised that what Roger Booth said was important. Until he said that, I had not quite believed that the Expressway *is* here now and will be part of the lives of people, birds and freshwater fish here, forever, or at least as close to forever as I can imagine. It is absurd that I thought the Expressway was not quite real when the vast concrete road was built, day by day, all around me, for three years. But until that meeting there was a small corner where I thought that one day I would wake up and it would not have happened. No dystopic movie scene where the Expressway would be crumbled concrete with sweet blue morning glory flowers growing over it. Just one day things would be different and what you feared simply is not there.

This thinking, which denies the full and permanent arrival of the Expressway, received a heavy blow from Roger Booth, but it did not die. Months after the residents' meeting about the noise,

I was looking back at old photographs of the Expressway under construction. Each time I saw the photographs from 2015, showing the new road as a rough track with no concrete to be seen, or the very early stages of the construction of the Waikanae River bridge, when you could still see the river with no bridge over it, I had that same doubled-up sense that the Waikanae River was still like that and, at the same time, a sadness rose inside me because I knew that it was not. I have not heard anyone else refer to the consolation to be found in all time existing simultaneously, but I think that multiplicity has kept me gently anaesthetised for these past few years.

'We're here because the matter [of noise] hasn't been sorted,' Roger Booth said. 'Our problem is that the rules don't seem to adequately cover our situation.' He explained that according to the rules, the east side of Kiwi Road is too far away from the Expressway to qualify for a noise-reducing wall, but that the houses and people there were getting the noise very badly. Booth said that the problem is worst for him at night, when the house is quiet and he is trying to go to sleep, and in the small hours of the morning, when the trucks are hurrying to get to Wellington early to avoid the morning rush hour.

Jonny Best, chair of the Paraparaumu/Raumati Community Board, said that he too thought that the Expressway would be found to be compliant with NZ Transport Agency (NZTA) standards for ongoing noise levels. He wants NZTA to go above and beyond the required standards for noise in the future, he said, and right now he wanted more noise mitigation here in Kāpiti. The community board had raised this matter with NZTA and was still waiting for a response.

Janet Holborow said that during construction Kāpiti Coast District Council had been dealing with the Alliance, the road-builders, who were much more responsive than NZTA, the road commissioner and funder.

Once members of the public began to speak, people described the forms of noise mitigation they thought would be useful, such as earth bunds and more planting and signs asking trucks not to use engine brakes. People talked about successful road noise reduction in other countries which use noise absorption panels instead of the noise reflection panels used in New Zealand. But by far the most meeting time was spent discussing NZS 6806, the standard which NZTA has chosen to adopt as the noise standard for the Kāpiti Expressway. According to this standard, noise is measured as an average over 24 hours rather than as a peak level. People at the meeting were angry because averaging, by definition, produces a number smaller than any peak figure. They said it was the peaks of noise that they could not sleep through, and an average figure does not give a fair representation of what the noise is like for them to live with. Nick Fisher, coordinator of the Expressway Noise Action Group and one of the affected residents, said he accepted that the Expressway noise complies with NZS 6806. He said it was irrelevant what the measurements say. 'It's too much. We can't sleep,' he said. The noise is about more than volume, he said.

Others spoke about vibration as a significant factor in obnoxious noise, and repeated patterns, like the *da-dum* noise a vehicle makes each time it crosses the **bridge expansion joints†** from one segment of a bridge to the next.

The people at the meeting, and I would guess there might have been a hundred, were mostly grey haired. Some were well dressed and spoke very confidently. There were a few younger couples and a child or two but grey heads predominated. Most of the people there, including me, were in the comfortable baggy clothes that Charles Brasch says characterise New Zealanders. No one shouted or wept.

They just described their situation, occasionally with a moment of wry humour, and they talked about their abortive attempts to contact someone in NZTA to put their concerns. After the meeting, I thought about what it would feel like to be one person, asking for help from NZTA, which is implementing government policy. In effect, you are asking for help from the government whose policy has caused your problem.

F o u r

This is what the mayor said
I am no expert in local body structures and roles, but I thought I detected a silence in this meeting where the Kāpiti Coast District Council's voice should be. A statement on the KCDC website about the purpose of the council makes its role in advocacy for the local community with central government explicit. However, it does not make clear which sorts of issues the council will advocate on, how that is done, and how far it extends in relation to small groups and even individuals. With Charles Brasch's letters to the editor of the *Otago Daily Times* in my mind, I wrote the following email to the mayor, K. Gurunathan, to ask about the council's role in the noise issue.

27 July 2017   5.12pm

Good afternoon Guru

Last week I attended a public meeting of residents adversely affected by Expressway noise. It was very distressing to hear individual people's situations. The message I came away with was that they have the sole responsibility for advocating with NZTA for improvement in noise by new or different sound barriers or a widening of the acceptable noise criterion. Janet Holborow and Jonny Best were at the meeting, but neither said anything about

being willing to advocate for people. On the Council website I see
that the Council joined the Alliance 'in order to better advocate
on the community's behalf'. I also see a note saying people affected
by the Expressway should take up the matter with NZTA direct.
Could you please explain to me where the Council sits, at this
post-construction stage, on the matter of ongoing problems for
ratepayers, such as adverse effects of road noise, arising from the
Expressway? Does Council or its staff have any role in advocacy?

On 17 August I received the mayor's reply.

It is a detailed letter, beginning with an expression of empathy for
the affected residents, followed by an outline of the council's role to
date. The mayor gives prominence to the council's role in ensuring
that the road complies with its consent conditions. He states that
these conditions cannot be changed. He also gives prominence to
the Community Liaison Group as the conduit between residents and
NZTA.

The letter does not say what options people have in this situation,
other than to put their names into a database and take part in
liaison. Nor does it refer to the period after the construction is
completed when the Neighbourhood Information Forums and their
peak body, the Community Liaison Group, will be shut down. From
that point there will no longer be any facilitated conduit from the
community to NZTA.

Kāpiti Coast
DISTRICT COUNCIL
Me Huri Whakamuri, Ka Titiro Whakamua

17 August 2017

Ms Lynn Jenner
█ Rosetta Road
RAUMATI SOUTH 5032

Dear Ms Jenner

RESIDENTS AFFECTED BY EXPRESSWAY NOISE

Thank you for your email of 27 July 2017. I empathise with residents who are being adversely impacted by vehicle noise associated with the new Expressway.

Council staff have been liaising with the NZ Transport Agency on this issue. The Council is responsible for enforcing compliance with the conditions of the Mackays to Peka Peka Expressway designation set by the Board of Inquiry under the Resource Management Act process. Under the designation conditions the NZTA is required to carry out operational noise monitoring within two years of the Expressway opening to traffic. In response to community concerns, Council staff liaised with NZTA to have indicative noise monitoring undertaken shortly after the road opened. NZTA also agreed to bring forward the formal compliance monitoring for the operational noise, to check that noise levels from Expressway traffic are within the acceptable range set in the designation conditions.

As a member of the Alliance, the Council worked extensively with other Alliance members to advocate for the community and reduce impacts resulting from the Expressway. The Council has actively supported various engagement forums and the chair of the Community Board was appointed chair of the M2PP Community Liaison Group. This allowed access to NZTA where Council has been lobbying for increased mitigation through the duration of the project.

In its regulatory role the Council has worked hard to ensure that the Expressway is built in accordance with the designation conditions, and that the effects of the Expressway are in compliance with the effects that the Board permitted in its decision. Part of this process has involved Neighbourhood Impact Forums set up to provide a platform for the community to voice any concerns or to highlight any impacts that the expressway has caused. These are required to still be run for at least a further six months. These forums directly report to an overarching Community Liaison Group that is required to monitor the effects of the project and allow an opportunity for concerns and issues to be reported to and responded by NZTA.

Council staff have met and spoken with numerous members of the public over this matter and have ensured that their complaints are recorded in the centralised complaints register which is held by the project. This is to ensure that no person who raised a concern was missed and that a centralised database of people with concerns was held, allowing for any trends, hotspots or analysis of the complaints to be undertaken.

3057589

K Gurunathan JP, MA, Mayor Kāpiti Coast District | Private Bag 60 601 Paraparaumu 5254 | 04 296 4757 | 027 205 3600 | k.gurunathan@kapiticoast.govt.nz

Information Council has at present indicates that the noise levels comply with the Board of Inquiry conditions. Legally there is no further option for appeal to the conditions set by the Board. The Board of Inquiry assessed noise mitigation with regards to best practicable option and imposed conditions accordingly.

Further steps can be taken by the affected residents to ensure they participate in the forums set up by the Alliance specifically for community members to raise concerns. Council will continue to attend these forums and advocate for resolution of the issues in our contact with NZTA and other M2PP Alliance members. At present we are awaiting the results from formal monitoring of operational noise required by the designation.

Yours sincerely

K Gurunathan JP, MA
MAYOR, KĀPITI COAST DISTRICT

3057589

F I V E

On 6 August 2017, I spoke to Nick Fisher

Nick Fisher's house is in Rata Road, at the closest point to the Expressway. He is the coordinator of the Expressway Noise Action Group. Fisher said NZTA should acknowledge the harmful health effects of broken and disrupted sleep and comply with the requirement to preserve the character of the area. He wants NZTA to build high-quality sound-absorbing walls, build bridge walls higher than truck exhausts, find alternatives to rumble strips, change the material of expansion strips on bridges, put up signs about engine braking, do more planting and pay for affected residents to install acoustic glazing. Fisher said acoustic glazing for his house would cost about $50,000, which he cannot afford to pay. In the absence of this, he has covered windows in one bedroom with plywood.

I asked Fisher if he had had any offers of support from either his local MP, Kris Faafoi, or from the Kāpiti Coast District Council. He said that Faafoi had called the community meeting and began the meeting by offering to advocate for affected residents 'if there was a will'. Faafoi had also visited him. Fisher said he waited for Faafoi to say 'If Labour is elected, we will do X about the problem' but nothing was said. Fisher and I had both noticed that the meeting on 17 July concluded with no specific offer from Faafoi to help the residents either individually or as a group.

Nick Fisher had always been opposed to the Expressway. He had made a submission to the Environmental Protection Agency's Board of Inquiry in 2012 (*see* **certainty†**). At an overview level, he objected to the failure of the transport policy to encourage rail, a poorly established case for the Expressway based on falling traffic numbers, the likely increase in reliance on fossil fuels, the consequent increase in foreign debt and an increase in the emissions causing climate change.

Fisher's 2012 submission did not accept that the Mackays to Peka Peka Expressway would reduce significantly journey times from Kāpiti to Wellington. He predicted that increased traffic would meet a bottleneck from Johnsonville to Wellington city. He objected to the tactics used by NZTA in consultation with the community and said that NZTA had not adequately considered alternative transport plans for Kāpiti. Most particularly he pointed to the Western Link Road, which was consented and ready to be built in 2010, had community support and included improvements to the existing State Highway 1 and to rail transport. At an individual householder level, Fisher objected to the establishment of a new motorway route which would be certain to reduce the value of some people's properties. He compared this with improvement of the current Highway 1 which he said would not change any property values.

Fisher also raised concerns in his submission about the possible adverse effects of dust, airborne pollution and noise. Like almost everyone, he saw dust and noise as problems that would happen during the construction phase, rather than after completion. The problem of *ongoing* noise from the Expressway at his own house and at other houses in Rata Road had taken Fisher by surprise. Prior to construction he had been reassured by an NZTA flyer dropped in his letterbox. He showed me the flyer. A diagram shows Fisher's house very close to the Expressway and it shows a noise-reducing concrete barrier between his house and the Expressway. A wall was planned, he said, but it was not built.

I did not ask Fisher what it felt like to be advocating for himself and his family with this government agency. I did not need to. We met on a Sunday morning. Fisher had gathered together papers ready to show me and we spent a couple of hours discussing the situation. The week before, on the coldest day of the winter, he and some other residents had installed fake signs on the Expressway asking truck drivers not to use engine braking in the neighborhood. In the afternoon of the day we met he was scheduled to meet two women from Aurecon, a consulting company retained by NZTA to be the communication channel between residents affected by Expressway noise and themselves. While we were talking, Fisher spoke calmly. He had done a lot of research into this local Kāpiti situation and the experience of other expressways in New Zealand, as well as solutions in other countries. He looked tired.

At one point Fisher said that he thought NZTA was planning to wait the situation out, hoping that the most affected and disgruntled residents would either die, or give up and sell their houses at whatever price they could, which would be less than the likely value if the Expressway had not been built nearby. He said he could not afford to sell for a reduced price so would not give up trying to improve the situation. There was an edge in his voice.

SIX

Noise is a short word. Say it slowly and it sounds a little like a dentist's drill.

On 14 August 2017, about 9.30 on a Monday morning, I walked along Rata Road. At its furthest point the Expressway might be 100 metres away from most of the houses, across flat land. Near Nick Fisher's house the Expressway is much closer. Beside Fisher's house the Expressway is above the level of the houses. On this particular day a light northerly wind brought the Expressway noise towards the houses. Northerlies and nor'westers are Kāpiti's predominant winds so this would happen often. Cars made up the majority of traffic on the Expressway. Cars make a high-pitched metallic sound. The word 'grind' gives something of the quality of a car-approaching sound, although there is also an element of 'swish' as a car passes. I imagine that these two noises are the engine and the noise of the tyres on the road surface. Twelve trucks passed in the quarter of an

hour that I was there. Trucks are much louder than cars and make a
different range of noises. I could always hear trucks coming before
I saw them. Trucks heading north on the Expressway come down a
small hill right near Fisher's house and I noticed that two of them
made a high-pitched squeal as well as their main heavy-engine noise
as they passed. The loudest trucks pulled tanks. I couldn't see what
was in the tanks, but those trucks made a low-frequency noise. As
I walked out of Rata Road and turned west into Raumati Road, I
saw a National Party billboard with the Expressway bridge behind
it. On the billboard were a smiling Bill English and Mana's National
candidate, Euon Murrell. Both men had had their eyes poked out
with ballpoint pens. The pens stayed there, sticking out of the
eyeballs, until election hoardings were taken down.

S E V E N

Noise update, 15 August 2017
NZTA has committed to installing advisory signs asking heavy
vehicle operators to limit the use of engine brakes. These signs will
be installed by the end of October 2017. They also say that truck
drivers do not necessarily obey signs.

Nick Fisher plans to put up a fake noise reduction barrier on the
Expressway, to keep the issue visible.

E I G H T

On noise and real estate values
Jonny Best is chair of the Community Liaison Group (CLG). He
also chairs the Paraparaumu/Raumati Community Board and
owns a house uncomfortably near the Expressway. He speaks a
little differently in each of these roles, but it all comes together in

his personal analysis of the situation. As chair of the CLG, he says that noise is the most difficult issue the group faces at present and the problem is not going away. After the road opened in February 2017, the CLG had to deal directly with NZTA, rather than with the Alliance as they did during the construction phase. The Alliance, Best says, was really good at helping people. Without giving any details, he says that by working with the Alliance the CLG was able to obtain some confidential settlements for people who were severely affected by the construction process. He does not say that NZTA is unwilling to help people, or even hint at that, but a contrast hangs in the air. He does say that a quieter road than this could be built, but it would cost more.

As chair of the Paraparaumu/Raumati Community Board, Best has written to NZTA following a motion from a board member. The letter asked NZTA to remedy the noise to stop further effects on people's sleep and on their health. NZTA responded by sending a representative to a community board meeting and telling the board that they had hired Aurecon as independent consultants to check that NZTA had met all the conditions of the consent and that the road is compliant with noise limits set in the consent.

In his private life, living in a house right near the Expressway, Best says he is taking a pragmatic attitude to the noise. From his house, he hears road-surface noise, the *da-dum* noise as each vehicle crosses segments of the bridge and the noise when a vehicle veers onto the rumble strip at the side of the road. His view is that the noise of the Expressway is compliant with the Board of Inquiry limit and therefore he cannot see why NZTA would want to do any more about the problem.

With so many people's stories in his mind, Best says that ongoing noise affects people differently, just as the construction noise affected people differently. Some people brush it off, he says, and some are badly affected. Best's theory is that a person can get into a spiral where they are upset about the noise, find it hard to relax and can't stop themselves from listening out for the noise.

I accept that there is some truth to the idea that people who sleep badly tend to be waiting to sleep badly when they go to bed, and are sensitive to anything that makes sleep harder. On the other hand, the argument that some people 'cope' with the noise and others don't, could very easily slide into 'it's all in your head', which has been used to discount many kinds of experience from sexual abuse to chronic pain. Best's 'individual differences cause varying responses to noise' theory also makes me think differently about the standard by which noise is measured. If noise is phenomenological, if people's reaction to noise is so varied, how meaningful is a single, averaged noise level figure as a standard?

The subject of noise from the Expressway causing a fall in property values came up in my conversation with Jonny Best as it had with Nick Fisher. Anecdotally, Best said, there had been some complaints about the impact of the Expressway on nearby property values. Prices may have 'stagnated a bit', he said, but the overall trend in the area was upwards. Best quoted one real estate agent who told him that houses near the Expressway are still selling for good prices, but are slower to sell. This unnamed local real estate agent had told Best that people like the convenience of being close to Expressway interchanges and houses further away from the Expressway on-ramps were taking longer to sell.

My own view is that proximity to Expressway interchanges is quite distinct from proximity to the Expressway itself, and I would expect those two situations to be differently reflected in house values. I emailed four local real estate agents about this and followed up with phone calls. Chris Parker of Tommy's was the only one of the four to respond. He said, 'The Kapiti Coast as a whole has gone crazy since Jan 2016. Houses near M2PP have not been affected at all in my opinion.'[2]

Nine

Noise update, 4 October 2017
On 4 October 2017, NZTA hosted a meeting at the Paraparaumu Community Centre for residents affected by Expressway noise. The meeting had been planned with some care. Tea, coffee, savouries, cakes and some reasonably senior staff were provided.

Craig Pitchford, the NZTA project manager for the delivery of the Mackays to Peka Peka Expressway, was there, as was Greg Haldane, principal environmental specialist at NZTA, Kiran Hira, senior civil engineer from Beca, and Alice Naylor, Mackays to Peka Peka environment manager. Sarona Iosefa, one of the consultants NZTA had appointed to liaise with affected residents back in July, and another NZTA communications manager were also present.

The meeting was described as an information session. The format was that residents could drop in between 4 and 8pm. What residents were to gain from dropping in was not so clear. NZTA had set out a long map of the Mackays to Peka Peka Expressway on tables and placed its experts behind the tables, along the route. There were no prepared speeches. Instead residents could approach and speak to one or more of the experts. Most people went to the place on the map nearest to their own property and spoke to the expert standing nearest to that, but if you wanted, you could speak to all the experts. There was a lot of noise from all the conversations happening simultaneously.

The description of the meeting as an information session did not specify who was to give and who was to receive information, or for what purpose. When I saw the residents talking to the experts I thought perhaps residents were giving information to NZTA's experts. But NZTA also gave out several handouts, so probably that was the information referred to. Handouts included four pages of frequently asked questions and single sheets titled 'Traffic noise – assessment, approvals, design and verification', 'Mackays to Peka Peka Expressway noise – what's happening?', 'Managing traffic noise – barriers', 'Engine braking noise' and 'Managing traffic noise – road surface'.

These documents contained very dense information, much of which I had not known before.

TEN

New facts of a technical nature
- The noises trucks make on roads are: tyre/road noise, aerodynamic noise, 'Body-slap', supplementary braking noise, and engine and mechanical noise. At higher speeds, the noise from tyres on the road surface is louder than engine noise.
- The type of road surface can affect noise levels by between six and ten decibels.
- 'Where required',[3] NZTA uses quiet road surfacing to reduce noise.

ELEVEN

New facts of a procedural nature
- NZTA has already decided to lay low-noise road surface along the northern portion of the Expressway, starting in December 2017.
- NZTA has appointed an Independent Review Panel 'to review compliance with noise approvals and also review the

reasonableness of noise from the expressway'.[4] The panel's findings will be available in November 2017.

• NZTA will then conduct an internal review of 'options to reasonably and safely address nuisance noise from rumble strip and bridge joints'.[5]

• NZTA will 'evaluate the findings and implement appropriate mitigation where it is considered practicable and effective'.[6]

Twelve

Degrees of separation
The Independent Review Panel is made up of two people, one of whom worked for NZTA as a principal environmental specialist responsible for noise and vibration, and simultaneously as a consultant, as recently as 2014. At the meeting on 4 October a member of the public challenged the capacity of someone with these close links to NZTA to be impartial.

She was told that a code of ethics for expert witnesses applies in this situation and that the New Zealand community of road noise experts is so small that all of its members have probably worked for NZTA at some point.

Thirteen

Trust update
On the trust side, NZTA had clearly invested time in preparing for this meeting. They had arranged for senior staff to be present, and they had brought these staff 50 kilometres from Wellington or from other places to meet with locals whom they knew were not happy. Information was given to residents by NZTA, both in conversation and in handout form. All NZTA's representatives at the meeting on 4 October had impressive qualifications in their own areas of

expertise. Everyone I met at the meeting from NZTA or the other companies seemed willing, on that day, in that situation, to listen to what the residents were saying. Some NZTA representatives took notes.

On the paranoia side, the meeting was not publicised and many householders living very close to the Expressway were unaware of it. One of the NZTA staff said to me that it would be good for these residents 'to vent'. That comment opens up the possibility that a meeting like this could be a form of 'going through the motions' of responsiveness to a community. Perhaps NZTA has evidence that a proportion of unhappy residents will say their piece at a meeting like this and, having let off steam, will then go home more willing to live with the noise from a road.

I notice that the independent review, to be followed by NZTA's decision about what mitigation is reasonable, is a typical government process. The powerful entity ruminates and announces its decision. The process of decision-making is all behind closed doors. All of this means there is little transparency about what weighting will be given to what factors.

At several points along the Expressway route, people waited, with varying levels of trust.

FOURTEEN

On 19 December 2017, the Independent Review Panel's report was released

The report was almost a month late and released only days before the Christmas holiday season. The review process itself was rigorous in a recursive, technical sort of way. The Board of Inquiry had consented to the Expressway back in April 2013 based on predictions of a certain level of noise which had been considered acceptable. The panel's role was checking the noise predictions against the noise data gathered after the Expressway opened, checking whether the Alliance had complied with construction requirements and checking whether decisions made by the Alliance during construction were reasonable. A lot of the report is taken up with comparison of noise measurements with the predicted noise measurements derived from computer modelling before construction. This is significant for subsequent projects, but does not address residents' concerns.

There are some criticisms in the report of the post-consent design process the Alliance used in construction of M2PP in respect of noise mitigation, and there is some dainty stepping out of the firing line by noise experts who make it clear that certain stages of the construction were not under their oversight.

The panel upheld some of the concerns residents had raised, especially the complaint about noise made by vehicles driving over Waikanae River bridge. From a resident's point of view the key recommendations are that NZTA should remove rumble strips from the left of the road in the vicinity of houses, offer ventilation systems for some specified houses so that they could keep their windows shut and therefore keep noise to an acceptable level, consider offering ventilation for certain other houses less severely affected, fix all bridge joints to reduce noise, fix the joints on the Waikanae River bridge in specified ways, maintain the low-noise surface of the road, install cameras to monitor engine braking and monitor traffic levels to see if they are higher than predicted, in which case the noise forecasts are too optimistic.

NZTA has the power to consider these recommendations and decide which it will act on.

Fifteen

The review panel's report

Near the end of the report is a summary paragraph where the panel shows some of its working assumptions.

> *Operational noise resulting from the M2PP has affected a number of residents in the vicinity of the M2PP. This is evident from the number of complaints about noise received by the Transport Agency. When a new road is built in the vicinity of PPFs [houses] where there were no major roads previously there is going to be an increase in traffic noise level and there will be people who are adversely impacted. NZ S6806 provides an approach to manage traffic noise levels. It is well known that people display different tolerance levels with respect to road-traffic noise depending on many factors and it is acknowledged that some residents will be* **annoyed†** *even when compliance with NZ6806 is achieved.*

> *The panel has found that while noise from the M2PP is clearly noticeable, including in areas that previously experienced minimal road-traffic noise, the noise is generally reasonable.*[7]

Interestingly, the panel was of the view that the noise complaints had been largely avoidable. Some complaints, deemed justified by the panel, were generated by entirely foreseeable problems with bridge expansion joints and their faulty construction. Other complaints came, the panel thought, from situations where the actual noise was very similar to what had been predicted prior to construction.

The panel was of the view that the Alliance had made a communication error. Residents had been told that noise would and did comply with the standard, instead of being told that there would be a change, sometimes a significant change, in their noise environment (*see* **honesty†**).

In other words, the residents might not have a point in legal terms, but NZTA should have told them what NZTA knew the noise situation would be and not spent so much energy trying to silence them with repetition of the legal situation. The panel thought residents would have adjusted better if this 'change' message, which fitted with their day-to-day experience, had been chosen in communications between the Alliance and NZTA and residents.

Sixteen

The mayor takes the noise standard 'upstairs'
In March 2018 I showed this record of the noise problem to the mayor of Kāpiti. He told me he had written to Phil Twyford, the Minister of Transport, urging him to accept that the noise standard NZS 6806 is not 'fit for purpose'. In his letter he makes the same point residents made at the public meeting in July 2017, that the noise from the Expressway is compliant with this standard but people cannot sleep (*see* **consent levels†**).

This advocacy may help people living near the Ōtaki to north of Levin Expressway, which is still in the route consultation phase, and I respect the mayor's efforts on their behalf. The mayor has moved on, and certainly it is his job to look ahead. It seems it is too late for the people near the Mackays to Peka Peka Expressway. Our road is built and it complies with NZS 6806 in most places.

If the road meets the noise standard, no matter whether it is recognised that the noise standard needs to be changed, there is nothing people living nearby can do except learn to live with the noise or sell the house, probably at a reduced price (*see* **losers†**). Each affected householder faces these choices alone.

Charles Brasch's Family History as a Painting, somewhat in the style of Colin McCahon's *The Canoe Tainui*

THE FIRST NAME is *Aaron*, and beside him, his brother *Moses*. Their names, alone on the first black panel, are the colour of sand.

After *Moses* and *Aaron* there are no names, no dates and no place names for something like three thousand years. This could be shown as eight panels of white canvas with the city of *Jerusalem* in the first panel, at the left-hand end. On the long white expanse, there could be a few wavy lines showing the *Mediterranean Sea*, the coast of *Cyprus*, *Athens*, *Thessalonica*, *Ephesus* and *Alexandria* and a single line which could be a road, leading through *Tunisia*, *Algeria* and *Morocco* to *Spain* and *France* and *Germany*. Eight panels of plain white canvas would also be possible, because really, we know nothing.

After this impenetrable white era marked with a tracery of possible journeys by people whose names we do not know, the background becomes black again. Black for silence. Names of the dead against black. Stories of the dead against silence.

Reuben Hallenstein is the colour of sand to show his direct connection to Aaron. Reuben Hallenstein married *Helene Michaelis* in 1825. They made three clever and fearless sons, *Bendix*, *Michaelis* and *Isaac Hallenstein*. Born as German Jews, the brothers passed time in *Manchester* where they began to speak English in the daytime. At night, in German, they talked of *Australia*, understanding as any Jewish trader would that there is more gold in supplying miners than in digging. All three brothers wanted to marry their housekeeper, *Mary Mountain*, but she chose Bendix, the lucky one. Bendix Hallenstein and Mary made four daughters, *Sara, Emily, Henrietta* and *Agnes*, but no sons. *Invercargill* is written in the colour of clay roads after weeks and weeks of sleet and rain, *Queenstown* in blue for the lake, *Dunedin* in yellow for the gold. Daughters all in gold too. Interesting girls, well educated and well loved, but the family business wanted men.

Sara Hallenstein married her first cousin *Willi Fels*. Willi Fels in thick gold paint and *Germany* in shiny red, close to his heart. Let's say Sara loved him, but the marriage was also practical. Yellow Dunedin sun shines on Willi Fels and fills his house, *Manono*.

Italian light surrounds Agnes Hallenstein. This light turns several corners, passes over a generation and falls on *Charles Brasch*, who needs it.

Willi Fels and Sara made four children, *Helene, Emily, Kate* and *Harold*. Harold is a soldier shape and then he is nothing but an empty bedroom full of model ships. Helene married *Hyam Brasch*, from *New Plymouth*. Helene's name is fine filigree gold to show that she does not live long. Hyam Brasch (later *Henry Brash*) is shiny black on black. Brasch by name, Brash by nature.

Helene and Hyam Brasch made two living children, a son *Charles* and a daughter *Lesley* (*Lel*). Charles with the Hallenstein deep-set eyes and seriousness of purpose. Charles with a ball of light from Great-Aunt Agnes on his left shoulder and his grandfather in his heart. Charles in gold, but not the son his father hoped for. Lel in fine filigree gold because, like her mother, she will die young.

After Charles and Lel, another long black panel with no names. If Helene Brasch and her third baby had lived and if that baby had been a son, Helene and Hyam would have given him an English-sounding name with no Jewish overtones. Edward, perhaps, or Cyril. The last black panel has space for him and all his descendants.

Indirections, Charles Brasch's (largely) Unloved Memoir

I HAVE HEARD *Indirections* described as 'reticent' and certainly it is
no Kardashian tell-all account of a life. Reading this memoir is more
like a friendship with a very sensitive, introverted English person.
You keep quiet and let them make the running. You keep paying
attention to what is being said, even if it takes a long time. You
assume that if they talk for a long time about plants or mountains
there will be a reason for that. You accept it all as the price of the
friendship.

Indirections was published in 1980, seven years after Brasch's death.
During those seven years James Bertram edited the manuscript of
the book down by about a half to the 424-page published version.
The year *Indirections* was published Charles Brasch was awarded
third place, posthumously, for the memoir at the Goodman Fielder
Wattie Book Awards. Despite this recognition, it is common to find
Indirections, unread and sometimes unopened, on the shelves of
literary people in New Zealand. When asked, some people say that
they started to read *Indirections* but did not finish it. I have found
multiple copies in second-hand shops and there is a copy on the
highest shelf of the bookcase at the Robert Lord Writers' Cottage
in Dunedin. I enjoyed finding it there and felt more at home in the
cottage as a result, but it did not look as if it was often used. I have
been asked, quite kindly, exactly how many unopened copies I have
seen on literary people's shelves, and, in all honesty, the answer is
fewer than five, one of which belonged to Robert Lord (of blessed
memory). The numbers are not compelling, but the point is I have
not found any fans of *Indirections*. By that I mean people with whom
I can discuss the book in detail. The cursor blinks for a long time

here to register the fact that after a lifetime of reading and writing, Charles Brasch, founding editor of *Landfall* and arbiter of literary taste, wrote a large book about himself that not many people are interested in. *I* like it though. I like it more than most of his poems.

I have spent quite a bit of time thinking about what causes potential readers of *Indirections* to leave it on the shelf or start the book but not finish it, and I think there are several possible answers. I cannot help but notice that Brasch himself is a figure that some people would like to leave on the shelf. I would prefer *not* to notice this, because I have a very typical Kiwi desire to avoid controversy, but it keeps forcing itself into my consciousness that among some bookish people I meet the best you could say is that there is not much knowledge of this man or curiosity about his work. I found this out by looking at their eyes. Here we are, talking books as we always do, and then I bring up Brasch and their eyes go dead. I don't mean to overstate this and I certainly do not have polls or statistics to back up my point, but I have been talking about Brasch for several years and I have had this 'dead eye' experience a number of times.

In the interests of balance I should say here that Brasch also has many loyal friends and supporters, as interest in the 2017 launch of the second volume of his journals has shown. Brasch has respect among people who knew him or know his poetry, are familiar with *Landfall* during his time as editor or are aware of his support for art and artists. People who knew him personally speak of his kindness and loyalty. Again without numerical evidence, my experience has been that attitudes to Brasch split roughly down generational lines.

Among younger writers the reaction at the mention of his name can be an irritated bristle, a pushing-away movement of the hands or some angry muttering about old white men who supported each other and failed to notice, spoke over or in subtle ways stifled diverse voices in New Zealand literature. Certainly the figures on percentages of male and female writers published in New Zealand in the years between World War II and the rise of feminism in the 1980s are stark. Given that Brasch was not just white and male but also wealthy, he might, with some validity, be seen as a person of privilege as well as power in the literary world. Perhaps a memoir which, by definition, is at least somewhat about its author, would fail to engage people who are just not interested in, or have antipathy towards, wealthy, influential, white males. I understand that position. But I think it is a bit too simplistic to equate Brasch with all the ideas of the literary nationalists or their times, especially when Brasch's own aesthetic could hardly have been further from their austere tone. He doesn't fit into any single category, and neither does his memoir.

Brasch's memoir covers the period 1909–46. Reading about that time, there is often an unquestioning acceptance of the dominant place of white people. It is distasteful when you encounter it, and you meet it quite quickly in Brasch's memoir. On page 19 there is a detailed description of how Willi Fels, Charles Brasch's grandfather, used to search for what the children called 'Maori curios' at Pipikaretu beach. These 'curios' were adzes, fish-hooks, flint knives, drills, stone sinkers, greenstone and whaletooth pendants. On the slopes above the beach, perhaps with a view down to where Fels was picking up his finds to take away to his own collection or to the museum, there was 'a dilapidated Maori cottage where we might see a few children, sometimes a cow or a rather sorry horse'. But, Brasch says, he never played with the Māori children. He was part of a large party, he says, and there were always children of friends or relations to play with. The Māori house and the children were part of another world and one which you could ignore, all the while buying your milk from the people in the dilapidated cottage.

Brasch's grandfather's archaeological practice enacts, albeit in a rather scholarly form, the colonial idea that whatever you could find in New Zealand was there for the taking. And it does not seem to have occurred to Brasch, even when he wrote the memoir as an older man, that these 'curios' might have been made by ancestors of the people in the dilapidated cottage. So yes, there are cultural perspectives in the memoir that are at odds with current ideas. The example I have cited is a singleton amongst all the content of the memoir, but it is there.

I have been thinking about why I was able carry on reading after this, and whether I would carry on reading a book if a writer described Jewish cultural objects with similar lack of respect or Jewish people with so little sense of them as people. Actually, this is a reasonably common experience. Usually it is in the way a Jewish character is described, or perhaps a brief snide comment about Jews, sometimes buried in a metaphor. Some of my favourite writers do it: George Orwell for example, and George Eliot. I read on, but there is a stone in my shoe for a few pages. If the snide comments about Jews are not frequent, I can still enjoy the author's craft and thinking, but there is an unease that never quite goes away. I think I put the racism I have described from *Indirections* aside a bit, as I do with anti-Semitism, and say to myself that this was of its time. I have a desire to examine the past, and sometimes I need to separate myself from aspects of it. But I am not usually tempted to pillory the past for its 'errors' because I can already feel myself and my present slipping away into the new past. However, glimpses of prejudices that other people may not see are very important and personal matters, so other readers may well have a different threshold for objection or resistance or see different problems from me. I choked and coughed a bit, but I carried on.

From page eight, when Brasch talks about his mother, how she died and how it affected him when he lost her just before his fifth birthday, I am, at least provisionally, 'in' this story. I found the little boy who lost his mother moving and I think most people would.

I choose to read a memoir for all sorts of reasons, but the proximity of another human being is certainly one of them.

Indirections was written many years after the events it describes. In between the events and the writing, Brasch had lived his life. He says he uses his journals to help him remember how things were, and *Indirections* is full of evidence of that. But there is a difference between the journals and the memoir. The man writing *Indirections* knows how things turned out. The narrator, you might say, is a man of the present and the past. Amos Oz once described the writer S.Y. Agnon as a man with several shadows. The author of this memoir is a man with several shadows too. I feel this when Brasch is describing **anti-Semitism*** in New Zealand. 'No-one of Jewish birth should count on being accepted,' he says on page 110. He is talking here about his father's anxieties about acceptance in Dunedin business circles, but that declarative sentence is much wider in scope than one Jewish man in Dunedin in the 1920s and '30s. To me this feels like a man who knows about the Jewish holocaust.

A memoir is about place as well as time. Charles Brasch travelled extensively in his adult life but his memoir makes it clear that, for Brasch, Dunedin, and more specifically a block of perhaps two square kilometres of north-facing hillside, was Ground Zero. Brasch grew up in an enclave of wealthy, mostly Jewish families, who all lived in big houses near each other in the Royal Terrace, London Street part of Dunedin. The houses themselves sometimes had colonial pedigrees like his parents' house, Bankton, which had belonged to Thomas Burns and Sir Robert Stout, or they were built on a grand scale, like **Manono***, Brasch's grandfather Willi Fels' house. Brasch continued to live in this area, although not in a grand house, until he died in 1973.

From their houses on the hill, the Fels/Brasch family drove, took trains, rode in service cars, walked and picnicked their way around

Otago Harbour, Dunedin's surrounding hills and Central Otago. Willi Fels adopted Dunedin as his home by walking its hills, brewing tea in a billy, building a house, making a garden where native and introduced plants were both encouraged, paying close attention to the family business and making donations to cultural causes. Charles's father, **Hyam Brasch***, wanted Dunedin to adopt him (*see also* **anti-Semitism***). He changed his name to Henry Brash, joined clubs and played sport and card games to seem adoptable.

Charles Brasch, the next generation, was born to Dunedin and remains its son. From the time he began editing *Landfall* until near his death, Brasch involved himself in civic and regional issues. At a time when the New Zealand government would sell a lake or a river for a song, and was doing exactly that in secret agreements with international companies to provide cheap power, Brasch saw hills and lakes and rivers as worth keeping. At a time when Dunedin's old buildings were seen as a burden, he knew that if those stone buildings were pulled down, nothing like them would come again. Brasch valued what was there, close at hand, and he did not soften his views for the sake of fashion, to please powerful people or because he was in a minority.

Brasch thought New Zealand had a propensity to choose quick and dirty solutions to problems. I challenge anyone to disagree with that, then or now. He wanted Dunedin and New Zealand people to think about how things *could* work and not just do the cheapest thing or the first thing that entered their heads. Sometimes he would get a polite but dismissive response, for example when he suggested that the University of Otago should develop an architectural plan for the campus to integrate old and new buildings. Other times the authorities kept quiet and proceeded with their plans, but Brasch never left off trying to get people to stop and think about how the country *could* be and how Dunedin could be. None of this is in the memoir, because the memoir ends in 1946, but for me it is another part of the context for the memoir and part of why I am interested in *Indirections*.

My own memory starts in the early 1960s so I don't have personal experience of time before that. But even in the 1960s, New Zealand could be pretty grim. There was less of some things in the 1960s, like cheap clothes and cafés and eating out, but there were many more sheep. Sheep were such a strong part of the consciousness that when I was a young teacher the father of one of the children in my class called me a 'two tooth'. I didn't know a two tooth was a maiden ewe and when I found out, I did not appreciate the reference to my reproductive potential. Sex wasn't a joke. If you 'got yourself' pregnant, your family was ashamed. If you lived with your boyfriend and were not married, your family was ashamed. Men and women could be forced into marriage. I saw that happen to two 17-year-olds in 1977. Regardless of your gender, it was lonely in Masterton or Hāwera or Cheviot if you did not watch rugby or cricket or play tennis or join in the after-match drinks at the club. It was hard to find people to talk books with. When I was in Masterton and Cheviot books were the light falling on a dark landscape. They were my necessary protection, but there were never enough of them.

Thank God, I say, for readers' and writers' festivals, for every government or philanthropic fund, every artist's residence, for the Whitireia writing programme that opens its doors to all-comers, for online writing courses, for all the schools of writing, for book groups and writing groups, for the university presses, for libraries, which are a wonder that does not belong in these times, for all the writers who wrote their books at night after the kids were in bed and never had enough money to get their teeth fixed, and for the thousands and thousands of readers who have created a larger literary community to which I can belong. I believe Brasch's activities helped to build that literary community. I am grateful to Brasch for his vision of New Zealand as a place that would one day be more than farms and draughty wooden houses. I am not suggesting that he was alone or first in these cultural activities, or that his activities could not be questioned or criticised, but I see him as having put his shoulder to the wheel, here, in New Zealand, as it was in 1946, and changed things. I see myself as a recipient of all that he and others did to make this a place where literary pursuits are legitimate, at least for me. That process of legitimisation is a long way from finished. Māori and Pacific writing is still greatly under-represented in New Zealand publishing and Māori and Pacific students are similarly under-represented in writing courses. These are the sorts of things I say at parties when people say they have a grudge against Brasch. My voice sounds distorted, even to me, and I hear the words falling into a generational and gender crevasse.

A memoir is a searchlight, not daylight. Although it describes the outer movements of Brasch's early life, *Indirections* is most of all a memoir of the development of his inner life, of the sensibilities which made him a poet and led him to the decision to return to New Zealand and begin *Landfall*. A memoir, like any book, is also a method. *Indirections* is unrelenting in its detail about the land, the sky, the sea and the botanical world of New Zealand. For all of us, family is the kindling of our consciousness, one stick laid at an angle to another, ready to burn, and experiences are the match. For Brasch something he saw in the natural world was often the match. The shapes and colours of the land, the sea and the plants sometimes had symbolic and metaphysical meaning but Brasch was first and always concerned with beauty.

As a reader, and as a person, I am not in close touch with the world of nature. The sheer volume of botanical detail sometimes caused me to fall into a deep trance in which I was dulled to the significance of what Brasch was describing. A friend put it more simply. It's boring, she said, as she showed me her copy of

Indirections, bookmarked at about page 50. If I were to avoid those deep trances, I had to find a method of reading this book. I found that if I slowed down and thought of *Indirections* as a big experience, like going to a 12-hour orchestral concert of a work you have never heard before, or entering a tall building and meeting a painting the height of 10 football fields, the book started to open itself to me, which allowed me to open myself to it.

Why would I persevere with a book that takes this much effort to avoid falling asleep? Because it is a bit weird that it is only half the book Brasch intended, and you can't help but wonder what is in the other half. Because, with its relentless David Foster Wallace-level of detail, there is nothing else quite like *Indirections*. Because, although it is more 'about' New Zealand than many botanical texts, it feels like a stranger here. Because the whole book is a **grass railway***. Because Brasch recorded moments of beauty and posed existential questions in his poems, but in *Indirections* flowers and colours appear in long complex sentences and paragraphs, ideas and emotions stretch out and connect with each other, and I cannot help but marvel at the precision of the engineering and the delicacy of the result. Because the man you meet in the memoir is brave in a Greek kind of way. And because Charles Brasch turned his cultural and artistic ideas into actions.

Brasch thought the New Zealand he returned to after the war was, to put it politely, a bit rough and ready. He thought this would be a better place if more questions were asked about our lives here. He thought that if our painters, composers and writers took more risks, if their work grabbed us by the throat with its intensity, they could force us to be less smug. Brasch thought that if artists were better supported they would be more likely to deliver the adventurous work that was needed for the task of examining of our lives here. He talks about this in the memoir.

In New Zealand it has always been dangerous to stand out. Charles Brasch knew that and he still wrote this unusual book. As it happened, he died before the public read it, but it might not have been that way.

The State of Things at the House

March 2017: The stucco exterior of Charles Brasch's house is presently painted white. Under that the original timber cladding shows signs of dry rot. Windows influenced by the arts and crafts movement and a dwarf maple outside the front bedroom are the only signs that beauty mattered here. When I arrived at 36a **Heriot Row***, late in the afternoon, two builders were packing their tools into their trucks. They clearly wanted to get away for the night but they could not leave while I was there. Even after I promised not to go inside, the older of the two builders followed me around while I took photographs of rotted rimu boards, nails from the 1930s and new interior pine framing for the apartments. As I was leaving, the builder asked me who the guy was that used to live in this house. I told him the owner had been a poet and had started a major literary journal. That was our conversation.

Later I heard, third-hand, that this same builder had told Travis **VanBrasch*** (*see* **Brasch, Braschi, VanBrasch**), a descendant of the American branch of the Brasch family, that he didn't feel entirely comfortable gutting the house of a famous man. I also heard that in the years since his death, Charles Brasch's house had been occupied by a painter who covered the walls with her work. My informant did not know the woman's name but said her work was impressive.

May 2017: At first glance not much seems to have changed since my first visit to Charles's house two months ago. There is still a skip outside, the porch and front lawn of the house are covered with chunks of broken concrete and scraps of timber, and there is a portaloo just outside the front door. But there are subtle changes. In March, there were pallets stacked with timber and GIB board in the garage. Now there is a tall stack of empty pallets. Last time the leaves on the maple outside the front room were just starting to turn red. This time the maple has a few red leaves left and all the rest are brown and dead. In March, there were two builders working flat out on demolition. This time the site seems to be quiet.

As I wander up the side path I notice that one of the panels of glass in the side door is broken. I'm thinking about how that pane of glass might have broken; about carrying long bits of timber, about strong winds blowing an old door. Thinking about vandals. Thinking about rats. And then I hear noises from inside the house. I consider making a hasty exit but decide I will look like a criminal if I run away, so I stand still and wait to see who or what is going to open the side door.

The guy who opens the door looks a little surprised to see me. I tell him my name. I say I am visiting the house because it used to belong to a famous poet, and I say the poet's name. I ask if he is the owner. He says no, he is the kitchen guy. He asks me when the poet lived there. I tell him. He says that he was *born* in 1973. Then he asks me if the poet died in the house. I say yes, I think so. He asks me to spell the name of the poet. Brasch must have been Jewish, he says. I look at the kitchen guy to see if he is Jewish, because why else would you say that? I don't feel like discussing the theist views or cultural identity of Charles Brasch with the kitchen guy so I say that the poet was from a Jewish family.

The kitchen guy looks at me and says, 'So are you kind of stalking this dead guy?' I say yes. He says, 'So you'll want to come and stay when the place is finished.' He does not say this as a question. Probably not, I say. I do not share with him the distinction which makes it reasonable, or even necessary, for me to visit the house but would not permit me to bring my overnight bag and sleep where the poet slept, because that would be a step too far. The kitchen guy asks me if the poet earned his living from poetry. I say no, not really. I guess he hasn't met many poets. Poets don't usually get new kitchens.

December 2017: The maple is covered in rich dark-red leaves. The side path has been smoothed and shingle laid where there used to be deep mud. The carport is empty. A retaining wall has been built half way up the slope of the front lawn and now there is a flat area beside the front door and a couple of chairs where you could, on a fine day, sit outside. I am standing half way up the path, considering these changes, when a woman greets me. She is the owner. I explain my interest in the house and she offers to show me around. She only has a few minutes, she says, because the first tenants are due to arrive.

We go in the side door to the kitchen. The benches and the cupboards are shiny and white. This was the original kitchen, the owner says. A new dining table and some chairs are already in place but there are door handles and light fittings and bits of packing on the table and little piles of plaster dust on the floor. I am a bit surprised that tenants would be moving in when this last tidying work has not been done, but the owner does not seem to notice the dust and the rubbish. I can tell that she is proud of how the house looks now. She takes me into a bedroom at the back of the house, with a sunroom opening off it.

The owner explains that the sunroom is not a very practical use of space in a rental property but she has decided to retain the house's original spaces. She had intended to keep the original internal walls of the house too, but when the builders took the lining off the walls they saw that in some places the walls had vertical studs but no horizontal dwangs. Builders told her there had been two separate fires inside the walls, but they could not tell when those fires had happened or what had caused them.

Liking the Local, a reading of Charles Brasch's poem 'The Clear'

The Clear

It is all the sky
Looks down on this one spot,
All the mountains that gather
In these rough bleak small hills
To blow their great breath on me,
And the sea that glances in
With shining eye from his epic southern prairies;
Working together
Time-long
World's way.[1]

The Clear* is a park in Dunedin's Town Belt. People play soccer there. Charles Brasch used to come to this park and look out across North Dunedin to the hills, and east towards the harbour and the sea. 'The Clear' is also a poem. Its title resonates with mysticism. It suggests a state of mind attained after many travails, or, in physical form, a place you might go to understand things that are normally obscured.

Right from the first line the scale of everything is cosmic. When 'all the sky looks down on this one spot' I feel a blast of Old Testament divinity. Pretty soon it is obvious that The Clear is a New Zealand place. I recognise its 'rough bleak' hills.

This is me now, liking the local. When I was younger, I was not
a fan of the local or Brasch's poems. In those days I was slightly
irritated by places like Waianakarua, a tiny town on the main
highway from Ōamaru to Dunedin which had never done anything
bad to me except not be 'sympathique'. New Zealand was mostly
made up of places like this, and in my mind the only thing to do
with all this nothing was to try to pass by as rapidly as possible and
hope you ended up somewhere urban before it got dark. I found it
annoying and also embarrassing that someone would try to make a
poem out of a place with nothing except sheep and a service station.
But that, as I say, was when I was young, before I noticed Dunedin's
yellow light.

I'm impressed that Brasch, writing this poem in the iconoclastic
late '60s or early '70s, would invoke something as close to the divine
as this sky, in such an unabashed way. Even at 64, there are many
topics I don't have the courage to write about, or perhaps more
accurately, stand behind. I wrote a poem once where a sky-being
looks down through the skylight of an apartment block on a young
man lying in a dishevelled bed. I loved the tube of light falling on
the young man whose pale skin and black hair seemed somehow to
be offset with a dash of crimson velvet. I liked the dust motes and
the young man's sleepy awareness of warmth and light. But I wasn't
convinced I had invoked a credible sense of a sky-being. Writing
about the divine, I decided, is as hard as writing science fiction.
Brasch suffers no such timidity. He makes the whole sky, the wind
from the mountains and the southern sea converge at this soccer
ground and engage with the place. Then he makes the wind breathe
on him. Not on the place, on him. I like the nerve of that.

The whole poem is small, fewer than 50 words in total, which
makes every word seem important. The word 'me', the only time
the writer appears as himself, is such a tiny inclusion, in one way so
modest and unassuming. And yet the word 'me' rings out like a bell,

calling me in to the scene. Poetry is not a rational thing, so I will just say, without explanation or justification, that because he is there, as himself, I can be there.

After the poet has felt the gaze of the sky and the breath of the mountains, the shining eye of the sea 'glances in'. Not the half-tamed sea of the inner harbour, the mirror-glass sea of the road to Aramoana. Not the safe-for-children sea of the saltwater baths at St Clair. The shining eye of the sea in this poem comes from the Roaring Forties, the 'epic southern prairies' of water and waves. I have seen this sea. It swirls deep and dangerous onto the rocks at the end of the spit at Aramoana. Gannets fall from the sky and selkies roll in and out of the kelp as if it was easy to live there. The best humans can do at the spit is build and rebuild a temporary projection from the shore into the sea. A rusting tangle of wood and metal that used to be a railway runs along beside the current spit. The wind here, the 'great breath', is strong enough to rock old railway sleepers bolted to slabs of concrete. The prairie of water that we glimpse here is never finished with its fierce coming and going.

The setting of this poem is much more specific than New Zealand. It is Dunedin. Once I had read that The Clear, in physical form, was a soccer ground, I knew without being told that there would be rough-mown grass and a caretaker's shed where the mower is stored. I knew it would smell of damp trees and mud. More importantly, I knew there would be sticky grey clay underneath that grass and that occasionally the clouds would part and blue sky would be visible over the grassy place. I know that circle of 'rough bleak' hills that surrounds the city, too, and the exact shades of green created by scrubby mānuka, macrocarpa and gorse.

Brasch and I share a fondness for the word 'rough'. 'Bleak', however, is a word I never use. When I was a child the wind that came from the mountains further back, behind the hills, cut through my woolly jerseys as though they were lace. Back then adults would use this word 'bleak' when speaking of the wind. But 'bleak' was much more than the wind. 'Bleak' was them, their brick houses with tiny windows, the grey prickles of their upholstery fabric, the meat you saved for tomorrow, the cold you felt on your back even when you faced the fireplace and, strangely, the brief appearance and rapid disappearance of the sun. I was afraid that if I emerged from my book, I would die of 'bleak'. To protect myself I tried not to look at telegraph poles sticking out of the mud at Waitati. Whenever we arrived at a new town I stayed in the car until the last possible minute and, above all, I never voluntarily touched the earth or allowed it to touch me. I didn't really know what I wanted the world to be like, but this bleak Dunedin and this bleak 'nature' definitely was not it.

I have heard of children who have a feeling they do not belong to the parents who are raising them. I had a feeling that I did not belong to the country I was living in. Along the way that has changed and now I feel that I do belong to Aotearoa New Zealand and to Dunedin. None of it belongs to me, and I don't think it should, but I belong to it. Last September in the Dunedin Botanic Garden I read a sign about the activities of the Otago Acclimatisation Society, which brought plants and animals from the old country and tested them to see which would thrive here. As I thought about that, a long pendulum began to swing inside me, which I understood to be a biological proof of successful transplantation.

My 64-year-old self is interested in whether 'The Clear' is an old man's poem, the encounters with the sublime sky and sea perhaps something akin to the awareness of white light that some people say they see in the moments before death. I don't want to jump to any hasty conclusions so I look back at older poems written by a younger Brasch. I see that wind and waves and hills and mānuka and time are all there in 1939, in Brasch's first collection,

The Land and the People, and Other Poems.[2] But here, in later life, the preoccupations of this poem, the sky, the light, the sea, the wind, the mountains and the work of time, have been reduced and reduced until the poem is down to an assertive and strongly flavoured essence. I detect an impatience with distraction or untrustworthy consolation in this poem, but however hard I try I cannot quite locate the place in the poem where I receive this message.

Although I do not live in Dunedin now, I remember the streets near the soccer ground well, which leads me to create, in my mind, a version of the poet's experience of walking from his house to The Clear. I start my hypothetical re-creation before the poem starts. As the poet walks into the Town Belt, along Queens Drive and Lachlan Avenue towards The Clear, he sees in his mind's eye how *the place* would be when he got there. How *he* would be. When you travel the same route often you know the places where you have doubts and where you can expect to be uplifted. I know for instance that sometimes in Dunedin at three o'clock, no matter what has happened before, yellow light falls over everything, creating a gold-edged warmth. This yellow light, which I first noticed through the kitchen window when I was in my late teens, struck me then as new and beautiful. It made me look out that window each time I passed by. It made me notice the trees on our section, and it made me notice light. I had not noticed light before. There is no yellow light in the poem 'The Clear', but I add some, because it could happen in the moment of the sky clearing. Then I take things a bit further because Brasch noticed 'the light on his face' in another poem,[3] because I know how it feels to have the sun shine on your face and because light is more than a colour. A clearing of the sky makes you want to take in warmth, take in every possible moment of it, because there are plenty of days and even years when there is nothing else as simple and benign as this feeling of warmth.

If it was one of the gold-edged days, I might, somewhat sheepishly, lie down full length on the grass, consciously put aside warnings about damp, and close my eyes. The slightest warmth on my face, a moment's separation between clouds through which the sun could warm me or even the briefest softening of the easterly wind would be enough to take me deep into the deep space between the sea and the sky, so deep that I could forget the shadow coming, miss the beginning of its crawl over the mower shed and across the grass, miss the sudden silence of the gulls and the long slow change of my trousers and shirt from chill to wet. I could lie so still, dreaming all, that a boy arriving for soccer practice might rouse me with a scooping-up, lifting kind of kick, saying later that he had mistaken me for a pile of dead brown leaves.

Despite my enthusiasm, my fall into this poem is, to an extent, a house built on sand. Alan Roddick, Brasch's literary executor, selected 'The Clear' for the anthology *Charles Brasch: Selected poems* from a folder containing unpublished poems. Roddick has given 'The Clear' an important place as the final poem in the collection. However, as Roddick says in the introduction, Brasch may not have been finished with this poem.

The final three lines of 'The Clear', dealing with time, are somewhat different in tone from the rest of the poem. The words are blunt messages, banged together and heavy footed. When I read this poem with a U3A group of poetry lovers they told me these three lines were the most meaningful parts of the poem. It is simple, they said. We pass quickly, but all of this – the sea, the sky and the wind – will always be here. That is the way of the world. They smiled kindly at me in the way older people often do.

The fact that The Clear was, in one sense, a soccer ground turned out to be no obstacle to moments of cosmic wonder. But of course I know that. You can find grand beings in muddy and mundane places, but you have to get out of the car.

The Lady Engine

ONE

A little boy and his dream

Charles Orwell Brasch was born in Dunedin in 1909. As a boy he
had a recurring dream of a train, which he wrote about twice, many
years later. Once, he made the dream into a poem and placed it in
his 1969 collection *Not Far Off*, and once he placed it in his memoir,
Indirections, in prose. By chance I read the poem first. Then I found
the prose version. After that I read the poem again. After that I
considered the context of the dream in *Indirections*, and in *Not Far
Off*. I looked up all the names of people and places I didn't know.
Then my heart melted. The poem 'On Joy and Other Obligations', in
Section Ten, records this moment of identification.

Once I could make sense again, I thought about why Brasch might
have written about the same thing twice.

TWO

The death of Helene Brasch changed everything

In his journals and in his memoir, Charles Brasch describes people's
looks in great detail. Their looks are their character in physical
form. Cousin Brightie, for example, is 'round-eyed, slightly doll-
like, conventional, wore rings and necklaces and pearl ear-rings and
dressed well; I see her colour as powder-blue'.[1] Brasch was also much
concerned with people's attractiveness. His insistence on this form
of analysis sometimes makes me uncomfortable because I cannot
help but imagine what he would have seen in me. But regarding
his parents, I am willing to join him in character deduction based

on appearance because, in an easy Californian way, it feels as if it has some validity and because Helene Brasch and Hyam Brasch are dead, so their feelings cannot be hurt.

Hyam Brasch, Charles's father, was handsome and sporty, a slim man with short-cut hair 'New Zealand fashion',[2] nine years older than his wife Helene. As a student at the University of Melbourne, Hyam Brasch rowed in a winning eights crew and was a competitive runner. He dressed better than most Dunedin people and often wore a flower in the lapel of his jacket. He 'carried himself with assurance and never lost his figure.[3] Did he really feel assured? Brasch thought so.

Helene Brasch, Charles Brasch's mother, was, Brasch says, 'small but active and strong, with long black hair thick and waving and parted in the middle, deep blue very bright eyes and dark lashes, pale skin without colour … and thought very beautiful.[4] A photograph of Helene, holding toddler Charles on her lap, shows her looking into the camera from under her rather bushy eyebrows and little Charles looking a bit wriggly and 'put upon'. Like the adult Charles, Helene has a long face, dark eyebrows and an intent expression. Something about her face says she is a serious person, but she has a lightness about her too.

World War I had not happened yet. A big family party, led by Charles's grandparents Willi and Sara Fels, used to take their summer holidays together at Karitane. Young women sang and laughed while they dried their long hair in the sun and boisterous young men played cricket and called to each other in their loud voices. There were bonfires on the lawn and potatoes in the embers and one night Charles remembers being carried up the stairs to his bed, held in someone's arms. He thinks this was his father.

Helene knew how to love. Charles describes his mother as 'unusually tender as well as happy, even among her warm-hearted family; she

Helene Brasch and Charles[5]

felt deeply and her face was always thoughtful. She lavished her tenderness on her children.'[6] Hyam Brasch's family was not so happy. His mother had died before he reached adolescence and after her death a rift developed between father and son.

What does love sound like? Charles remembers lying in bed one night hearing his father calling his mother for dinner. 'He-*le*-ne!'

Hyam called. And from his father's voice Charles knew that they were happy and that his father adored her.

Everything seemed set for Charles and his younger sister Lel to have a wool-clad, late Edwardian, upper-middle-class, German-Jewish, New Zealand childhood. But when Charles was four, his mother Helene died while pregnant with her third child. She was 31. In his memoir Brasch says, 'Her death was the first blow to shatter the family. It also, I see looking back, ended my childhood proper, shortly before my fifth birthday.'[7] After Helene died a rift developed between Charles and his father, just as there had been between Hyam and his widowed father a generation earlier.

A few years after his mother died, this little boy, separated from his father by complex and painful emotions, had a recurrent dream about a Lady Engine. And many, many years later Charles Brasch, a man in late middle age, wrote about the dream he had as a boy. Twice.

Lady Engine

The Lady Engine steamed across the road.
Quietly, black-shining.

Pavement, hedges, houses
Drew back to give her way
Through afternoon, no one about.

Slowly passing, she looked at me,
Not turning her head.
Grave, kindly, silent. Looking.
I gazed back. We gazed at each other.
Nothing said.

What did we feel, Lady Engine?
Only felt; no words. Gazing.
Gazing took our breath.

Gazing till she drew away,
Not looking now.
I followed with my look.
Past the hedges, past the houses,
Out of day.

Gone. Vanished.

No sound, no smoke in air, no rails crossing the road,
No sign of stain anywhere.
Houses, hedges, pavement, all as before.

Gone, gone.
Where?
No where?

Here or
Therewhere –
Lady Engine:

Under the world.

THREE

The Lady Engine poem
I came across 'Lady Engine' in the 2015 *Selected Poems* collection. This poem seemed different from anything I had read of Brasch until then. It is fragmented, like a piece of discordant music. The line 'Only felt; no words. Gazing' is an example. I wondered why Brasch had chosen this effect. He often uses questions in his poems. The three questions in this poem are a direct challenge to any sense of fluency. When I tried reading the poem out loud I couldn't decide how to intone 'No where?' Near the end of the poem, among other fragments, there is one of Brasch's made-up words, 'Therewhere'. I marked this poem 'Strange!' in the Index of Titles and First Lines.

Brasch often writes about places and people, but this poem is 'about' a machine. The words 'Lady Engine' themselves set off little bells. As a child, I was taught to refer to any woman as a 'lady', the term indicating respect and gender. I might have imposed this later, once I knew about the little boy who had a dream, but I heard something child-like in Brasch's use of the word 'lady'.

At this stage of my life, the term 'lady' is first and foremost part of the shorthand of English class structure. A description Brasch wrote of a woman called Anne showed me that, in 1940 anyway, he also used the word 'lady' to make a distinction between different sorts of women.

> *No, I do not take to Anne; she has no grace & gentleness of either speech or movement; an almost harsh forced laugh; no poise & no reserve. She is not only not a lady (appearing rather to emphasise that she isn't) but does not seem womanly ...*[8]

The engine is a 'lady' then, not just female. She has grace and gentleness; poise and reserve. When you add 'engine' to 'lady' you arrive at a composite refined female being, who is both human and machine. Her 'black-shining' body is literally like any steam engine and less literally like Helene Brasch's hair.

In 1969, when the poem 'Lady Engine' appeared in Brasch's collection *Not Far Off*, steam engines were outdated technology, but when the dreams took place, steam engines were the most powerful machines on land. As a little boy, Charles Brasch would have seen steam trains at the Dunedin railway station, caught glimpses of flames inside the firebox, seen sparks fly out of the chimney as the engine built up pressure, and heard the pistons hiss. The 'Lady Engine' both is and is not like other steam engines. Off track and steaming across a road, she is not where she is supposed to be. And she is not noisy. She is 'grave, kindly, silent ...'

I have to confess I thought of Freud as soon as I read 'Lady Engine', because the engine is such a powerful image. Using the Freudian idea that dream objects and events are symbols of what they resemble, the 'Lady Engine' might 'be' Brasch's mother because both disappear. She might also be male, because she emits steam which could stand in for ejaculation. She might be other things, too, beyond my amateur psychoanalytic imagination. Brasch was interested in his own dreams, and recorded other dreams in his journals. Sometimes he analysed them himself, but not this time. The 'Lady Engine' poem is the dream pure, with no added commentary.

In the poem, the 'Lady Engine' appears, she and the dreamer say nothing, but they gaze at each other with such intensity that 'Gazing took our breath away'. The words 'gaze' and 'look', in different forms, are repeated nine times in this short poem. We could not have any clearer indication that this exchange of looking is at the core of the poem. It is in the exchange of looking and feeling that the poet knows the engine's kindness and her seriousness. Then she draws away, and he continues to look after her. Everything in the ordinary world is just as it was before she arrived. That seems important too. The poet knows that the Lady Engine has disappeared from view, but exists still, 'Under the world'. This is the last line of the poem. It is too simple to say her existence is some consolation for her absence, but it makes a difference to know that she is somewhere.

FOUR

The Lady Engine in Indirections

There was a recurrent dream about a Lady Engine. I was walking up Royal Terrace with Miss Darling. As we turned the corner into Cobden Street, the Lady Engine steamed slowly from among the houses and gardens on the shady side of the street, passed across

*it, and disappeared behind the hawthorn hedge that enclosed the
garden of the Tower House – the old wooden house with the tower
room on top, part of St Hilda's School. We stood quite near, waiting
to cross the line. The Lady Engine seemed to turn, as she slowly
passed, and looked down at me – to her, clearly, I was alone. It was
a kindly look; not because of any smile or movement of the lips, or
any tenderness in the eyes, but because she, the Lady Engine, knew
I was there and gazed calmly down at me as she passed. Waiting
before she came, I had been frightened, my heart beat unnaturally,
my head grew tight; but now I had no fear. I stood and watched
her, not moving, simply there.*

*I cannot tell what she was like. Being an engine she was of course
dark – blue-black and shiny; and being a lady she must have had
eyes and a mouth and hair, but I do not remember them. The loud
hissing steam and the muscular pistons that I feared before she
came into sight did not frighten me once she was actually there.
I did not notice them. So she turned to me – with no movement
of the neck and shoulders or inclining of the body – and slowly
passed, looking, and was straight again as she disappeared. Her
grave expressionless look as she passed by said plainly that she
would return, and that I would be there again waiting for her, in
fear before and after but impassive in her presence. Not, of course,
that this had been her first coming. There was no first. I had always
known her.*[9]

FIVE

I had always known her

The dream in prose form is much more grounded than the poem.
In *Indirections* the Lady Engine appears in a specific place – Cobden
Street, Dunedin – as Charles and his nanny, Miss Darling, turn
the corner from Royal Terrace. The Lady Engine appears from the
houses and gardens and steams across the street as she does in the

poem, but in the memoir version she disappears behind a hawthorn
hedge into the garden of St Hilda's school. So many things are still
there, in Dunedin, from Brasch's time. When I went to Cobden
Street, hoping for a Lady Engine reenactment, the streets Brasch
walked with his nanny, the houses he lived in and visited, St Hilda's
school, even the hawthorn hedge, were still there, exactly as they
were when he had the dream and when he wrote about his dream.
These days there is a pedestrian crossing in Royal Terrace, just
before the intersection with Cobden Street, about where the Lady
Engine would have crossed. I peeked behind the hawthorn hedge
just in case there was a black and shining steam engine waiting in
there, but she had not come for me.

As with the poem, the Lady Engine's 'kindly' gaze, directed at the
boy, is at the heart of the dream. Brasch is at pains to say that this
look was not made up of smiling lips or warmth in the eyes, or any
of the usual ingredients in a kindly look. The Lady Engine just 'gazed
calmly' at the boy as she passed. A calm gaze does not promise
redemption or even consolation. It is a kind of witnessing, a gesture
that acknowledges the nature of a situation. In both the poem and
the prose, descriptions of the gaze are about stillness and being able
to bear, or contain, what is happening.

Apart from its specified location, the prose version of the dream
has several other elements that are not part of the poem. First, the
reader is told that the Lady Engine is part of a recurring childhood
dream. Once you know this, the poem is still strange, but it is a great
deal more comprehensible. Secondly, the Lady Engine in *Indirections*
knows the boy is alone. In a literal sense, he is accompanied by Miss
Darling. But in an emotional sense the dream acknowledges that
this little boy feels alone. He has a father, fond grandparents whom
he sees almost every day, many cousins and uncles and aunts and
a sister. But he does not have a mother now. The man writing the
memoir does not remember his mother's hair or eyes. Nor does he

remember much about what the Lady Engine looked like in the dream. Her 'lady' qualities, her hair, her eyes and her mouth, have faded from his memory as have his mother's hair, mouth and eyes. When, as an older man, he thinks back to childhood, all he has of his mother is a few photographs, his father's voice calling her name and her genetic imprint on his face and body.

In prose, the dreamer knows the Lady Engine will come. Waiting, he is terrified. But once she is really there, he is no longer afraid. She is still herself, still an engine, but her 'hissing steam' and 'muscular pistons' are not so terrible once she arrives. In the prose account the Lady Engine's body is present. She is an engine, so she is rigid. But somehow, without moving her neck or shoulders or inclining her body, she turns to look at the boy as she passes, and then is straight again after she has passed him. This is spelled out carefully. I am not sure what it means.

Finally, and most importantly, in the prose version the dreamer knows that this is not the first time the Lady Engine has been there. 'There was no first. I had always known her', he says. This goes to the same metaphysical territory as 'Under the world', the engine's destination at the end of the poem, but reveals more. The Lady Engine has no beginning and Brasch's knowledge of her has neither beginning nor end. That is the crux of the prose version of the dream.

This greater elaboration alone draws me to the prose version. But there is more, too. I could say that since hearing what Einstein said about time, I have been convinced that time past and times present and future are all happening at once. But the truth is much less theoretical and more undisciplined. I just feel, as Brasch does, that the barrier between this world and the past or the future is very very thin. He does not need to persuade me that there are no beginnings and no end.

Six

Lady Engine as a lament

Returning to the poem after reading the prose, knowing now that the poem is the record of a child's dream, it makes sense that the poem would be fragmentary. Thinking of the dream as a child's experience makes me pay more attention to the puzzlement and questioning in the last third of the poem, after the Lady Engine has drawn away. It is so easy to imagine that moment from a child's point of view. Something awe-inspiring was there. Then it is not. The Lady Engine is 'Gone. Vanished', like the pretty girl in a magic trick. The Lady Engine is so strongly absent that she almost leaves a negative image of her presence. But with 'Gone, gone' the tone changes, away from surprise and towards lament. The questions 'Where? / No where?' feel plaintive and perseverative, as a child's questions sometimes do.

After 'No where?' I think the poet, as a grown man, takes over from the child. He provides the answer, such as it is, to the child who had the dream. The Lady Engine is still there, 'Under the world'. Can you comfort your child-self? Perhaps.

Seven

The significance of context

Up to this point I have been comparing the two texts of the dream and thinking about what they contain. But some voice from many years back keeps saying this word 'context'. As a psychologist, I was trained to think about the pressures and influences on any person. I decided to be a psychologist again for a few minutes, to stop listening to what the poem and the prose version of the dream say as individual texts, in isolation, and start listening to the voices all around them.

[A DISCLAIMER: The following description and analysis is based on the published version of *Indirections*. Because the published version of *Indirections* has been edited down to about half its original size, the amount of space or the level of detail cannot be assumed to be exactly what Brasch intended. I have not read all of Brasch's final manuscript to compare it with the published version, but my impression, based on a comparison sample of 50 pages and what Bertram says in his editor's notes, is that the edit mostly removed elaborations of points Brasch had already made to the editor's satisfaction.]

EIGHT

Lyrical, factual and reflective

Indirections is made up of 50 numbered pieces of text. The first opens with this dreamy sentence which locates the writer in time, physical and emotional space, and class.

> *For a few years before the first war, my grandparents used to take Dr. Truby King's house at Karitane each summer.*[10]

It continues, placing the young Charles in his family as the first-born 'man-child' in his generation and therefore belonging 'especially' to his grandfather. It places Charles Brasch in his whakapapa as the descendant of Bendix Hallenstein, founder of the family's fortunes in New Zealand, and it places the wider family in their houses, all near each other in the London Street/Royal Terrace area of Dunedin. There are three lyrical, factual and reflective pages of this context to Charles Brasch's early life before death came into his world.

Section 2 tells the story of Helene Brasch's death and the circumstances which led up to it. In typical Brasch fashion it is detailed, lyrical and contains a hint of the mystical. In the winter of

1914, Miss Darling, the nanny, took Charles away to Middlemarch, where it was thought that the dry atmosphere would help his weak chest. Charles did so well in Middlemarch that the family decided that they wanted him to stay on there once Miss Darling's own winter holiday was over, so they told her they would send another person to take over caring for Charles. But, Brasch says, 'something kept telling [Miss Darling] she had to take me home'.[11] Miss Darling, whom Brasch describes as 'fair-haired, wide-blue-eyed and **ardent**',[12] obeyed this feeling and took Charles home to Dunedin. Miss Darling was right. Charles was at home one day before his mother died of a haemorrhage.

A sad and silent memory picture ends Section 2.

> I remember walking with my father and Lel into the side-garden, and on the winding paths among the rose-beds. It must have been very soon after she died, when the business of death was clearly over, yet before we tried to begin normal life again. I do not recall that any of us spoke or showed emotion, but my father's silence was heavy as he steered us along the paths, between the low box borders.[13]

In Section 3 Brasch moves closer to the dream. First though, he describes his 'puzzling over the nature of things'.[14]

> My mother's life on earth had come to an end, she had disappeared, and for ever, as I understood. Was there a time, earlier, when she had not been? Or a time when I had not been? I could not remember or imagine such times. I had a strong sense that everything I knew, and everything that existed now, had always existed, and because it existed, must exist always in the future. My mother's death did not necessarily contradict this. It made existence more complex, however, added a dimension to it, and suggested that one should not judge too readily by appearances. That sense of the beginninglessness of things, of

*their permanence whether they are present or not, and although I
cannot tell how they persist, remains with me still.*[15]

The dream appears after this as an imaginative working out of these
ideas from this time in Brasch's life. You could look at the dream
itself, like his poems, as 'flashed off' from his life, 'like a spark from
steel.'[16]

The description of the dream is just over a page long, finishing
with the sentence 'I had always known her'. Clearly that is
intended to connect with the paragraph which explains the idea of
beginninglessness* and claims it as a lifelong tenet.

Section 4 sets out the important parts of life for Charles after his
mother's death. His own home, Bankton, was 'shadowed by our
loss.'[17] His father tried to be 'both mother and father to us'[18] but
could not make up for what was lost. The paragraph Brasch writes
about his father is painfully careful, as he tries to think fairly about
the pressures on his father, but between the lines, he judges his
father's parenting efforts a failure.

Most of the rest of this section is devoted to matters of religion and
spirituality. There is description of the religious past of the family
and of its spiritual present. The patriarch Bendix Hallenstein is
described as keeping up 'a few Jewish observances all his life.'[19]
His wife was Anglican. Their four daughters, 'given the usual
instruction of Jewish girls',[20] lived in a world of these 'two creeds and
observances; and following their own bent and some intellectual
interests of the time, Grandmother and Aunt Emily came to things
Japanese, Chinese, Indian, to Max Müller and Madame Blavatsky
and Mrs Besant'.[21] Over time Grandmother's interests 'centred in
theosophy',[22] which led to Charles being taken to the Theosophical
Society's Sunday school. This, he says, was the only formal religious
instruction he had as a child, and he says it 'left no impression on
me that I can discern.'[23]

Brasch may be right that he never entered again the sort of 'general mist of sentiment and intensity woven around esoteric doctrines of a colourful, implausible, flimsy, flummery sort …',[24] but the general interest in comparative religions, the commitment to try to live without hurting other creatures, and the acceptance that human awareness might be larger than science describes, all seem to me to have followed Brasch out the door of that Theosophical Sunday school and into his life and his poems.

As a young child, Brasch says, he knew nothing of Judaism, or Christianity, and 'no one in our family circle went either to church or to synagogue'.[25] I don't very often find myself thinking that what Brasch says is just plain silly, but this is one instance. Even if the two generations after Bendix (three if you count young Charles) were not observant Jews, the men amongst whom Charles Brasch lived looked out at the world through a Judaism-shaped hole.

Young Charles Brasch was living in a family which, on one side, was Jewish, tending generally towards assimilation and secularity. The other side of the family contained a strand of comparative religious study and openness to spiritual enthusiasms. All of this was taking place in colonial New Zealand, with its generally Christian history and culture, and in Dunedin, with its Scottish Presbyterian flavour. It was a complex and relatively open environment from a spiritual point of view. If you found yourself believing in beginninglessness in this family, I don't think you would feel an outlaw. If you chose the right person, maybe you could even talk about that. Families are unknowable though so perhaps I have this sense of openness wrong.

Section 5 is about place in a geographical sense. Here Brasch describes the way his family explored and appreciated the land around Dunedin. Parts of this section are very lyrical, for example his description of the green and silver everlasting daisies, his chosen native flower. There is also a description of the Māori people the family saw living near sites that had been occupied by Māori in times gone by. The expeditions of walking and swimming and boiling the billy for tea were happy times for Brasch, and his description of the smell of the mānuka and lupin fires and salty air and of coming home sunburnt are memories lots of older New Zealanders would have.

Section 6 is about the life of the boy with no mother. He had asthma, people worried about him, he spent a lot of time in bed and he played elaborate imaginative games. He drew maps of made-up worlds, made a railway out of grass stalks, saw hidden meanings in the colour of marbles. After a long description of the grass railway game he explains that it gave him 'aesthetic and imaginative pleasure of a sort I found in no other game … Only the arrangement of words, audible, tangible words set side by side to strike out new unsuspected meanings that came from who knows where, was to give me, later, any comparable satisfaction.'[26]

Chapter One of *Indirections*, with the dream of the Lady Engine embedded as one of a string of brightly coloured experiences, is the most sophisticated setting-out of context that I have ever seen. It has a little boy, coming into consciousness at a certain time. It shows the boy's place of belonging, his family culture, his families' religions. It shows the boy's family in nature and in relation to Māori culture. It shows the boy's curiosity about life and death. At the end of the chapter the author pins his colours to the mast as a person for whom the inner life of beauty and imagination is as important as his heartbeat. This is the little boy who had the dream and became the author of the memoir and all the poems.

N I N E

The themes and mood of Not Far Off

The winter of 2016 was one of the moments in my exploration of
Brasch's work when I knew exactly what to do next. I would spend
however long it took to read the poems in *Not Far Off* to absorb the
context of the Lady Engine dream. I sat in a warm room. I absolved
myself of all responsibilities except to be present for these poems. I
did not feel in the least guilty. It was my job to walk into this word-
pool and be there. My method was simple. I read the poems over
and over. If there were names I did not know, I looked them up.

Brasch usually wrote his poems slowly. He assembled his collections
slowly too. I think it would be fair to assume that nothing about the
collection *Not Far Off* is an accident. In the first poem, 'A Closed
Book', a worm speaks. The worm's message is that there is no such
thing as 'a life earth holds of no account'. Then there is 'Lady Engine'.
After that is a short and rather cryptic poem called 'One Starless
Night' which seems to be an old soldier's acknowledgement of the
power of a supreme being.

> [...] There is nothing, you said, in all the world
> That does not show us a way
> To fear him and to serve him.
> Every place is his.
> All is commandment.
>
> So I learned at Kobryn
> Passing your house one starless night.
>
> And put off my shoes.[27]

Kobryn is a town in Belarus, which used to have a Jewish population
of perhaps 10,000 people. At the start of World War II, Kobryn, then
part of Poland, was occupied by Russia. In 1941, when Russia and
Germany declared war, Kobryn was taken by the Germans, after

which a ghetto was established, buildings burned, the Jews fined and forced labour set in place. In 1942 the ghettos were emptied and most of the Jews killed. The Russians took control of Kobryn again in 1944. There are no Jews there now. There is no mention of Kobryn in the index of Brasch's memoir or journals; nothing to tie him directly to the town. I am not even sure if this Jewish history was what connected Brasch to Kobryn. The old soldier who speaks in the poem could be from any army. In the absence of anything more authoritative I am left with just the name Kobryn, and a sense of weight and sorrow.

The instruction to take off your shoes on holy ground has biblical origins. In Exodus God said to Moses:

Draw not nigh hither: put off thy shoes from off thy feet, for the place whereon thou standest is holy ground.

Kobryn is holy ground then for Brasch. Given what the worm says, perhaps everywhere is holy ground? With this sense of weight and sorrow, ground made holy by suffering and the picture of Brasch metaphorically taking off his shoes and standing in the mud, his thin white feet exposed, I started to get a sense of his openness and courage in facing the legacy of Kobryn, whatever it was for him. This poem is not in the *Collected Poems* collection, so perhaps it has not spoken to other readers as much as it did to me.

Brasch writes several times about the feeling that a poem is near and could be born if he is able to sit quietly and help it to arrive. Reading all the poems in *Not Far Off* I had that rush of feeling that tells me a poem is nearby.

'On Joy and Other Obligations', the result of my week-long séance with Charles Brasch's 1969 book of poems *Not Far Off*, is my summation of the context in which Brasch places the 'Lady Engine' poem.

TEN

'On Joy and Other Obligations'[28]

If you open a book that has been closed for forty-four years, if dust
floats in the sunlight, if the book sold in 1969 for $1.60, and you buy
it second-hand for $10, that might be your good fortune. If there is
a tiny segmented weevil in the dusty space between the binding and
the cover, if the worm lifts its head, if you raise your hand to kill the
worm but pause instead, that might also be your good fortune. There
is no such thing as a life that means nothing, the worm says in its
airy voice.

I see that I disgust you, the worm says. Do what you must. But in
the blood, the blood, the stream, the river, I am you and you are also
me. Every life contains the memory of countless other lives; lives we
knew, deaths we mourn and those behind the door. Perhaps, after all,
a cosmos binds and holds us all together, whatever death may report?

Bend your neck, pause long enough to say your own name, and raise
your head again. In the presence of the river, of pieces of bone, of fish-
hooks and the skeletons of tiny glassy fish, this movement is required
of you. Also, near towns where your ancestors died, take off your
sandals so that mud and blood and salt water will soak your skin.

Light will slowly fade as winter comes. Clouds will cover the moon.
Winter of earth, winter of sky, winter of hope, winter of loss, winter
of exile, winter of silence, winter of anger. Winter of such faint light,
winter of waiting, winter of longing. In these short days, people will
travel together for safety but will be beaten down by soldiers and
armies of words. There is no forgiveness. Rain never stops, rivers run
to flood, run underground and swell the sea. To endure is the thing.

Ah, but joy has a new shoot. In the bush, cabbage trees flower and
a breeze blows their sweet pink perfume along your path. Someone

of ninety makes marmalade, there is a yellow bowl of persimmons and three blackbirds on the table outside. It *doesn't* always come back to you, Rilke says, Brasch says, the worm says. Leaves of giant flax rattle and clack. Green is dark and wild. Joy is a single tūī, two fantails, a cloud like a child's drawing. On your last day, you may see a vermillion sky.

Speak like Auden of humankind in all its endeavours, of all its want and weakness, speak when it seems there may be a new war and everything is advertising and resignation. Pain and love through dark glasses, that is your business. Or, like Blake, go inside the vault of your head to where the visions start. Walk with the dead, hold their hands, dance until you cannot tell them from yourself. Record an image, a young woman stepping down from a bus. Can you call her back? To name, to try, to do, is the thing.

Eleven

A returning of life upon itself
In this journal entry, dated Wednesday, 9 July 1952, Brasch describes writing part of what will become his memoir.

> *Wrote this morning a couple of sentences which might serve as an opening for the autobiographical sketches I've thought of so often. They seem to strike the kind of note I must aim at; for these sketches, I see now, have a purpose, a use for me: they will remake me, create an image of myself, & so give me in my own eyes a reality & a stability that I scarcely possess even yet, & a continuity which I have never achieved. They may offer me a* **centre*** *to write poetry from, possibly a hint of direction too. They should be simple & flowing to read yet suggest richness and complexity – the constant turning & returning of life upon itself in reflection & speculation, in dream & fantasy.*[29]

The Human Hand

ONE

The road over the river

In Dunedin, one winter morning in 2017, five Pākehā baby boomers sit around a wooden table, drinking very good coffee from Crown Lynn cups and discussing the construction of roads in places where there are said to be taniwha. Someone says they don't believe in a Christian god, a Jewish god, Buddhist gods or taniwha but other people can believe what they like. Someone says when a road is being build you can't have equal respect for everyone's views because either the road goes over the river where the taniwha lives or it doesn't. Someone thinks the taniwha might be a metaphor. I mention the Golem of Prague which someone says isn't the same thing at all. Someone says the road should just go somewhere else. Someone else says why should it go somewhere else to avoid a thing that is a myth? The conversation becomes a little heated. A couple of people don't say anything about the taniwha and the road. Later I realised they were the only ones with direct experience of such matters.

We talked then about archaeological methods. Otago picnics where well-dressed Edwardian ladies and gentlemen boiled the billy, dug trenches, picked up things they noticed and took them home. Willi Fels and his party at Karitane before World War I. Fels dragging his walking stick behind him as he walked up and down the beach looking for 'Maori curios' to add to his collection. Later groups who sluiced surfaces with water to expose objects. The destruction of sites. The fact that these days **archaeology†** in New Zealand is almost all paid for by developers or required as part of an infrastructure project. The notion of 'collecting'. What each kind of collector thinks of those who went before. Objects bought and sold. Objects on the walls of spare bedrooms, their origins now unable to be traced. Heads that used to be on display at Otago Museum a few decades ago, but aren't now.

Two

To take others with him

It never takes long in any discussion of collections at Otago Museum for the name Willi Fels to come up. The Fels Wing, opened in 1930, was named after him in recognition of funds he donated and raised from other sources. All together, Fels donated 7900 objects from his own collections to the museum. Some of those are on display now and some in storage. After Fels died in 1946, his family presented a carefully chosen Willi Fels Memorial Collection to the museum. In addition to objects donated by Fels and given to commemorate him, there are also objects bought by the museum with money from the Fels Fund. These links are acknowledged on cards beside each object. In June 2017 the Fels Trust Fund amounted to $862,937. That is a *very* substantial footprint.

Fels was such an important figure in the growth and development of Otago Museum that when he died in 1946 the museum's director, H.D. Skinner, wrote a small monograph about him. It is 14 pages long, elegantly typeset and begins with a poem 'In Memory of Willi Fels (1858–1946)', written by Charles Brasch. The book has a laudatory tone, as one might expect for a book about a major financial benefactor, but it also brings together information which places Fels' contributions to the museum in the context of his life. Skinner provides a fascinating peek into Fels' modus operandi. When I read it, I thought for a moment that I was reading about Charles Brasch, despite the actual fields of endeavour being different.

According to Skinner, when Fels was at school he was keenly
interested in history and in the classical languages, hoping for a
university career in these fields, but he followed his father's wishes
and entered commerce. If this is right, and I think the family would
have intervened if it was not, Fels found himself, as a young man,
in a somewhat similar situation to the one his grandson Charles
Brasch faced many years later. Fels' education and interests led him
away from the family business, but the business needed him. Unlike
his grandson, Fels capitulated to the pressure. Instead of becoming
bitter about that, he worked hard and successfully in what Skinner
calls 'commerce'. In Skinner's mouth, I hear the word 'commerce'
as pejorative, but perhaps I am wrong. Though his activities were
successfully diverted into another field, throughout his life Fels'
reading 'remained predominantly historical and classical'.[1]

In his private life Fels collected things, by finding them himself and
buying from dealers. According to Skinner, Fels started to collect
Māori and Oceanic material in the early 1890s, soon after he became
a New Zealand citizen. After that Fels began to collect Oriental
arms, ceramics, objects from Persia, India, Japan and Burma, books
by early Italian printers and some English writers, coins and plants.
One of the privileges of wealth is that your hobbies can be bigger
than other people's. They can grow and grow and take up money and
time and space and no one will call it hoarding because everything is
neat and tidy and valuable. Nevertheless, I find it impossible to read
this list of collections without wondering what all that collecting was
about. Was it a form of art practice? A hedge of beauty and craft to
protect him from the working world? Charles Brasch has an answer.

In his memorial poem Brasch says of his grandfather,

> He watched a distracted world
>
> And studied in all things to draw men and peoples
> Together, that, each should learn the others' ripest

Wisest creations, and, by beauty persuaded,
Cold envy, false fear forget.

O not that human folly, inhuman hatred,
Be covered up, or discounted, or forgiven;
But that in each the best be discerned as truest,
The final expressive form

In which it is most itself, and speaks most clearly
To those who would hear, as he, the quick and eager,
Everywhere sought and heard. Yet he was never
One to delight alone,

But loved to take others with him into the shining
Kingdom of joy, where understanding transfigures
The meanest features, and strangers are strangers no longer,
For all life breathes as one.[2]

This poem grew on me slowly. The first thing I noticed was that the poem is full of Brasch's ideas about the significance of beauty and people being better from exposure to beauty. When I read the words 'human folly' and 'inhuman hatred' I started to feel that Brasch was talking about a man who saw the nastiest parts of human activity clearly but was not paralysed by that knowledge. I remembered that the poem was written in 1946, that in the weeks Brasch sat beside his dying grandfather, survivors of the Holocaust were trying to find their way to the places that had been their homes and searching for their families. News of what had happened was in the newspapers, even in New Zealand. But still, this is a poem about Fels as Brasch knew him, not about Brasch or the Holocaust. It celebrates Fels' faith, or at least hope, that the best of human craft brings people together. I think I understand the compulsive collecting a little better for reading the poem.

Skinner says that after Fels' son Harold died at the Battle of Broodseinde in 1917, Fels decided that his collection should be 'given to the community'.[3] Harold, his heir, was gone. I can imagine a questioning of assumptions, a review of the purpose of all plans and activities, set off by grief. Maybe Fels could imagine his three girls in houses with husbands and children but not with all these thousands of precious objects? Maybe Fels wasn't thinking so personally but more about building up the cultural resources of the city of Dunedin? Maybe the two ideas worked together. But for whatever reason, in the 1920s Fels chose Otago Museum as the home of his gifts to the community.

THREE

Fels the strategist
Skinner's outline of the way Fels went about helping the museum to be ready for his collections is a fascinating glimpse into Fels' planning skills, applied in this case to a cultural endeavour.

> *His first step was to find a keeper for the Department of Anthropology, which he was virtually creating. Having provided finance and made the appointment, he founded a new fund, the income of which was to be used for the purchase of picked pieces for exhibition in the Museum Galleries. He then began the orderly handing over of his own collections, ethnographic material and Oriental arms coming first. The need for new galleries in the Museum was evident at once, and he cheerfully undertook the task of collecting funds for them. With the aid of a Government grant of £25,000, a sum of £56,000 was secured. Building and furnishing the new wing cost £30,000, and the balance was paid into capital, income from which was used for maintenance.*[4]

No step is taken without consideration of how it will work in practice. If a new initiative is to happen, it is supported with funding both for day-to-day operations and in **money*** to support its work in perpetuity. The Willi Fels Wing was opened on 15 October 1930, just over a year after the Wall Street crash that precipitated the Great Depression. Museums have changed character a lot since the Fels Wing was built and its elegant Greek shape doesn't seem a very good match now for some of what goes on inside the museum, but the wing itself is still graceful and white on the outside, calm on the inside and full of treasures of many kinds.

Fels didn't just stand outside and give money and objects to the museum. He involved himself in its activities. Again, Skinner's description is a vivid evocation of the man and the way he did things.

> *In the Museum he was keenly interested, critical, genial, making a point of meeting and knowing every member of the staff. He had an instinctive appreciation of quality in Museum material and he gave no quarter to mediocrity in quality or method of display. Tireless industry, conspicuous feature of his business success, was apparent also in his collections, each of them meticulously catalogued in neat handwriting. Every piece was described, measured, localized, and many were sketched … Most important of all was the careful localization of every piece in his extensive and important Maori collection. In this case his care will leave its permanent mark on all research work in Maori material culture.*[5]

It is interesting to imagine this as a description of the establishment and operation of *Landfall* under Brasch's editorial control. The cataloguing, measuring and localising. Think of all Brasch's travelling to meet prospective contributors and his confidence in his own capacity to recognise quality in visual art works or in writing. Perhaps it is drawing too long a bow, but the concept of localisation seems to resonate with the idea that place matters, and with the desire for literature and commentary that is from here and about here.

Willi Fels was chairman of the Museum Committee and of the Association of Friends of the Museum from their inception until his death. He was a member of the Otago Branch of the Royal Society of New Zealand for 50 years, serving on its council as treasurer and vice-president.

Four

The Royal Society's dig at Little Papanui

In 1929 and 1930 a party from the Archaeological Section of the Otago Branch of the Royal Society excavated a site by the mouth of a stream at what they called Little Papanui beach on the Pacific Ocean side of Otago Peninsula. H.D. Skinner was in charge. In an article written many years later, in 1960, Skinner describes the process by which the archaeologists got access to the site in two information-packed but oddly unsatisfying sentences.

> *In 1928, the Karetai family, then in occupation of the farm land at the back of the beach, were approached by the Archaeological Section of the Otago Branch of the Royal Society of New Zealand, and generously gave permission to set up camp and to excavate, the artefacts recovered to be the property of Otago Museum.*

> *Members of the two parties who excavated at Little Papanui at Easter, 1929, and in January, 1930, have the happiest memories of the co-operation and hospitality of the Karetai family.[6]*

The passive 'were approached' obscures so much interesting detail. I would like to know much more about how the 'approach' happened, who spoke on behalf of the Royal Society, and who spoke on behalf of the Karetai family. I would like to know why Skinner uses the phrase 'in occupation of' to describe the relationship of the Karetai family to this piece of land. I would like to know exactly how the proposition that the artefacts would belong to the museum was phrased and what the Karetai family thought about this. I'm not likely to find these things out because the digs happened 30-odd years before Skinner's article appeared. The article is a window but a very cloudy one.

There was no direct road access to the site, which meant the parties were dependent on the Karetai family for access in the literal sense as well as in the sense of permission.

> *The main body of each party was brought by bus to the nearest point on the Lighthouse Road, and tents and stores were taken by sledge to the camp site, sledge and horses provided by the Karetais.[7]*

There is a brief reference in Skinner's article to the Karetai family's hostility towards curio hunters.

> *When I first saw it this area was a shoulder of bare clay from which the top soil had been stripped by the wind. This wind erosion was doubtless consequent on the united scratching of collectors and rabbits, to both of whom the legal owners were understandably hostile.[8]*

Perhaps, in the light of this damage, the Karetai family viewed the Royal Society's expedition as an improvement on earlier more lawless collectors? But again, time, Skinner's own interests and the conventions of academic writing style have obscured all the detail.

Even though the artefacts were to come into the museum's collection, there was no money from Otago Museum to help with these expeditions, so members of the expedition paid for the food and any other costs themselves. Eva Skinner, H.D. Skinner's wife and a founding member of the Association of Friends of the Otago Museum, was quartermaster.

> *Quartermaster duties, discharged by Eva Skinner, were onerous, since there was much coming and going of personnel. The day*

began with a hot meal in camp. A cut lunch was provided on the excavation site, with billy tea, and a hot three-course meal was served at camp each evening.[9]

The party drank water from the One-paipai stream which ran through bush, and they watched the local wildlife. Although these digs were early in the year, conditions were not summery.

The beach below the camp was perfect for sea bathing, with the reservation that the current from the south resulted in a water temperature less attractive than some might desire. Seals and sea-lions sometimes hauled ashore there. Bush gave shelter from westerly and southerly wind to the five tents pitched on the terrace. At the excavation site a tent was erected for shelter from the occasional shower accompanying southerly weather.[10]

Skinner concluded that Little Papanui, like a similar area in Kāpiti where the bones of a woman were found in 2014 (*see* **Waikanae River Woman**†), was a place people visited to find extra food supplies rather than a permanently occupied site. His evidence for this conclusion was partly the list of things he did *not* find.

There were no stone fireplaces, and nephrite, though it occurred at all levels, was rare. Adzes were few and uninteresting, and there was no evidence of canoe building. There was no evidence of European contact. Occupation seems not to have been permanent. Little Papanui was presumably the site of an important summer fishing-camp.[11]

F I V E

Little Papanui Woman: her short life and the long life of her bones

Skinner found no buried human beings in the 1929 and 1930 digs. But according to Helen Leach and Philip Houghton writing

in *The Book of New Zealand Women*,[12] during a later dig, on 6
September 1932, Skinner and Roger Duff found the skeleton of a
woman at Little Papanui. The woman's body was found at the mouth
of a small creek at the south end of Little Papanui beach, where there
was a camp or small village. Leach and Houghton say the woman's
body had been trussed and buried with her head facing north. Leach
and Houghton named her 'Little Papanui Woman'. Skinner and Duff
named her 'Skeleton #3'.

Leach and Houghton say Little Papanui Woman lived about 1600
CE, and died when she was approximately 35 years old. She was
161 centimetres tall and had little degeneration of the spine. She
had had one child. Attempting to understand something of her life,
they said that at Little Papanui she had access to the sea, to creeks
and to coastal forest, which meant she could eat penguins, seagulls,
fur seals, pāua, mussels, albatross and dogs, as well as ocean fish
like cod. Little Papanui is too far south to grow kūmara, so Leach
and Houghton thought Little Papanui Woman would probably have
eaten beaten bracken roots and cooked cabbage tree roots instead.

I asked an archaeologist how Little Papanui Woman might have
spent her days. This person said Little Papanui Woman would have
collected wood, prepared food, woven baskets, mats and perhaps
cloaks, and looked after children. A few days later I heard it said that
descriptions of the division of labour in pre-European Māori groups
bear a strong imprint of patriarchal ideas from European culture
and that we might be imposing our own gender roles on these
people.

Little Papanui Woman's bones, together with remains of other
human beings from Little Papanui and other Otago sites, are in
boxes now, behind a heavy steel door, in the Wāhi Tapu at Otago
Museum. One box per person. Boxes from one place grouped
together. The remains will, in due course, be returned to local iwi,

but for the time being the bones of Little Papanui Woman are in the museum, where they have been for 86 years. In 2017 I went down, with a guide, to the steel door at the entrance to the Wāhi Tapu room. The person who showed me to the door and told me about the protocol for the Wāhi Tapu said that she keeps the room dusted and clean. This is a small service she performs for these people, she said. These are her people and she enjoys caring for them.

Six

The steel door and the little plastic bags

In the basement of Otago Museum there are miles of corridors and rows and rows of shelves on which sit boxes of objects from Little Papanui and other digs around Otago. Some of the showiest objects found at Little Papanui are on display upstairs in the public areas but the majority are in the basement, in boxes. Some of the objects are tiny, like the backbones of very small fish and fragments of fish-hooks. These are placed in little plastic bags. Larger stone objects, like knives, sit on foam inside their boxes.

Even the tiny, commonly found objects bear traces of what has happened to them, such as little nicks along a bone, or marks of a fire. There are lots of diagrams in Skinner's article showing the fish-hooks and knives his parties found at Little Papanui, and there are lots of awe-inspiring objects on display at the museum. But I learned most from the sealed door of the Wāhi Tapu and the humbler objects in the little plastic bags. When I saw the door that a relative could enter but I could not, I understood that the bones were all that was left of a real woman, and that, in this period of her existence, she has people looking after her. She belonged to a place and some people when she was alive. Then she did not. Now she does again. When I saw the individual nicks along the edge of a piece of a fish-hook I understood that a person had made every chip that made an edge on a knife and smoothed every piece of a fish-hook – a person who knew what sort of hook would catch what sort of fish, who knew that if the fish slipped off the hook because it wasn't shaped right, people might go hungry.

If I had stayed up on the gallery floors I would not have learned this. I would have noticed beauty or artisan complexity but missed the human hand behind the skill. I see **archives*** of letters and manuscripts and fragments of poems and thoughts on torn bits of paper as the exact equivalent of these shelves of tiny plastic bags. The practices of excavation, display and preservation change, what is valued changes, but the objects themselves have power for those of us who are inclined to look back.

On the Unshapely Present

THE PAST IS EASY, or at least you can pretend it is. The past does not protest at what you include and what you leave out. The past is in museums. It sits still, in vitrines, while you look at it. The past is in books. It is alive in your head but dead on the page. The past is right there, so close behind you that you can feel its breath and its pain. All you have to do is turn and watch its shapes changing colour and form. The past is itself. It does not perform for you. Its legacy is alive, but the past is indifferent to that legacy. The past is inside everything. The past is earth and bone.

The present is carbon too but the carbon of new leaves and tiny silver fish that we catch at the river mouth as they arrive from the sea. The present is 17 tiny silver fish from the genus *Galaxias*, washed in fresh water, dropped into beaten egg, fried in butter and served with crusty bread. Seventeen fish for me. Another 17 for you. The future could have been 34 tiny silver fish waiting for the spring in a clear stream. The present is me and my friend and our Friday-night fritters. The present is nets drying on the lawn and the bacterial count of the river. The present is the road through the wetland. The present is our four-wheel-drive cars and all our agitations. The present is never still. It shouts and grumbles and argues and you can't tell who is right. The present doesn't know. It cares about a thousand things and nothing. The present has no shape. Does anyone even know when the present began? The present is me in the moment before I become the past. The present is happening today. The present thinks that is what matters.

When I decided to write about the building of the road through the wetland, I thought my story would begin in the present and have an ending. I thought I would catch a few pieces of the present as they rushed by. The narrative would be simple. *There is no road there. Someone decides there should be a road there. People build it. Then it is there.* The end of my story would be the opening of the road. But there were three openings. One was for dignitaries, one was for the populace, and only the third and last was for cars.

I thought that after the opening, the road would have been transformed into the pliable, indifferent past and I would walk away, having made my little record. But the openings came and went and the story of the road shattered into hundreds of pieces. There is the story of the people who used to live in a quiet place, with birds. Now those people wake in the night to the flap and hiss of trucks. I say the names of the birds. Now that is all I can do. There is the story of the road noise standard which may or may not be reasonable and the story of the Alliance and its proud engineers. The story of the benefits of the road to the local economy. The story of the jagged hole left in the hill after the yellow rock was removed to make the road; the story of one Māori land-owner who gave her land away rather than sell to the Crown. Her name is Patricia Grace. There is the story of the woman whose bones were found crouched in a sand dune. I do not know her name so I say the name of the river, Waikanae, because she would have known that word. I say 'kanae', the fish-word inside the river-word. Words. That is what I have. There is the story of the longfin eels, lamprey, banded kōkopu, giant kōkopu and red-finned bullies rehomed in streams made by bulldozers. There is the story of the pavement meant to last 18 years and the water that rose up and destroyed the sleek black surface; the story of the couple still fighting for a fair price for their land, four years after the road was built on that land; and the story of the road that was so important to one government and might not have been built in the same way by the next. Stories. That is what I found.

The road through the wetland is *absolutely* the present. The stories of its construction are in the past, but its legacies are with us now. Our

memories of dispute, of the occasional win. Its due processes, its
hubris, its cones, its polite people, its Independent Review Panel, its
noisy bridge expansion joints and its 'significant change in the noise
environment' of certain houses. All those are with us now.

Stories of the present, I have learned, do not end with a velvet
curtain coming down on a final tableau. There are no retrospectively
visible moves toward stability or resolution. Stories of the present
resist endings. They are toddlers who won't go to bed. They
wave their little white arms in front of your face and tell you that
tomorrow will be even more interesting than today. For now, I am
seduced. I'm keeping up to date with the lobby groups. I'm still
writing occasional letters to politicians, but I am tired of reading
their clever replies. Tired of all the ways they have to make you be
quiet or just not matter. One day soon I will give up; I'll stop looking
at the road and just drive on it, as other people do.

My record of the road could end with an incomplete sentence,
followed by an ellipsis and a big white gap. But that is a cliché. My
record ends with an incantation. I take off my shoes. Then I say the
name of the river, slowly. Waikanae. I say the names of the grand
trees. Pōhutukawa, Pūriri, Kohekohe, Tōtara. Each name a comfort
and a light. I say each name seven times. I say 'Harakeke', I listen to
its leaves rattling in the westerly wind. I look for the biggest, blackest
tūī, the one who sits high in the Pūriri tree. I watch his flight path,
imagine his purposes. I do not know the name of the woman buried
first in sand and now in peat, but I say a blessing for her.

GLOSSARIES

One Starless Night
A glossary of my acquaintance with Charles Brasch

accent, deliberately cultivated: In his memoir, *Indirections*, Charles Brasch says that during his secondary school years he admired the way his aunts and two cousins, recently come from school in England, spoke. He decided then to try to speak like them. After reading that I wanted very badly to hear his voice so I listened to a 1961 recording of an unnamed female interviewer from the New Zealand Broadcasting Service asking Charles Brasch about the state of New Zealand writing.[1] When the interviewer greets Brasch his reply sounds a little awkward or reluctant but then he seems to warm up and gives expansive replies to the interviewer's questions. He sounds downright enthusiastic about the history of *Landfall* and the state of New Zealand writing. There are noticeable pauses, which these days would be edited out, as he thinks out his answers to the interviewer's questions, one part at a time. I like that because it feels as if he is arriving at his view in real time.

In terms of his physical speech, Brasch makes a big round 'ow' sound like the queen in words like 'now' and 'about' and there is a slightly prolonged 'a' in the word 'exactly'. The first-person pronoun 'I' veers towards the royal family's 'eh' but doesn't quite go that far. The 'r' in the word 'very' and 'literature' has something like a 'd' sound and 'literature' becomes 'lideratchure'.

The interviewer asks Brasch how well New Zealand writing reflects the New Zealand scene. You can't look for a direct or in any sense a general picture of New Zealand life in New Zealand writing, he says, but you *can* learn a good deal about New Zealand life from it. Why, for heaven's sake, didn't she ask him what he had learned about New Zealand life?

accent, New Zealand: I have heard it said that Charles Brasch hated
the New Zealand accent. 'The New Zealand accent' is not a topic I hear
discussed much these days, although it was a hot topic in my childhood.
While I was thinking about what Charles Brasch's accent would have been
like, I heard a man speaking on RNZ National about what he called 'agri-
business'. This man said the first-person pronoun 'I' as 'oi'. In the 1960s, as
my family moved around rural towns of New Zealand, my parents worried
that I might have caught that 'oi' vowel sound from the other children. The
'oi' sound was rural or working class, and in the case of a daughter might
limit her chances of marrying someone of probity, like a lawyer.

Another undesirable speech marker at that time was the use of the
interrogative 'eh?' at the end of sentences. This was understood as a Māori
influence.

acceptance: Brasch dedicated his memoir to his grandfather Willi Fels.

*Grandfather was the most constant figure in my life, its rock and centre …
He bore no grudges, he did not keep trying to get at me, he accepted me,
finally, as I was. There was peace between us. There was no such peace
between my father and me.*[2]

The word 'Fels' means rock in German but this description of his
grandfather as a rock is not just an amusing pun. For Charles Brasch 'rock'
and 'stone' were 'words of intimate meaning'.[3] In these three sentences
Brasch tells the reader whose version of love helped him live and, by
implication, what poisoned his father's version of love.

'acclimatize':

*I see it as Grandfather's consistent aim, always to acclimatize in the new
country which as a young man he had chosen for his own the best ideas
and products of older countries, especially of Europe, and above all of
classical Italy and Greece.*[4]

The word 'acclimatize' was used from early in colonial times to refer to
efforts to establish plants and animals from England in New Zealand. Here
something less English is being introduced. When I look at 'acclimatize'

on the page the energy and will built up inside the word cause it to emit low-frequency vibrations. Brasch says that his grandfather Fels hoped that New Zealand was 'fresh soil, unencumbered by the trammels and shadows and prejudices of the past'.[5] The optimism of this is poignant, and to me it has a Jewish flavour and a refugee flavour. It misses the shadows of colonial Aotearoa though.

Although he lived more than half his life in English-speaking countries, Willi Fels spoke English with a strong German accent.

> *But he had made New Zealand his own and thought of himself as a New Zealander by adoption. He knew more of the country and more about it than most New Zealanders, and loved it deeply, especially Dunedin and its surroundings. Here was his home, here he had put down roots, here he expected his children and grandchildren to succeed him.[6]*

anti-Semitism, and prejudice, in New Zealand:

> *No-one of Jewish birth should count on being accepted. Prejudice waited everywhere, and might declare itself at any time, if not too blatantly. It waited, as always in New Zealand, for anyone who excelled – or excelled in any field except sport. Be too successful or too intelligent, too outspoken or too well-spoken, and on every hand the mediocre and complacent will prickle, and hold you an object of suspicion. My father may have been all of these on occasion, until he grew wary and learned more complete conformity. He was not ashamed of being Jewish, but resented anti-Jewish prejudice, and was unable or unprepared to ignore it or brazen it out. That prejudice was not overt in Dunedin and my father was too friendly and too normal in every way to excite it; but it showed from time to time.[7]*

The pages in which this quotation sits bring together Hyam Brasch's reasons for sending the young Charles to Oxford; Hyam Brasch's experience of anti-Semitism in Dunedin; and Charles Brasch's own views of prejudice in New Zealand, and anti-Semitism in Dunedin in particular. Oxford, Hyam Brasch thought, would give Charles a status that could not be disputed – in the father's reasoning, this would lead to social acceptance. Here Charles Brasch makes it extremely clear that, in his view, being accepted is never to be expected for a Jewish person. It is a stark and uncompromising view. The context of the sentence is Dunedin but the sentence itself reads as if this is his opinion about anti-Semitism everywhere. It is one of those moments in a memoir when you feel an abrupt change in tone, when the narrative or tone of the memoir cracks and something intense pokes through.

After the opening sentence Brasch starts to explore 'prejudice' in New Zealand in a way that includes much wider versions of prejudice than just anti-Semitism. The mediocre or complacent will be suspicious of the conspicuous, he says. He specifically excludes sporting prowess from this. The propensity of New Zealanders for prejudice against high achievers has been widely reported so this hardly breaks new ground.

Brasch then considers his father, Hyam Brasch, in relation to the New Zealand form of prejudice, which brings us closer to Judaism again. The picture of Hyam Brasch that emerges between the lines here is of a man who might have fitted the common Jewish stereotypes of talking too much and being too brainy or too pushy – and maybe his clothes were too fancy – until, over the years, he learned to camouflage himself better to suit Dunedin. I find it sad but not surprising that he felt he needed to soften the edges of his identity. Brasch says that in the private clubs his father belonged to there was always someone who, during a dispute, would say that his father was 'the first and last etc. etc. to be admitted', but Brasch's description is hard to follow. I think Brasch means that in the heat of the moment someone said Hyam Brasch was the 'first and last [*Jew*] to be admitted'. But the word 'Jew', which would allow the comment to make sense, is missing. It is as if this word cannot be said, even here, when the subject is anti-Semitism. The names of the clubs are also missing and so are the names of the people who said these things. I would have liked less discretion from Brasch here. I would have liked him to name names and describe scenes at the club that might have embarrassed prominent Dunedin businessmen or their descendants, even decades later, but that is not the Brasch memoir style.

Hyam Brasch's reactions to these events is difficult to see from the description. Brasch says that his father cannot or would not ignore this prejudice, which must mean that Hyam Brasch had or made some response to it. But what exactly was his response? The next part of the sentence says he could not 'brazen out' the prejudiced statements boldly, but again, this does not tell me what happened.

I find it interesting that Charles Brasch says that anti-Jewish prejudice was not 'overt' in Dunedin. Immediately after that he says that his father received anti-Jewish comments. As Charles Brasch says, anti-Semitism (my choice of term) was not *commonly* overt. But nor was it absent. My mother, who grew up Jewish in Dunedin about 15 years later than Brasch, said that Jews of the ordinary sort tried not to stand out. The Hallenstein/Fels family were not Jews of the ordinary sort, but Brasch's description of his father's experiences shows that even someone connected to the wealthiest Jewish families sometimes tried not to stand out. Having a degree from Oxford, though, was a form of standing out. There is a paradox here that I can't quite untangle.

archives: On 6 March 2017, at the Hocken Collections in Dunedin, I opened item MS-009-004/051, a folder of Brasch's loose papers relating to his memoir, *Indirections*. My intention had been to look at the difference between the 424-page published version of *Indirections* and Brasch's own, much larger, manuscript, but in the face of the enormity of the number of files in the Brasch archive, I started with this slim folder containing unclassified loose notes of additions or changes to *Indirections* that Brasch wanted to remember, written between 1970 and 1972.

The first thing I noticed in the folder was lots of different sorts of paper. The first page was from a pad of the cheapest sort of lined notepaper. There were two handwritten sentences on it.

> *The first part of this book formed itself in my mind over many years, until the vividness of its memories forced me to write them down. The rest followed similarly, with some ~~extraneous aid~~ help now from diaries and notebooks.*

I felt a stab of empathy for the man whose memories were so vivid that he had to get them out of his head and onto paper. I think I actually said 'Oh!' out loud, as if I had felt a short sharp pain. I remember realising I had made this sound and looking up to see who else was there, in the reading room. There was only one woman. She didn't react, but I did make a mental note to keep my emotions under better control in the library.

I felt that Brasch was speaking to me in this first sentence, explaining, in a matter-of-fact and direct way, that the vividness of his memories 'forced' him to write a memoir. Joseph Brodsky, remembering with 'mesmerizing clarity' a scene from his childhood, wonders why these remembered moments have this 'unnatural, high-resolution-lens clarity'.

> *The only answer that occurs to me is: So that this moment exists, so that it is not forgotten when the actors are gone, myself included … And by the same token, in order to make clear what moments are.*[8]

If Charles Brasch were alive, and willing to talk with me, the first question I would ask is whether, like Brodsky, he was interested in recording both the existence of moments and the nature of moments. Later, if we had more rapport, I would ask why, having been 'forced' to write his memoir, he wrote it in this enormous, ornate form.

The second sentence in the handwritten note, about the process of writing the book, doesn't pack such a punch, but is still fascinating, because anyone who has looked at *Indirections* will wonder how a writer could remember the detail that is in this book. Just two sentences on that first scrap of notepaper started to tell me why and how Brasch wrote this book, and brought me, the reader of this little note, right up close to the writer and the process.

On a physical level, the paper in the folder remained of great interest. Some of the paper had been used before. On page 10 there were two paragraphs about great works of art, including this sentence:

> *To participate and to reflect, these are the chief effects of a work of art: to bind and loose and bind again.*

There was a diagonal line through other paragraphs about the effects of art, as though they had perhaps been included in something else and were no longer needed, but this sentence, with its emphasis, and its dangling

verbs, remained. Perhaps Brasch rejected it? The paper had been turned
over and a single sentence handwritten on the other side.

There I think I first heard the sea in a shell.

This tiny sentence, so different in tone from the abstraction about the
effects of art, took my breath away.

The folder also contained a half sheet of green paper so thin you could see
through it. Later, when I asked older people about thin green paper, one
said you might use this paper for making a carbon copy. In *An Angel at My
Table* Janet Frame says that Frank Sargeson told her that green typing paper
was easiest on the eyes.

There was half a page of expensive creamy paper, the sort you might use for
the most formal pieces of letter writing, and there was a strip of very ugly
grey unlined paper of medium quality. There were several pages of that
cheap lined notepaper you used to buy at the corner stationery shop when
letter writing was common. One note was written on the back of a packing
slip from B.H. Blackwell Ltd, a bookseller from Oxford. One of the half
sheets had been cut with scissors. The others had been torn along the edge
of a ruler.

Among other things, these torn and cut pieces of paper tell me Brasch did
not waste paper. How else would you ever know this? Why aren't hundreds
of people waiting every morning to get into the Hocken to find out things
like this? A small section of a lecture Charles Brasch gave in 1971 shows
that he understood the way archives speak to certain people:

*The Hocken Library collects both verse and prose manuscripts of all kinds.
This in years to come will be an invaluable continuing record of the work
of New Zealand writers; it is exciting and often moving to see manuscript
versions of poems, stories and novels one knows and to be able to follow
them through successive drafts; in a different way; it brings one as close as
letters and portraits to the man himself, the man at work ...*[9]

Yes. It does.

ardent, from the Latin *ardere*, 'to burn', is a Brasch word. To be ardent is a very good thing indeed. Ardent people include Miss Darling, his nanny, and the young artists drawn to Ursula Bethell by her gift for friendship. I happen to have been reading *Middlemarch* again recently and I have been surprised to find that Dorothea, Will Ladislaw and Dr Lydgate, the three most important characters in the book, are repeatedly described as 'ardent'. 'Ardent souls, ready to construct their coming lives, are apt to commit themselves to the fulfilment of their own visions,'[10] Eliot says of Dorothea. For one reason or another, each of Eliot's three ardent souls is born an outsider. They get themselves in tangles because of their ideas, but they fizz with energy, they are fundamentally benign and they change things. Brasch does not see much ardency in himself. I do.

art: as provocation, artists as bees: This is a concise summary of several Brasch opinions and some Braschian logic.

> *If Toss [Woollaston] survived, then other artists too would appear in time and perform – whatever the cost – their essential fertilizing, civilizing work; work that before it could be received must disturb and unsettle a society so timid and shallow, so loosely settled on the surface of the country in an order so easily set up and so little questioned. The country had not searched its foundations, nor had it fought for its liberties; such beliefs as it professed had scarcely been tested.*[11]

If you had been part of the campaigns for workers' rights like the Waihī strike in 1912, or the Great Strike in 1913, or the unemployment riots in 1932, you might not agree with Brasch here.

art, receptivity to:

> *… there is no New Zealand artist so commanding who can force us to see ourselves.*[12]

I do not usually think of the relationship between artists and their audience as involving the words 'commanding' and 'force'. But in a speech to students at the University of Otago in late March 1969, Brasch explained that New Zealanders are generally not receptive to works of art, 'new' art particularly, because they 'are not used to seeing reflections and embodiments of themselves in works of art'. Brasch's logic is that if New Zealand artists were more 'commanding' we could not help but take notice of the way they show us to ourselves, and if we had seen this kind of reflection of ourselves in our schooling, we would be more open to 'new' art. He thought artists could become more 'commanding' only by experimentation and by having time to spend on their art practice.

artists and writers, in need: In 1969 Brasch took advantage of the presence of the Minister of Internal Affairs at the opening of a major exhibition of the work of Frances Hodgkins to lobby for government support for 'New Zealand artists and writers in need'. He is not talking about the capacity to apply for grants. He is talking about poverty and hardship that are the result of a lifetime of putting creative activity ahead of financial security.

> *Frances Hodgkins had often to struggle in great hardship and had at one stage appealed to the New Zealand Government for a small pension. To the country's shame, this had been refused, Dr Brasch said.*[13]

Often when I read Brasch I think that not much has changed.

attachment, to a place:

> *Poplar rooted in one plot of earth, swallow free of the air and yet true, it also, to a single home and nest: must one range the skies for one's proper food, or will everything come to him who remains fixed in one place, alert to every least stir of life? I tried for years to put questions such as these into poems, and did not speak of them.*[14]

My friend and I discussed this at midnight one night. Having left New Zealand, she is in Edinburgh, in search of her 'proper food'. I am fixed for now in the Kāpiti coast. She is exposed to the white nights and seas of a new blue, whereas I am digging deeper and deeper into the things that are happening near me.

Brasch seems to have created his own mix of being fixed in one place listening for the stir of life, and ranging, presumably also to listen for the stir of life. After finishing at Oxford and after he stopped working on archaeological sites in the Middle East, Brasch decided to stay in Europe to try and become a poet. England was nominally his home but he travelled to the eastern edge of Europe and all around Western Europe. Within England he travelled a great deal to visit friends in different parts of the country. After he returned to New Zealand he travelled constantly around the country, visiting friends and making new connections. When you read about his travels around New Zealand in the journals, it sounds exhausting. Being away so much would surely change the character of your belonging in your home place, too.

aunt, frigid:

> *How can the country be expected to take an intelligent interest in its affairs while that frigid, terrified maiden aunt, the New Zealand Broadcasting Corporation, keeps its entertainment at a level of saccharine triviality and clamps down on discussion of matters of real concern to us?*[15]

At the time of this 1969 letter, Brasch clearly believed that the country did NOT take an intelligent interest in its affairs, but citizens were not to blame for this. The fault was with the state broadcaster, New Zealand Broadcasting Corporation (NZBC), which did not allow contentious topics to be aired. Brasch thought the government had far too much influence over the NZBC. He was in favour of university radio stations and university television stations, because he thought they would be much more likely to challenge the government and other institutions. I am pleased Brasch never saw television news and current events since the government passed over this responsibility to the marketplace.

The same day that this speech about Aunty NZBC was reported, the *Otago Daily Times* reported that the Minister of Health told parliament that the possibility of requiring cigarette manufacturers to include a warning on cigarette packets about the dangers of smoking was being considered. Regulations requiring such warnings came into force 38 years later, in 2007. I am increasingly persuaded that change in New Zealand takes about 40 years after the need is first identified.

aunt, slang term for (generally women's) lavatory:

The cottage has no water, but there's a stream nearby, & it makes the
only sound to be heard as one stands outside. No aunt either – they use
the fields; which is uncomfortable in this bitter weather & must be much
worse when it is wet.[16]

austerity: I read that Brasch shopped and cooked for himself and carried
his groceries home in a string bag. His friend and *Indirections* editor James
Bertram says Brasch 'lived with a simplicity and disregard for personal
comfort most people would regard as austerity … Unfortunately for his
digestion, he wasn't a very good cook.'[17] Once he served a chocolate fish as
a dessert.

the Baal Shem Tov (Master of the Good Name), in Maori Hill: In Brasch's
library, now a special collection at the University of Otago Library, I
noticed Martin Buber's beautiful translations of the stories of the Baal
Shem Tov, a teacher who was born in Ukraine about 1700. The Baal Shem
Tov's stories are brief and slightly enigmatic. Heady with the fumes of pine
forests, they catch fire in your mind. Warm and loving and terrifying, they
are a cocktail direct from Eastern Europe.

Brasch, in middle age, decided one day that an old wreck of a house on the
edge of Jubilee Park in Dunedin was the setting for one of the stories of
the Baal Shem Tov. I wish I had been there beside him as the Master of the
Good Name rose up from the depths of history, imagination and Jewish
identity to visit Brasch at a park in Dunedin. I wish I knew which of the
Baal Shem Tov's stories was in his mind that day. I wish Brasch could point
out that house to me, even if now it is just another expensive house with a
well-tended lawn.

Brasch called these moments when art fused with a physical location
'identifications'. They had happened since his youth and he saw no reason
to apologise for them. They happened 'unconditionally, immediately, under
the joint spell of poem and place, both of them holy and enchanted'.[18]
Brasch has me in the palm of his hand with this because I have
'identifications' too, times when a spark joins one piece of wire to another
across space and time. Probably lots of readers, writers and artists have this
experience. I have never asked.

If I met Brasch, I might be unable to stop myself telling him about the day the smell of kawakawa and river clay fused into the possibility of a golem, like the Golem of Prague, but come to save the Waikanae River from the Expressway. I believe that even if we were awkward with each other on a personal level, he would understand if I said that on that day, a place from here merged with a story from 'over there'.

Immediately after talking about the Baal Shem Tov, Brasch does something which I have come to think of as a Braschian side step. He starts by describing some bushes, 'sprouting intrepidly' at the edge of a chasm, 'as if defying destruction by their very confidence and serenity'. Then he pauses, seems to rise into the air, changes direction and gains momentum. The bushes, he says, 'flourished, as if grown proud and strong in extremity of danger'.

And then the real point.

> *This was the normal condition of all living things, to have no certainty except of oneself, to live in calm disregard of what the future might bring. It shamed me that I in similar or far less danger, personal and public (for these plants and trees returned to my mind again and again in the thirties, forties and fifties: I saw them at least once in each decade), should be so shaken and fearful and vacillating, so little able to compose myself, to live as if it made no difference whether I and my world would endure forever or be cut off abruptly and calamitously tomorrow.*[19]

His journals and memoir are full of self-accusations like this. As a reader, my first impulse is to follow him sympathetically and argue with him that he has done okay. Occasionally, but not here, I feel impatient with his anxious sensitivity. Brasch's late poems have stoicism in spades and other beauties besides, so when I read about this anxiety from his youth, I think that he sometimes found exactly the strength he talks about here.

beginninglessness:

> *That sense of the beginninglessness of things, of their permanence whether they are present or not, and although I cannot tell how they persist, remains with me still.*[20]

Brasch makes up words, especially abstract compound words. 'Beginninglessness', which sounds like an English version of a German word, has such a horrible run of sibilants at the end that I wonder if Brasch ever tried to say it out loud.

books, absorbed through the fingertips: I have noticed that biographies of writers and writer's memoirs often have a photograph of the subject sitting somewhere, reading. The front cover of Charles Brasch's *Journals 1938–1945* is a picture of a young Brasch sitting on a couch, reading. His glasses dangle from his right hand and the fingers of his left hand, spread slightly apart, rest on the page as if he is absorbing the book through the tips of his fingers. A later photograph in *Journals 1945–1957* shows Brasch in dim light, reading, in a hut somewhere between the Matukituki and Wakatipu. Again, one hand touches the page. A second book sits beside his bunk. This was a tramping trip, so presumably he carried these books in his pack when every extra ounce mattered. In both photographs Brasch looks to be concentrating so deeply on his reading that he does not notice the photographer's presence.

books, to use: Brasch did not collect books out of a wish to collect.

I wanted books to read and use, not to admire for their age and rarity and preserve in cases.[21]

Brasch, Braschi, VanBrasch: Down at the Hocken library, in 2017, there was a sudden rise in excitement the day Travis VanBrasch turned up from America. As far as I know there was no karanga, no wero and no waiata, but after they showed him all the best things in the Brasch collection, Travis responded with his own gift, which took the form of news that Pope Pius VI, born Count Giovanni Angelo Braschi, was one of the family. While it was a bit of a shock that Giovanni Braschi was not just Catholic, but as Catholic as you can possibly be, it was generally agreed that the Brasch pope's well-known enthusiasm for the Vatican museum was not a surprise at all.

Travis VanBrasch stayed at a rather upmarket B&B near what some people still call 'Charles's house' in Heriot Row. One of the builders renovating the house told me that VanBrasch is an architect, so they let him look inside at the gutted shell of the house. Travis is reported to have said that if he had been in Dunedin 18 months earlier he would have bought 'Charles's house' and preserved it as a memorial, but no one says much about this because Dunedin people do not get excited about something that could have happened but didn't.

Travis also paid his respects at all the Brasch shrines. He met Brasch's literary executor, called in at the Brasch library at the Hocken, and bought a copy of *Indirections*. After that there was only the crib at Broad Bay to see. There, Travis is reported to have exclaimed at the sheer beauty of the beach and made a comment about the temperature of the water.

When I visited Dunedin two weeks later, the real Travis VanBrasch had left the building, but echoes of his visit could still be heard. The name Travis slipped in and out of people's memory because not many people in Dunedin are called Travis; his Dutch 'van' sometimes appeared in conversation as the noble German 'von'; but the Brasch pope was still there, blowing people's minds.

Brasch, Charles Orwell, appearance: Charles Brasch was a slight man with bushy eyebrows. His eyes and eyebrows looked very like those of his mother, Helene Fels Brasch, and he had the same long jaw as his father, Hyam Brasch. Left to bring up two children after his wife died, Hyam Brasch followed his own theories about how to keep a delicate boy healthy. He dressed Charles in wool. First, a heavy singlet or combinations done up to the neck. Then a warm flannel shirt. Over that young Charles had to wear one or two jerseys and a jacket. For outdoors, an overcoat and a scarf completed the outfit. The weight and heat and constraint on movement was torture to the little boy inside.

Once he gained control of his wardrobe, Charles Brasch liked his clothes to be 'few and light'.[22] He appears in most photographs in a shirt, a tie and either a suit if the occasion is formal, or Oxford bag trousers and a tweed sports jacket. Occasionally he wears what might be either a vest or a jersey.

Brasch, Charles Orwell, attitude of New Zealanders towards: James Bertram thought New Zealanders might look at Brasch differently if they knew more about his life. *Indirections*, he says, 'will prove that one who seemed in later life, in the small world of New Zealand, to be unusually favoured by fortune and family background to lead the apparently sheltered life of an artist and connoisseur, had in fact a longer and more testing private struggle to assert and justify his poetic vocation than many of his fellow writers'.[23]

Brasch, Charles Orwell, elegant: Vincent O'Sullivan describes Brasch in a poem published in 2011:

> *Wild Flowers of Greece* was a volume given me
> by a poet I admired, an austere, elegant
> arbiter of taste ...[24]

Brasch, Charles Orwell, favourite tie: In his poem 'The Gift', dedicated to Allen Curnow, C.K. Stead describes Brasch's voice, his tie and his relationship with his journal.

> Brasch in his velvet
> voice and signature
> purple tie
>
> complained to his
> journal that you had
> 'interrupted'.
>
> I wasn't sorry.
> That was Somervell's
> coffee shop
>
> nineteen fifty-three.[25]

My father would never have worn a purple tie in the 1950s, or ever, actually. Purple would have marked you out as 'one of *those*', a phrase he used when telling me about Oscar Wilde sometime about 1969. Whenever he said 'one of *those*', my father used to let one wrist drop and assume a worldly air. I had forgotten about this term for gay men until I read it recently in *No Fretful Sleeper*, Paul Millar's biography of Bill Pearson.

Brasch, Charles Orwell, on the mode of address: Mostly I think of him as 'Charles Brasch', a literary person. Initially I thought of him as a person of another time, but now he is present with me. He is around that corner, under the world or in the radio, close by, where the dead are. Not that the dead are literally watching us, or eating from our plates, but more that they have left behind a warmth. Things they thought and wanted matter to me and I want to find out what those things were. A mix of historical distance and affectionate respect applies to my use of 'Charles Brasch'.

I also think of this man as 'Brasch', a shortcut that helps a sentence move along. My father told me that gentlemen might refer to each other by their surnames if there were some degree of intimacy between them. I am a woman and therefore liable to make mistakes in the world of gentlemen. I hope I will be able to say 'Brasch' without causing offence.

When I corresponded with Charles Brasch, I called him Mr Brasch and I thought very carefully about what I was saying. The *Otago Daily Times* uses the honorific 'Dr' after Brasch's honorary doctorate was conferred in 1963, but I do not use that title.

Brasch, Charles Orwell, his family, back to Moses: Some people's eyes glaze over when faced with genealogy, but mine focus intently. I suppose it is all to do with what you think all these names mean. Now that I am older and have become the custodian of several of those folded papers with their spidery family trees, I see them as containing important information in encrypted form. Names stand in for people. People stand in for cultures. Marriages stand in for property and sometimes for bonds of love. Children stand in for everyone who went before and for the future.

Brasch, Charles Orwell, the spear side: In terms of space and the warmth of his descriptions, Charles Brasch gives much less to the Brasch family than he does to the Hallensteins. I am going to pay some attention to the Brasch side of the family because an absence, or a turning away, is a form of significance, even if the nature of the significance remains obscure.

Charles Brasch's paternal grandfather, whose first name is not given in *Indirections*, was born in the village of Schwersenz, near Posen (now Poland, but previously part of the German Empire). This grandfather subsequently lived in New Plymouth where he worked as a tobacconist. Brasch compares this grandfather with the three 'decidedly energetic and enterprising' Hallenstein brothers and concludes that his grandfather Brasch did not 'do very well' for himself.[26]

Hyam Brasch was born in the village of New Plymouth in New Zealand in 1873, the second of four boys. Hyam's mother died when he was about eight. In his memoir Charles Brasch never mentions meeting his Brasch grandfather, says nothing about his nature, nothing about the way his father was brought up and nothing about how his father was able to get from New Plymouth to Melbourne to study law. Charles Brasch does say that at some time after his mother's death Hyam 'seems to have fallen out with his father'.[27] The author of the memoir has drawn a curtain here, perhaps over something painful, something that could hurt living people or something potentially scandalous or explosive. But he does say that there were two dead mothers and two boys alienated from their fathers in this family. In the case of Charles Brasch and his father the result was painful in the extreme. Very likely the same was true for Hyam and his father.

After a careful description of his father's professional life, including his strengths and some deficiencies, Charles Brasch concludes that as a barrister, his father was 'perhaps in the second rather than the first rank'.[28] I find this ranking of people unpleasant, but then I am the granddaughter of a pharmacist, a mechanic and two shop assistants. By my standards, a man who has come to a new country and found a way to support himself has done well. Similarly, a man who was born in New Plymouth to a family with no spare money, who has acquired a university education at a time when only the wealthy could manage that, and who then became a barrister, has also done well. Whether they were kind, sad or bitter men is another matter.

Certain colourful possibilities in this family *did* interest Brasch. One was that the Brasch name was a version of Ben Rabbi Asch (BRSH), meaning son of Rabbi Asch. Another was that the family could have been Hasidic

Jews, part of the same world as the Baal Shem Tov. Brasch also enjoyed the story of two London-born Jews, John (Israel) Hart and Benjamin Hart who were part of his father's mother's family. These men, it seems, ran away to sea, later earned their living as conjurers, volunteered or were pressed into the English navy, and fought at the Battle of Trafalgar.

Brasch, Hyam (later Henry Brash), appearance, anxieties and temperament:

> *Handsome, well-built and lean, with a compact, well-made head and features, he carried himself with assurance and never lost his figure, although his hair went white early – he wore it, in later years, very short, New Zealand fashion; and since he always dressed with quiet care in good taste (he had one whole big drawer full of ties, more than I have ever seen before or since), often wearing a flower in the lapel of his jacket, he made a distinguished figure in a community where most people, men and women, disguised themselves as sacks or bags.*[29]

This is a complex sentence, a flower arrangement of subordinate clauses and phrases. I tried reading the sentence aloud, slowly, as if it were a poem, and after doing this a few times, I found a rhythm and began to enjoy each element and the way they all come together to make a whole story and a portrait of the man. The indictment of sack-wearing is a rare moment when Charles aligns himself with his father against the rest of New Zealand. When it comes to describing his father's nature, Charles says:

> *His temperament was not in doubt; he was energetic, self-confident, rather impatient, and not in the least introspective.*

> *He and I were certainly very different by nature. Our temperaments might have been thought complementary; but my father wished me to be like him in all things, only, with my greater opportunities, much more successful.*[30]

According to Charles, the flip side of his father's brashness was that he was always anxious about whether he would be or had been accepted in Dunedin society, 'as a lawyer, and a Jewish one at that.'[31] Charles Brasch places his father's occupation first as the source of his anxiety over acceptance, and his Jewishness second. I might argue with him about the order. In general though, I appreciate the way Brasch deals with Jewish matters. With the exception of the description of anti-Semitic comments made to his father, he seems to me to look the subject in the eye. Hyam Brasch tried to gain acceptance by changing his name to Henry Brash and by playing what I would call sports but Charles calls 'games'. In his father's circle, he says, games, 'were an expression of social solidarity'.[32]

Charles Brasch's Ten Commandments, as I imagine them:
i   Do something strong in artistic terms, something local which is also innovative, or something that brings the rest of the world's art and New Zealand art closer.
ii   Better to fail than be timid.
iii Engage yourself with the community.
iv   It is good for people to live in a rich environment of amenities and beauty. Test every idea against this principle.
v   Think ahead and make a start now on projects that will take decades to fully show results.
vi   Plan the money side of things properly.
vii Think of local artists as contributing to the community in a real and important way, and not as bludgers.
viii Preserve the human past.
ix   Preserve trees, lakes, mountains, rivers, birds, fish and people. Everything is connected.
x   You *must not* think in expedience. You must not.

cadet corps, at Waitaki Boys' High School: Brasch hated the compulsory military drill in the cadet corps at Waitaki Boys' High School.

causes, liberal: James Bertram says that 'In Dunedin [Brasch] was known as a staunch supporter of liberal causes'.[33] Charles Brasch was a member of the Dunedin committee of 'Save Manapouri', the campaign to prevent the government from raising the level of Lake Manapōuri to generate hydro-electric power that would be sold cheaply to Comalco, the operators of the aluminium smelter at Bluff.

He was opposed to New Zealand's participation in the American war on the people of Vietnam and later to the careless haste with which a project to build an aluminium smelter at Aramoana was being developed.

'He wrote strong letters to the newspapers, with a vein of Swiftian indignation when he was deeply moved,'[34] Bertram says. This is the only reference I have seen to Brasch's letters to the newspapers. It suggests that Bertram saw at least some of these letters. I wonder if Brasch sent them to him, since Bertram did not live in Dunedin.

Central Otago, 1920:

> *In the hotel near the lake, our small rooms opened onto the garden with its rare old mulberry tree, its beds of poppies blazing in that clear hot sun, roses that rushed into bloom and died almost in a day, delphinium and clarkia, hollyhock and nasturtium. With Carty and our hotel acquaintances we spent much of our day beside the lake, in the green shade of the small thick willow trees along the shore, which rose in low ridges of pale shingle formed by the different levels of the water.*[35]

I can picture Brasch sitting somewhere quiet, perhaps in the late 1960s, thinking back to a Wanaka holiday when he was a child. I can imagine that the light and the heat and the trees by the lake might have stayed with him over the years. But when I arrive at the list of flowers, doubt creeps in and I wonder if there really was an 11-year-old who not only noticed these flowers but knew them well enough to be sure of their names. This supra-real moment, which happens nearly a quarter of the way through the book, and others like it, changed my view of *Indirections*. Initially I read it as a literal memoir but with this flower-painting, supposedly remembered by a child, I started to see it as a self-conscious and deliberate work of art.

When I was 20 I spent the summer working in Central Otago. Mostly I spent my days pouring beer into jugs, gathering up trays of glasses and warding off hairy, sun-burnt arms, but on my days off I saw the crimson flowers people with settled lives had planted beside their stone houses. I smelled wild thyme and touched the rocks people said were so hot you could fry an egg on them. When I read the passage in *Indirections* I remembered the lacy lime-green willows. I am grateful for the description of the shade as green and for the memory of crimson flowers and for Brasch's moment of Central Otago heat, connected for me to the swish of the steriliser and lying under the irrigators in the wee small hours, looking up at the moon.

centre, and periphery:

> *It is true that New Zealand is a long way from Europe. But it is also true that the European tradition can take root here and grow, if we wish it to do so. To think of this country as a mere province, a poverty-stricken outpost where nothing original can be expected to arise, is false and stultifying and the best way of ensuring that in fact nothing will arise. Every province has something to contribute to the centre – provided it continues to welcome what the centre can give it; every province can be a centre in its own right – provided it does not imagine that it can be self-sufficient.*[36]

If you think immediately of Great Britain as the centre of a colonial empire, and New Zealand as one of her far-flung provinces, if you think of the contributions made by the centre as pigs and pox and colonialism and the contributions from the periphery as wealth, trees, water, meat, blood and clever young people, you will start to get angry. But Brasch's concept of the centre is very different from the one you might expect.

> *Working in his own place and time he [the artist] is drawing on a tradition which has been formed in so many places and times that it now belongs to none exclusively but to all. In one sense he is working on the periphery, wherever he may be, even in London or Paris or Vienna, because at the same time the tradition belongs to and is being reincarnated in a dozen other places as well; but inasmuch as the tradition is alive for him it has become localized and he is working from a centre [Brasch's emphasis]. There is no single centre; the Yugoslavia of Mestrovich, the Finland of Sibelius, the Ireland of Yeats, are as much centres in respect of the work of these artists as the Italy of Dante or the France of Cézanne.*[37]

The male pronouns are still a bit of an obstacle, but the idea that each artist is on their own periphery feels right.

Maybe the centre/periphery dichotomy was part of every colonial childhood? As a schoolboy during World War II, C.K. Stead learned that if Europe is the centre, New Zealand must be at the fringe. Stead remembers learning this from the map which hung over the blackboard at the front of the classroom.

> *It was a Mercator's projection, and because of the way the world was laid out, with the international date line to the far left and far right, New Zealand appeared twice, once in the lower left-hand corner and again at the lower right. I don't remember that this repetition was ever pointed out or commented on, but I was struck by it. It seemed to suggest our insignificance. We were so unimportant we could appear twice and it didn't matter, made no difference.*[38]

If you think, as the young Stead did in the 1940s, that 'all the world's significant events, and everyone of importance in it, were remote from us, away mostly *up there*, or if not, then *over there*, to our left and to our right',[39] then logic dictates that what happens here is less significant, and is therefore worth less. If you write about *here*, will people think that is less significant than if you wrote about *over there*? I ponder this with reference to a book about a road in provincial New Zealand.

centre, working from, as a condition of good work:

> *… the first condition of good work here is that for the artist the tradition must be localized, in himself or in a group to which he has access, so that he may feel himself, just as an artist working in Europe would, to be working from a centre, and can see his subject matter, which will be local at least in the sense that he belongs to this particular time and place, quite naturally in terms of the tradition. He must at the same time reincarnate the tradition in a local form, and embody his local and personal material in terms recognizably of the tradition, however modified.*[40]

certainty, sad: Janet Frame on the emotional attitude of Brasch's poems:

I remembered [Brasch's] poems in the Book of New Zealand Verse: they were mysterious poems, questions addressed to the mountains, the sea and the dead, with the sad certainty that there would be no answer.[41]

certainty, of tone:

However the arts may develop in New Zealand, they will still be working within and must still depend on the European tradition. Of that there can be no question. But the European tradition is not static, and there are many branches of it; all the branches depend on the main tradition, but all are constantly adding to it and modifying it, and there is no apparent limit to their number and variety. In every good artist in every European society that main tradition is reincarnated.[42]

Both the tone and content of this pronouncement from the first *Landfall* cause me to recoil. I have heard Brasch's pronouncements described as 'magisterial', a description that brings with it a stamping out of the possibility of contrary voices. At the same time as I am distancing myself, I respect that Brasch has a position which he has thought through and is willing to stand behind. I can also imagine the mix of anxiousness and brio that might have been swirling around in the lead-up to the launch of *Landfall*'s first issue, but, 70 years on, I do not see all New Zealand art as belonging within the dynamic European art tradition or New Zealand itself as a 'European society'.

Charles Brasch *see* **Brasch, Charles Orwell**

china, using the good set: In 2017 I inherited a set of *Landfall* journals, starting from the absolute beginning in March 1947 and ending in 1994, when the owner stopped his subscription because the work in the journal stopped being of interest to him. I have been wondering if I should open these 70-year-old journals, press the pages flat, put other books on top of them and put them on the table next to my computer, as if they were ordinary books. It is the same sort of decision as whether to use your good china or whether to keep it in a cupboard where it is less likely to be dropped or broken. My decision is to read the journals, and work with them, because I think that is what they were made for. So I take them out to the lounge, four or five at a time, put them on the table beside my favourite chair, and read them in the afternoon sun. I don't fold the pages down but I write in pencil in the margins and leave Post-it notes in them, just as I do in every other book. The binding is a bit fragile, and a couple have made a cracking sound as I opened them, but I believe they want to be opened, even if it hurts. I don't have room for them all in my bookcases so I keep my *Landfall* collection in the spare room, on the bedside table and on the chest of drawers. It is still possible for a guest to sleep in the room, but there is a dusty old-book smell which might not suit everyone, and there is no room for makeup and hair brushes because all the flat surfaces are covered with stacks of *Landfall* journals, in chronological order. Sometimes in research it is hard to locate information. In the case of Charles Brasch, the opposite is true.

The Clear, also known as Prospect Park: The day I visited Prospect Park for the first time the whole city was in a misty cloud of rain. It was March but the temperature outside was about eight degrees. I had a sore throat, a runny nose and about half my usual energy. Nevertheless, I was determined to walk up the hill to The Clear that afternoon. When I arrived at the park I looked around to see if I could find what Brasch might have found so special about the place. I discovered the wooden bench that his friends had put there after he died and I sat on it, thinking that his friends loved him very much. I wondered whether he liked to look over North East Valley, towards Aquinas College, or south, across the city? At some point, I noticed that the mown area of the park is roughly a circle, the hills in the distance are almost a circle and the blue sky above the park that day was a circular hole. I knew then that I should have trusted Brasch more.

coffee cups:

> *My favourite coffee cups belonged to a simple shapely Doulton set, plain white, fluted, narrowing downwards, with gold handles, small enough to allow one to drink two or three cupsfull (black or with hot milk, and brown sugar crystals) without seeming greedy.*[43]

colonial, as in 'a job only a colonial could do':

> *I see dear old (as you say) Karl [Wolfskehl] at least once a week, and he's been here several times. He went into the sea once and looked like*

an intellectual porpoise. I have a notion he may be doing me harm. After all, I'm a colonial and have a job to do that only a colonial can do, but intercourse with him is so damned attractive I'm losing my grip. I'm degenerating into a second-rate European, all subjective, when I ought to be trying to draw the subjective out of objective colonialism ...[44]

Frank Sargeson included this description of Karl Wolfskehl as a porpoise in a 1943 letter. Wolfskehl, a German Jewish refugee from Hitler who lived in New Zealand during World War II, was an eminent poet and scholar. He was also a big man, and in the light of Sargeson's often quoted description, I picture Wolfskehl as pale and fleshy in the waves.

I understand that Wolfskehl could stand for the seductive power of European culture. After all, it would be nice if you could enjoy the scholarly, musical or literary culture of Germany, here. I understand too that if you try to emulate European ways from here, you would end up with kitsch. I understand that someone from here could write stories about here that a visitor could not and that this might be the job 'only a colonial could do'. I *don't* understand 'trying to draw the subjective out of objective colonialism'. Does Sargeson mean 'draw out' as a poultice draws out malignant humours? Sargeson later withdrew from his friendship with Wolfskehl.

conscientious objectors, treatment of: In recording his own life in journals and in his memoir, Brasch also recorded his personal contact with other circumstances of the day in which he was just a minor player. For example, both *Indirections* and Brasch's journal contain descriptions of attending Military Service Tribunal hearings for conscientious objectors in Britain during the early part of World War II. In January 1940 Brasch and his friend John Crockett wanted to know what happened at the tribunals because they were thinking of going through that process themselves. In April 1940 Brasch attended a tribunal with Crockett on the day his friend's case to be recognised as a conscientious objector was heard. The anxiety and fear of the hearing are vivid. 'I went as though to my own execution,'[45] Brasch says, no doubt aware of the harshness with which pacifists had been treated during World War I, both in Britain and New Zealand, and wondering if this war would be different.

The tribunal scene is described in detail. There is an apparent arbitrariness to the outcome as different tribunal members express their views and then vote on the decision. Crockett, an artist, was given the alternatives of working in Air Raid Precautions, which seldom accepted conscientious objectors so was a phoney option, or working in agriculture or forestry, far from London. 'So the old world ends for him', Brasch writes in his journal. In *Indirections* he spells out a bit more what has ended for John.

> *He had his orders. His freedom was now limited, he had no longer to make ultimate decisions, his life being prescribed for him. It would be my turn next.*[46]

There is dread in that final sentence. I think I hear a squeak of envy too, for Crockett who no longer had the responsibility of deciding what to do with his life.

In the months between September 1940 and May 1941 Germany bombed England night after night as a preliminary to invasion. In his journal Brasch documents his movements from flat to flat and his visits to various friends, some of whom sleep with their children in the garden in their cold bomb shelter. Some sleep under the kitchen table and some stay in their beds because they are too old to sleep in a makeshift bed. Brasch tells us where he sleeps, where the bombs fell and what he sees from the window, but emotion is, perhaps deliberately, restrained. George Orwell's journal of the Blitz is much darker, more chaotic and more frightening, but both men think a German invasion of Britain is imminent.

By early 1941 Brasch had decided he could not be a pacifist conscientious objector in these circumstances and would comply with the call-up into the armed forces when it came. Brasch's description in his journal of his army medical examination in February 1941 is clear, and at the same time tense with the pressure of feeling behind it. The physical arrangements could have been written by Kafka. Four doctors, each in a separate cubicle, examined the men. The first looked at eyes, feet and reflexes. The second measured height, weight and chest. (Brasch was five foot eight and three-quarter inches, and weighed nine and a half stone.) For the third doctor you made fists, whirled your arms and then dropped your trousers while the doctor felt one ball. The third doctor asked a question that Brasch did not hear, but to which he 'answered instinctively no'.[47] For the fourth doctor, you 'passed water' into a bottle and then he inspected your ears while his assistant tested the urine. In between you waited, fully clothed, in a room with a big blazing fire. At the end, a fifth doctor reviewed all the information, asked you what you wanted to do in the military and then told you what would happen next.

Brasch, who had seen a drawing at the National Gallery of men standing around naked at a World War I military medical examination, had been afraid of being humiliated, cold and shouted at, and afraid of how he would cope with the fear of being a soldier in combat. But the process was not as terrible as he had imagined. He was only naked for one doctor, the doctors all spoke quietly and the rooms were warm. Despite this relatively humane treatment, the outcome was still disturbing. The second doctor told Brasch he had slight emphysema in one lung but did not explain what that was. Because of the emphysema, the fifth doctor gave Brasch a card saying that the army did not consider him fit and he would not be called up for some considerable time. Afterwards, Brasch had an hour to wait for the bus home so he spent time in a cathedral. Rooks, which mean death to me and maybe to Brasch, flapped off the tower. Then he noticed other birds singing as if it were already spring. 'It almost seemed that with these announcements of spring, and my release, the war was over for me,'[48] Brasch says. Once home he worried a bit about whether 'emphysema' was a euphemism for Tb and looked up 'emphysema', comparing what he found in the dictionary with what he had read in Thomas Mann's *The Magic Mountain*.

dictionary, personal: In 'Dialogue on the Art of Composition', Milan Kundera talks about each of his novels having 'theme-words' at its core. As well as each of his novels having certain key words, he himself has key words. Sixty-three, to be precise. Those words are his personal dictionary. 'One Starless Night', this glossary, is not Brasch's personal dictionary. It is mine.

distortions, Frank Sargeson on:

> *… we New Zealanders are European, and the great majority of us have our recent origins in some part of the British Isles – but we live at the other end of the world. I imagine I can hear listeners saying, How obvious!, and How tedious to listen to what is so obvious! Yet it must be repeated again and again – a sort of mental pinch as it were, to wake ourselves up – otherwise we shall go on to the end of time, representing snow storms in our shop windows at Christmas, when the sun is melting the asphalt pavement … I fancy that one of the very first things the New Zealand novelist must be aware of, is the large number of distortions which he has to deal with.*[49]

Ever since I read this, I have been looking out for other distortions. The first distortion I saw was in the opening sentence of this quotation. We New Zealanders are not 'European'. We were not European when Sargeson wrote this and we are even less European now.

In a recent essay, Tina Makereti points out that a literary world and a publishing industry that does not include stories from large parts of the community is a distortion.

> *So let me ask directly: Where are our immigrant stories? Our stories of poor communities? Our stories of growing communities of street people? Our queer stories? Our stories of people with disabilities? Our stories of Pasifika communities? And while you can probably name more than one Māori writer, the statistics on publication of Māori writing might continue to surprise, since they aren't even half way to proportional. Yes – these stories and these writers exist, in small quantities, often in small presses. But how many stories from any of these communities might the average New Zealander encounter in the average year?*[50]

Makereti calls for people from all these under-represented groups to write the stories that matter to them, and hopes that in this way there will be more stories for the next generations to see themselves in. These stories will have the double attraction for their readers that *Man Alone* had for C.K. Stead in 1949: 'It was dealing with a known world and using language in ways that broke with older, more formal, essentially British and middle-class conventions.'[51]

domesticity: Commenting on housekeeping at the home of a family he often stayed with while London was being bombed, Brasch says, 'This house is cleaned incessantly, remorselessly. How I hate the domesticity that enslaves one to one's possessions ...'[52] Balancing dirt with effort is a hard balance to find, I admit.

Dunedin, and Brasch: A woman smiles at me as I come in the door of the Allpress café. She knows my name before I say it. She tells me she had heard there was a woman in town who was interested in Brasch and then last week she spotted me in Everyday Gourmet talking earnestly to someone who is *very* interested in Brasch. After so many years away, I had forgotten that in Dunedin there are no secrets. I moved my friends, my teapots and my long conversations about Brasch to a table at the back of Everyday Gourmet after that, but nothing much changed. From my table at the back, I saw that woman several more times, standing outside Knox Church, waiting for the bus.

In Dunedin, being *very* interested in Brasch is seen as completely understandable. I was not prepared for that either. The way people helped me with their ideas, their warm cakes, their connections and their houses was a surprise too. All of that made me feel grateful and hopeful, both of which are as powerful for a writer as strong coffee. That they did not out me as an imposter made me pink and sweaty with relief.

duty: It is clear from Brasch's letters to the editor of the *Otago Daily Times* and from his reported speeches that he thought any formal organisation had, or should have, a purpose, a role and a set of operating policies and procedures. Its duty then was to fulfil that purpose by enacting the policies. This framework was the sort of thinking Brasch would have heard from his father and his grandfather as they went about their financial and philanthropic business. If Brasch saw disparities between the purpose of an organisation, its policy and its behaviour, he would point them out, along with what he thought should happen to fix the problem.

endurance *see* **the Baal Shem Tov**

everlasting daisies: Known to Brasch as 'everlastings'. The flower most associated with his grandmother, because the pale green and white colours of their leaves and petals 'went naturally with the ivory and dry cool green of her tussore silk veils and parasols'.[53] Identifying a person with a colour, or in this case two colours, is a Brasch thing. It is interesting to be told in *Indirections* that Brasch kept the phrase 'the honey eyes of the everlastings' for years while he waited to find the right poem to put it in. The further you take the word away from the daisies, the more it starts to sound like one of those abstract compound words that Brasch liked.

friends, at boarding school:

He[Peter Shand] had a circle of devoted friends; no boy in the school was more courted. A few of those friends might seem to be hearties and nothing else, but some romantic streak drew them to Peter.[54]

Charles Brasch was drawn to Peter Shand, who was big and strong and a capable footballer and cricketer. Peter seemed unafraid and 'his combination of seriousness and waywardness, of gaiety and melancholy, made him a delightful and unpredictable companion'. Tony, who was 19, and not very clever, was drawn to Peter so strongly that 'it affected his work and even his games'.[55] Peter used to treat Tony with a mix of neglect and affection. This caused Tony distress and he used to ask Brasch's advice. Brasch was fond of Tony but Tony knew that although Brasch was attached to Peter, they were not rivals. Tony had a motorbike and he used to take Peter into Ōamaru to one of the tea rooms. Peter and Charles used to talk poetry. Once, when 'his fascination held me most strongly', Charles wrote a poem in which he described the pale fine tussock as silky like Peter's hair.

friends, as readers:

I continued to ask friends (James [Bertram] later and almost regularly, as a matter of course; later still, Ruth Dallas) for an opinion of poems before I ventured to publish them.[56]

friendships, thought to be undesirable: Hyam Brasch thought a short spell at home was desirable, between his son's time at Waitaki Boys' and starting Oxford. Charles Brasch speculates about the reasons for this. He says that his father might have wanted to give him exposure to the business or 'to loosen undesirable friendships'.[57]

generosity, and gentle remoteness: The man who gave me the set of *Landfall* journals explained that he remembered *Landfall*'s short stories from his school days. These stories stood out from the rest of the set texts because they were written by New Zealanders. After studying in Europe this man returned to Dunedin, decided to subscribe to *Landfall* and, remembering those early stories, set himself the additional goal of collecting the journal back to the beginning. Hearing about this, Charles Brasch gave the man his own copies of some early issues to fill gaps. These issues have the letters 'Cb' on the top-right corner, the same mark Brasch made inside the cover of some of his books. The man had appreciated Brasch's generosity, and it seemed only right, he said, that he should continue the chain of generosity Brasch had started. He also told me that Brasch had a gentle remoteness about him.

I would like to thank the man who gave me the *Landfall* journals. The stories, poems, book reviews, sociological writing and even the covers remind me of the adults I used to hear talking when I was a child, except that now I understand their preoccupations better. Now I also know how much work would be required to write each story and poem and to fill, edit and sell every issue of the journal.

Germany, March 1930: Brasch found some of his Hanover relatives a bit disappointing.

> *Uncle Richard had a family likeness to Grandfather, without his industry and intelligence; he was small, kindly, correct, a little insubstantial, and collected stamps. He held some grey clerkly job which just kept him and (perhaps with help from Grandfather) allowed him to go walking in the mountains in summer with friends; if Grandfather on visits to Europe took his relatives to Italy or elsewhere, it was at his own expense.*[58]

As with his attitude to his Brasch grandfather, Charles Brasch's attitude to this man is condescending. For Brasch, if you had a 'grey clerkly job' and did not lead an enterprise or create art, you had failed. Maybe this man created a small world in which he was kind to people and they were kind to him?

girls, second best:

She [Lel] was more cheerful and easy going than I, sturdier, more adventurous, with more of the boy in her then, and readier to be his companion. Yet she was only a girl, and girls are second best.[59]

I think these statements are meant as an ironic version of what Hyam Brasch thought. I hope so.

grass railways, building, compared with the arrangement of words:

One [activity] that absorbed me still more deeply for a long time was building grass railways ... On top of the bank grew tall strong cocksfoot grass, its long stalks brown and dry; the season must have been a dry one. I broke off a stalk, making a clean break, and stuck one end carefully into the clay bank. The other end I fitted into another thicker stalk, which I made sure not to split; the two had to fit exactly. I then cautiously bent these two attached stalks along the face of the bank, a few inches out, and anchored them by sticking the farther end into the clay. So I had the first loop of an aerial railway. Beginning thus, I was able to construct an intricate network of lines running both up and down and along, with two or more loops starting from one point in the clay, and covering a bank perhaps twenty feet long by four or five feet high ... I can still recall the deep content and satisfaction of this game. I think it gave me aesthetic, imaginative pleasure of a sort I found in no other game then or indeed at any other time. I was making something visible and tangible in the real world, yet something as light, graceful and fragile as the tracery of a bird's flight, fantail or swallow, or the motions of fish in a stream. Only the arrangement of words, audible tangible words set side by side to strike out new unsuspected meanings that came from who knows where, was to give me, later, any comparable satisfaction.[60]

hair, long: At the house in Karitane, where the family spent their summers when Brasch was a boy, there was a flagpole. Some way up there was a platform.

There my aunts and their friends used to climb and gaze out, laughing and singing as they dried their long hair in the sun and wind.[61]

This scene, much elaborated, also appears in 'Karitane', the second part of the poem 'Otago Landscapes':

> On the tall platform under the flag
> Laughing girls climb
> To take the air and gaze,
> And over the sea's breast
> Peering through blown hair
> Feel their breath come faster,
> Launching into the wind
> Thoughts that sigh and swell
> With amber tresses of the sea,
> Drawn to the green caves under
> The fluted wave,
> To the singing among the rocks,
> The echo in the twilit shell
> Of distant bells and muted thunder.[62]

In the Foreword to *Indirections* Brasch says that his memoir contains recollections he 'was not able to shape into poems'. This does not seem to be correct. *Indirections* contains a number of recollections which were already poems, like this one, or became poems. Often, as in this case, I like the prose version better.

head piece, university as: The *Otago Daily Times* usually reported Brasch's speeches, in detail.

> *Dr Brasch said the community could not exist without the knowledge and special skills which the university inherited, revised and taught. The university was the head piece or the thinking organ of the community. The community expressed its multifarious interests in the university; the university was thus the community expressing itself and speaking to the world at large.*[63]

hearties: A group Brasch identifies at Oxford.

There were a number of large loud hearties about too, who rowed, some of them, and spent a good deal of money, and were often drunk.[64]

Brasch was not large, or loud. He did not row, spent money judiciously and did not drink much. There had been hearties at Waitaki Boys' High School too. I saw some in Hyde Street in 2017.

Heriot Row, 36a: What is there now is a simulacrum of Charles Brasch's house. For me, a latecomer with no memories of the man in the peacock chair, afternoon teas in the drawing room or, more importantly, the man who worked so hard in a messy room further back in the house, 36a Heriot Row is not Charles Brasch's house any more.

The owner of a second-hand bookshop told me that from his point of view Charles Brasch is still 'there', in Dunedin. Artists and writers had told him over and over about ways that Brasch had supported them in their creative work, he said – a residency or a fellowship at a critical time that helped them to take an imaginative leap in their work. Brasch is there, behind those projects, he said. I agree. Brasch is there, in Dunedin still, looking after the Hocken, the university library and Otago Museum. In a less direct way, he is looking after me. He does not need to look after the house.

home ground, New Zealand as: This sentence on the inside blurb of Charles Brasch's 1969 collection *Not Far Off* places Brasch firmly in and of New Zealand:

Because he lives in New Zealand, this country is the centre of the world for Charles Brasch; as the poems in this book show, all his experience begins and ends on home ground.

The next sentence opens the door to a wider world.

But his world knows no boundaries of place and time: he shares the lives of men here and elsewhere – wherever they may be, whatever their experience, it is Not Far Off.[65]

The person who wrote this blurb might have felt that Brasch needed to be branded as someone for whom New Zealand was 'home ground', even though he was born here and had lived in New Zealand for more than 20 years. After that, in second place, comes the sentence that recognises Brasch as a person who can connect with people everywhere. Blurbs are full of meaningless things, but still, it feels a bit sad to me that Brasch's claim to be at home here needs to be restated so late in his life.

I, first-person pronoun: During his years at Waitaki Boys' High School, Brasch and his sister Lel spent holidays each summer at Frankton, now a suburb of Queenstown, but a separate township then. He speaks of these times in the first-person plural: 'we' bathed once or twice a day in the lake; 'we' lay in the sun and ate wild gooseberries.

> *We walked about the Flat, climbed trees, fetched the cows for milking, played cards, and I wrote poetry.*[66]

But only *he* wrote poetry.

indirection: If you were Hyam Brasch and you had a son who never wanted what you wanted, how would you get him to do something you thought was important?

> *I do not think he [Hyam Brasch] gave any reasons for sending me to Oxford, except of the vaguest, most general sort; I had to deduce them. Possibly he was trying to get his way by indirection, knowing my stubbornness already and realizing that open opposition to me would be ineffective.*[67]

Indirections, reasons for writing: In 1953, in his 40s, Brasch was already thinking about what he called 'autobiographical sketches'. His working title was *Finestra a levante, A Window to the East*:

> *... it expresses or suggests as much as could be got into a title, probably: the return to childhood, my own origins, & the origins of the human race (& the Jews), the dawn which is the beginning of all things, the perpetual renewal, the new day.*[68]

Finestra a levante lasted a long time as a working title, but in the end *Indirections* won out. The return to childhood is still central, but with the title *Indirections* existential doubt and hesitation take centre stage along with what James Bertram, who edited *Indirections*, called the 'Growth of a Poet's Mind'.[69] 'Above all,' Bertram says, 'this is a poet's testament.' I agree.

The manuscript Bertram worked with had been 'in part revised by the author, but was of a length and almost Goncourt density of detail that made immediate publication unlikely'.[70] The 'major problem', according to Bertram, was deciding 'for whom Brasch was writing'. If it was for Brasch's 'scattered friends and fellow spirits' in Europe and America there should not be too much detail about New Zealand. And New Zealand readers, interested in the childhood of a famous man, might not be interested in European art and the archaeological dig in Egypt. I find it hard to empathise with Bertram's editorial dilemma. Nearly 40 years later, I want to resist the idea that New Zealand readers would not be interested in European art and literature.

My own theory is that Brasch wrote *Indirections* first and foremost as an aesthetic project, for which *he* was the primary reader. The text had to have European and New Zealand art and literature in it because he had both inside him. Recently someone suggested that the ornate and detail-heavy text is in some way Brasch hiding from the question of his sexuality. I don't know if that is a factor in Brasch's chosen style. Whatever flaws *Indirections* has as a piece of writing, I wish it had been published as its author envisaged it.

Indirections, sequel: When *Indirections* ends, Brasch's grandfather has just died.

> *Two days later a bellbird in the trees sang him out of the garden, through clear light and shadow.*
>
> *At last it was time for something new to begin.*[71]

That new thing was *Landfall*.

> *The true sequel to this introductory memoir then becomes five volumes of verse, twenty volumes of Landfall, and the anthology* Landfall Country ...[72]

Jewish, as in 'How Jewish was Brasch?': Whether explicitly or implicitly
everyone who writes about Brasch deals with this question. My experience
has been that New Zealanders brought up in a Christian framework
minimise Brasch's Jewishness. Maybe they don't see it? I am not saying that
Jewishness was the only or even one of the *most* important influences on
Brasch's life, but I think the case is very strong that it was important.

Bertram, one of Brasch's oldest friends, says, 'Both [Brasch's] parents were
of Jewish descent, though on neither side had they been practising Jews
for a couple of generations.'[73] The subtext here is that Jewishness is at some
distance from Brasch. Bertram is technically correct that Brasch's mother
is of Jewish descent rather than Jewish herself. However, looking at Charles
Brasch's parents' cultural identity, it is strongly Jewish on both sides.

In the editorial note to *Indirections* Bertram calls Brasch 'a New Zealander
by birth, Jewish by origin, and European by cultural inheritance ...'[74] This
layering of heritages, of which Judaism is one, makes more sense to me
than Bertram's earlier description, although I think that the separation
between Jewish and European is artificial. Steven Sedley and Leonard
Bell both join the two concepts together. Sedley, writing from a Jewish
perspective, includes Brasch in his chapter on Jewish writers in New
Zealand. He describes Brasch as having a 'supressed sense of Jewishness'
and points out that neither the word 'Jew' or the Holocaust appear in
Brasch's poems.[75] For Sedley, Brasch is a 'cosmopolitan Jew, at home in
Italy, France, Australia and New Zealand'.

Leonard Bell describes Brasch as 'a secular, Central European Jewish
intellectual',[76] born in New Zealand. He goes further, too, drawing a
parallel between Brasch and other sons of continental European Jewish
businessmen who became alienated from their fathers. He cites Walter
Benjamin, Theodore Adorno and Karl Wolfskehl as examples. According to
Bell, Brasch in New Zealand was 'an intermediary, and a mediating figure
between the local, British-shaped and the alien, Continental'.[77]

It seems to me that the key words 'European', 'New Zealander' and 'Jewish'
want to join into some composite word that starts to capture the texture
of Brasch's cultural identity. I do not fully agree with Bell's description of

Brasch as 'secular'. Yes, he was secular in that he was not an active member of any religion. He was not observant in a Jewish sense, but no, he was not secular. He saw the world in spiritual as well as material dimensions.

In 1938 Charles Brasch was conscious of his own Jewishness and some of the hardships being faced by Jews in Europe when he wrote to Ursula Bethell that his 'Jewish blood' made him 'too heavy with guilt'[78] to return to the safety of New Zealand. Around this same time, he describes his awareness of the personal menace of fascism.

> *Hitler made me keenly conscious, intermittently, that I was of Jewish descent and that Nazis, Mosleyites and their kind must hate me as such and want to kill me.*[79]

But in 1940, as the Nazis invaded country after country and invasion of Great Britain looked likely, Brasch's 'Jewish descent' description of himself disappeared and he called himself a Jew.

> *The terrible humiliation of realizing that though one might repudiate war one is [Brasch's emphasis] dependent on the issue of it, utterly dependent – at least as a Jew I am.*[80]

Brasch's library and his poems show that he had what might be called a cultural sympathy with Jewish writers, but his mind was open to non-Jewish writers too.

> *I loved the Old Testament, or parts of it. The Gospels drew me like a chant, a haunting plainsong groundbass sounding continuously behind and within daily life and history. I took a certain relish in being descended from Aaron and so able to consider Moses an uncle. It pleased me too that I might claim kinship of a sort with Montaigne, Spinoza, Heine, Pissaro, Buber, Kafka. But I felt as close or closer to many others who were no such kin, from Piero and Bellini to Wordsworth and Shelley.*[81]

In February 1947 Brasch records that he read a description of the 'Hebrew Consciousness' and saw himself.

> *Tonight I read the chapter on The Hebrew Consciousness in Macmurray's The Clue to History, & found there described my own attitude to life – an inborn attitude for which I can take no credit – life as a seamless garment,*

religion as total, as informing everything, & not an external nor a mere single aspect. To be religious in this sense does not mean to be better than others whose religion is different or who have none; it has nothing to do with morality.[82]

I noticed that Brasch saw this Jewish 'attitude to life' as a positive thing, something he valued in himself. He can appreciate it, but has done nothing to cause it.

In March 1947, the same month as the first issue of *Landfall* was published, while Brasch was visiting Christchurch often to supervise the preparations, there was an outbreak of anti-Semitic correspondence in Christchurch's *Press*. It scared Brasch, as it would any Jewish person.

A correspondence about the Jews is proceeding in the Chch Press; those who write against them use pseudonyms; one of these brought out as 'evidence' the Protocols of the Elders of Zion, & when an editorial note pointed out, not very clearly, that the Protocols had been exposed, another wrote that this was 'very interesting' but that he supported the first correspondent, & went on to say that Jews had accomplished the first part of their plan 'to overthrow the existing social order, & to substitute chaos for civilization' because 'Central Europe lies in ruin.' For whose benefit, one wonders, when several million Jews died in the process.

All this gives me a sense of foreboding & nausea.[83]

Brasch's recorded response to this has rational elements, such as his questioning the correspondent's conclusion that Jews had partially succeeded in taking over the world. But the physical reaction he describes suggests he has more than an intellectual involvement in this issue. He has a sense of foreboding. In other less restrained words, he has a sense of apprehensiveness, disquiet, trepidation, unease, worry, fear and alarm.

No discussion of Brasch and Judaism could omit his poem 'Bred in the Bone' from his *Ambulando* collection, published in 1964. Bertram calls this 'the most intensely Jewish poem Brasch ever wrote.'[84] This segment from stanza I is addressed to a deity, as psalms often are. It asserts the writer's right to identify with the deity and the people who belong to the deity.

And was I not free also
Who did not know you except through them,
Free to breathe of that dark and day,
To tread, without obligation, your chosen land,
To drink of your streams, hearing songs that sought you,
Count myself of your people?

The writer of this poem does not expect to become wise or resolve the questions of the universe.

I have been ashamed, I have drunk humiliation
In my youth and in my middle years; I shall drink it again
As I grow old. Waiting on you
I shall surely drink it, as befits
The callow servant of your office.
[...]
So I shall end my life not knowing
Either myself or you.
Receive my humiliation,
Fulfill this ignorance
In which my words go out
To seek you, heard or unheard,
And never turning back
Denying or confirming,
No trace, no echo and no consequence.

At the end of stanza II there is a credo that moves a long way from the psalm form.

I neither believe nor disbelieve,
I expect the rising moon
And the dissolution of empires;
A tree in which the winds nest,
Knowing and knowing nothing.

The writer of this poem does not fit in with any formal religious structure. The element of Macmurray's description of the Hebrew Consciousness that Brasch identifies with is its totality. It is not genealogy, although ancestry plays a part. It is definitely not external observances or any single aspect of thinking. The religious is everywhere and in everything. This world-view is not chosen. It is 'bred in the bone'.

Keats, cause of a family row: Brasch was 16. He had been reading a pocket selection of Keats' poems that had belonged to his mother. Friends gave him a life of Keats and then, naturally, he wanted the complete works. His father, and probably at this stage Willi Fels too, thought Charles's destiny was to work in the Hallenstein business. Strip lights shone at the edges of the path from Manono to the warehouse, the factory, the offices and the shops. Joining the business was not just Charles's destiny, it was his duty. Hyam Brasch – who, by the way, did not join the family business when he married Helene – saw Charles's preoccupation with poetry and his request for this book of poems by Keats as taking him away from his rightful path, so he asked the family not to give him any more books of poetry. In the way of parents, he was half right. The call of poetry *did* take his son away from the business, but the process could not have been stopped by forbidding a hundred poetry books. One evening at Manono the subject came up, Willi Fels changed sides, Hyam was outnumbered and out-argued and Charles got his Keats.

know, as in 'I came to know it':

> *The whole world before me seemed my possession; I had never before, alone, held such a vast scene in my eye and mind, had never been subjected to and penetrated by one so grand, so rich. All I had ever known of the visible creation was gathered there in my sight: no matter that it was country in fact new to me: it was not strange, that day I came to know it, and it was made mine for good.*[85]

This paragraph, which dates from a trip to Minaret Station on Lake Wanaka in Central Otago before Brasch left for Oxford, is one of those heightened moments that Brasch could have written a poem about. I asked myself who or what was this 'one so grand, so rich' that he was 'subjected to' and 'penetrated by' and decided it was the 'scene'. *It* came to know him and, in the process, he came to know *it*.

Lady Engine *see* **beginninglessness**

Law Courts, Dunedin: Each time I see something new happening in Dunedin I try to decide whether what I am seeing is something Brasch would approve of, or not. In May 2017, on my walk down to Toitū Otago Settlers Museum to visit my tupuna whose picture hangs in the room which is the museum's heart, I passed the Law Courts building. I don't mean the pub opposite the *Otago Daily Times* office, I mean the actual court building.

Back in 2011 the Law Courts had been declared an earthquake risk, and the future of the building was uncertain for some years. There had been a campaign to preserve it – not only as a heritage building but as the working court. One of the arguments for saving it was that its value was made up of more than just its beauty. The business of justice would be better done in a building that made everyone aware of the seriousness of the situation, the campaigners said.

In December 2016 the refurbishment began. In May 2017 the Law Courts building was covered in scaffolding; the main front doorway was just an arch-shaped hole that opened into the gutted foyer, and from across the road I could see straight through the building. The inside of the building was dark and the workmen had set up a couple of extremely bright halogen lights to work by. The men were dark shapes, their faces were grim, the wind was cold and the whole scene resembled hell, but that wasn't the point. The point was, would Brasch have thought this building should be saved?

In general, he liked things to be preserved, whether it was a line of poplar trees, the shape of a hill or the town hall clock tower. But in the case of buildings, he campaigned to save only the ones he saw as having some architectural merit. I looked this Law Courts building up and down to see if I could see architectural merit. It is a big, heavy, rather block-shaped building, mostly made of that dark-grey Port Chalmers stone Dunedin builders used for serious buildings, with one slightly stubby tower in which a statue of Justice stands. The side of the building nearest to Cumberland Street is made of red brick with a veneer of the grey stone along the Stuart Street face, but the rest of the building seems to be made of stone.

I did not see grace but I did see age and gravitas. Together with the Law
Courts Hotel, the Best Café, the old prison, the *Otago Daily Times* and the
Evening Star newspapers, the Law Courts used to form a busy and highly
interconnected world, but some of those links are gone now. At present
the scaffolding obscures the lines of the building like braces on a young
person's teeth, but after considering the world of which it was the centre,
I think the Law Courts building would fit Brasch's definition of a 'public
building', outlined in relation to the Bank of New South Wales building.

> *It is a public building in that it imposes its character on the street and the
> neighbourhood, and exerts a strong if intangible influence, through its
> proportions, its dignity, its restrained decoration, on all who work or have
> business in it and who pass it day by day, who in fact live with it in one
> way or another.*[86]

I wondered whether the red brick wall would mean the building could
not be considered a 'good building' like the Bank of New South Wales,
but decided that the bricks are just part of the evolution of the building;
something to conserve rather than object to or replace. I think Brasch
would have been in favour of restoring the old Law Courts building, for its
contribution to Dunedin's strong 'character' and 'dignity', but that is only
a guess. Based on his view that University of Otago buildings reflected
and influenced teaching and learning, I think he would have supported
the argument that the court building could affect the processes of law
enforcement. My own capacity to distinguish a sham-Gothic nineteenth-
century building which deserves no sympathy, from a building we should
keep for the sake of its mana, is not great. I have Brasch's words 'sham' and
'muddle' and 'formlessness' in my mind, but I am still not convinced that I
can recognise these in practice.

libraries, access to books: Brasch records that the library at Waitaki Boys'
High School contained 'some of the standard English poets, historians
and novelists (novelists from Scott and Thackeray to Wells, Bennett and
Galsworthy), and a miscellany of recent works of all kinds'.[87] There were
prints of famous paintings on the walls and these were a library also; more
informal, and not even good prints, but 'they formed a wonderfully rich
pasture for boys to browse in'. There were magazines and newspapers too,

catering to diverse interests. But Brasch's interest does not stop at telling the reader what was there. Boys were encouraged to use the library, he says, and 'expected to take out one book a week at least'. Like a fussy prefect, Brasch notes that some boys may not have read the books they took out. The failure of these boys to appreciate the easy access to books must have struck Brasch as all the more wasteful in the context of the family row over whether he would be allowed to have a book of Keats' poems.

life, public or private? In England, late in 1945, Brasch met Jan Solecki, a Pole, born in Manchuria, who had been taken to Japan as a prisoner. This young man, well placed to have a subtle understanding of such matters, knew that America and Russia were enemies now and thought they might do battle by proxy in China.

It bore in on Brasch that even though the war in Europe had ended, tensions between Russia and America undermined any naïve idea that peace had arrived or even the hope for peace in the future. Brasch was planning his return to New Zealand to launch a New Zealand quarterly literary journal, but Solecki's perspective 'overwhelmed' him and forced him to reconsider his moral right to live 'a private life pursuing private ends'.[88] Should he force himself into a life of political action? he wondered.

> But there is only one answer: the world must go on: political action is never a complete answer to the earth's disorder, & as a life is an answer only for the few; for most people the indirect way [my emphasis] is inevitable, & probably far more effective. To bring some form of order out of chaos is the most that a man can achieve, whether it be in personal life, in artistic creation, or in society; & even now I believe that should be one's aim. If only I can keep this clearly before me.[89]

Less than a month after meeting Solecki, on 10 December 1945, Brasch set sail for New Zealand. By the time *Landfall* was launched Brasch was able to set out a vision of literature that gives it a role in social, political and economic issues of the day. When a writer uses a word in the text that is also the title of his book, you pay attention.

local: Is there such a thing as too local? Poets might write about a moment or a single tree and look for universality. If I write about a road, and how it came to be here, can that be interesting to people who live 50 or 500 kilometres away?

long sentences: Brasch often wrote long sentences in his prose. He may have learned this from Giacomo Leopardi. In Florence, in 1929, the poetry of Leopardi 'sank into'[90] Brasch.

> *It is by his masterly control of the rhythm sustained through long sentences in which every word is lovingly, unerringly placed to carry the burden of his anguish and compassion and penetrating insight into the human condition, that Leopardi makes felt his incomparable sense of the beauty of the world and the ultimate calm to which overwhelming despair leads him.*[91]

man, as in 'make a man of me': At the beginning of 1923, Charles Brasch was sent to boarding school at Waitaki Boys' High School, which he always refers to as 'Waitaki'. With his typical attention to language Brasch notes that the name of the school was said 'English-fashion', with the emphasis on the second syllable. The 'hard, assertive, even aggressive second syllable rang with the strength and independence which the school was believed to instil into its boys'.[92] Writing his memoir in the late 1960s or early 1970s Brasch knows that there was another 'Waitaki', the river, with a Māori name which he says means 'sounding water'. He wishes he had known that as a boy, he says. Brasch believes that his father chose Waitaki Boys' High School for him because that school would 'make a man'[93] of him. This, he says, was one of his father's 'lasting cares'.

Often stories of boarding schools are full of loneliness and bullying, especially for slightly built boys who write poetry instead of playing rugby, but Brasch was happy at Waitaki. When Brasch writes about Waitaki Boys' High School, the buildings, the grounds and the surrounding countryside glow. In his last two years there he was happier than at any other time in his life, he says. He made friendships that lasted his whole life and he was beginning to find his 'own special interests'.[94] The headmaster encouraged him to write poetry. He had a place within the school. Once, while Brasch was speaking in a debate, some boys at the back laughed at his accent. The headmaster stepped in and, with a light touch, stopped the ridicule.

Waitaki didn't make Brasch the man he became, but it kept him safe and encouraged him in the things that were important to him. That's a pretty good result for a school, then or now.

Manono, house built for Willi Fels and his wife Sara in the early twentieth century: Willi Fels lived at Manono until his death in 1946. After Fels died, Brasch records that Miss Welsh, the housekeeper, got up at six one morning to help Brasch with the exhausting and sad job of packing up the contents. Miss Welsh's niece, now a woman in her late 80s, is the mother-in-law of one of my friends.

In Brasch's childhood Manono was set in extensive gardens, but these have mostly been built on. Not only that, but there is a very raw, ugly and mean dwelling between Manono and London Street. I hope Brasch never saw that.

Manono attitudes: Charles Brasch employs the term 'Manono attitudes'[95] as shorthand for all the interests, practices, priorities, habits and beliefs of his grandfather. The life of the Fels family at Manono was expansive and confident. Value was placed on hard work and on education and history. The arts were an integral part of life, as were enjoyment of the outdoors and exploration of the local environment. Connections to family and to Europe were actively supported, and at the same time New Zealand was home. Brasch contrasts 'Manono attitudes' with the attitudes of his father, who placed great store by sport and whose world-view was narrower.

Māori: The following sentence is part of an article, published in 1946, about the relationship between landscape and literature in New Zealand. The article has nothing to do with Brasch but I have included it as a small piece of the New Zealand environment to which Brasch returned and in which he started *Landfall*.

> *Leaving the Maori out of the count, we may say that every settled piece of our land has its story, and it is the business of the historian and the geographer to join hands to interpret it.*[96]

'Leaving the Maori out of the count' is placed at the front of this sentence, where you put your assumptions.

Maori, as in 'big old Maori woman'[97]: A Mrs Harper, who was said to have carried sailors in from the sea in the whaling days, supplied the Fels family with milk at Karitane.

mind-scanning, and mind-scan blocks: When a human male is abducted by aliens, he is taken on board the UFO, his clothes are removed, he is placed on an examination table and his sperm is harvested, using a small machine which attaches to the penis. After this, aliens run their fingers over the man's whole body, paying particular attention to the brain and the spinal column and the eyes. While this is happening one alien looks directly into the eyes of the human from a distance of only two or three inches. This is referred to as 'mind-scanning'. During mind-scanning the alien uses the optic nerve as a conduit to the brain. This staring, from close up, allows the alien to see and feel everything important to that man. The abductee is unable to close his eyes or avert his gaze during this time.

When Charles Brasch read a book, he mind-scanned it. The traces of his reading that Brasch left in Frank Sargeson's 1965 novel *Memoirs of a Peon* show the process. On the flyleaf, he records that the book was reviewed in the *Times Literary Supplement* in 1965. On the next page there are four page references for particular pieces of information or topics in the book. For example, 'M.N. his appearance 48'. (Michael Newhouse is the protagonist.) On the next page Brasch has made a chapter contents list that could be used for returning to a particular part of the story.

> *1. childhood with his grandparents in Wynyard St, 7*
> *2. boyhood in Hamilton: family, Margaret, Ernie, 19, [etc.]*

Inside the book is a long thin strip of recycled paper with rough edges, probably torn with a ruler. On the paper is a list of eight words and the page on which each appears.

copaiba	*109, 110 para 2 / 1*
jerry riddle	*110*
faggot	*113*
strabismic	*121*
camp	*206–7*

curette	*213*
opsimath	*239*
torticollis	*240*

It isn't immediately obvious to me why each of these words is of interest. The only man who knew why each word was important has a mind-scan block in place. It takes the form of this denial.

> I know how I feel, what I do,
> But how true my feelings are
> And why I perform a particular
> Act is quite beyond me ...[98]

money, clear thinking about: It was not enough for Brasch to read in the paper in 1960 that the government had established a cultural fund. There is a big difference between the money that can be disbursed from an *income* of £60,000 and the income from *capital* of £60,000, and Brasch wanted to know which scenario applied. He thought the *Otago Daily Times* should have been clearer in its description of the fund and he told them so.

> *The Otago Daily Times would do its readers a service by providing more information; in particular, by making clear whether the £60,000 is to be the fund's capital or its income, and what exactly the money is to be used for. Readers would then be in a better position to judge the value of the scheme ...*[99]

This is a typical Brasch telling off. The newspaper has not done its job to the standard he expected and that just won't do.

munificence: I have always thought of this word as having a halo of irony, but the irony turns out to be my own contribution. On the bronze bust of Charles Brasch in the de Beer Gallery which leads to the University of Otago's Special Collections is a caption illustrating the correct use of the word.

> *Charles Brasch 1909–1973*
> *Poet, founder of Landfall, patron of the arts and benefactor of the University.*

His generous donations enhanced the Library's collections, notably in modern literature. His munificence also extended to other areas of the University's cultural and artistic life.

New Zealand, 1941: A bloody brutal barbarous environment, according to Frank Sargeson.

Glad you've met Brasch, never met him myself, but they say he's a nice fellow, and I like his verse. There have been extraordinary developments in recent years, but what will happen next is a question. You have to be out here to realise the N.Z. writer's dilemma. Any truly indigenous literature is hardly past its embryo stage. It's damned hard to accept this bloody brutal barbarous environment for better or worse. In my stories I've tried to do this, but of course I've had to go to Europe and America for technique.[100]

Orwell, George: If Charles Brasch was interested in a writer, he bought their books. In his collection of 6854 books, there are 'runs' of certain authors both from New Zealand and from around the world. Rilke, for example, or Forster, or Huxley, and many others. Of George Orwell's work there is only the novel *Burmese Days*, published in 1934. No *Homage to Catalonia*, no *1984*, no *Animal Farm* and no essays. It would be drawing too long a bow to say that this is evidence that Brasch didn't like Orwell's writing, but it might be reasonable to say that Brasch does not seem to have been very interested in Orwell's writing. If that is true, that is a difference between Brasch and me.

Paradise Lost: Brasch was 16 or 17 when he spent two weeks at Minaret Station at mustering time. One day he climbed up to a hut that was used as a musterer's base, several hours away from the homestead. It sounds very beautiful, with snow visible in frosty moonlight. For the hired men, there was work every day, but for Brasch there was poetry and water play.

While the men went out to prospect I stayed behind, reading Paradise Lost *and damming the stream ...*[101]

poetry: Brasch used poetry as a form of exploration. I notice that his poems contain actual questions as well as explorations of questions in his mind.

poetry, Brasch's own, 1927: 'I wrote most of the time, if seldom to my own satisfaction …';[102] 'Shelley and water, Keats and water, sometimes Yeats and water, but mostly water …'[103]

poetry *is* the message:

Hyam Brasch: If you're a poet, you must have a message. What's your message?

Teenaged Charles Brasch: Silence.

Hyam Brasch: You haven't got a message! All right. Then you can't be a poet.

The answer, the only answer, that poetry is the message, did not come to me until long enough afterwards for it to be of no use; and I doubt whether I could have delivered it with sufficient conviction in face of his assured scepticism.[104]

poetry, voluntary and compulsory: Charles Brasch's grandmother Sara loved poetry. She used to hold evenings dedicated to a particular poet. Willi Fels read poetry in English, but seemed to get more pleasure from returning to Goethe, Schiller and Heine. During school holidays his grandfather required Charles and a family friend to read the *Odyssey* and the *Iliad* aloud to him after midday dinner on Sundays. The boys were bored and protested, but Willi Fels just laughed 'tolerantly'[105] and made them carry on. Later, in the six months before leaving for Oxford, Charles and his grandfather read poetry together again, this time voluntarily.

politics, keeping out of: In 1946 Orwell was of the view that 'In our age there is no such thing as "keeping out of politics." All issues are political issues,'[106] he says.

The opinion that art should have nothing to do with politics is itself a political attitude.[107]

Brasch is in conversation with Orwell about this in the editor's notes to the first issue of *Landfall*, in 1947. Brasch is a little condescending, I think, describing Orwell's view as 'one of those desperate simplifications which, in a desperate age, we are all prone to make', while making it clear that he has not fallen for this desire to make things simple. There is, he says, 'a certain truth in it' but only insofar as 'all issues are far more closely related than we have been accustomed to allow and all in some way or another both affect and are affected by politics'. The assertion that all issues are political is, Brasch says, 'wholly false'. Despite several attempts I don't understand the distinction he makes between his own view and Orwell's 'desperate simplification'.

I always want political thinking in writing. I feel comfortable reading writing by, and selected by, anyone who sees literature as part of political ecologies and I feel uncomfortable if there is nothing of this connection. But not everyone agrees. Writer James McNeish saw Brasch's view that 'philosophers, historians and men of letters' sometimes bring 'valuable new perspectives' to social and political questions as 'eccentric'.[108] 'Curiously he [Brasch] insisted that a literary journal must have a political dimension', McNeish says. However, by the time McNeish has finished a section on the contributions to *Landfall* from India, China and central Europe, he has talked himself around, and he concludes with this sentence:

There was usually a reason for Brasch's eccentricities.[109]

prose, like a window pane: Good prose is like a window pane, according to Orwell. One of the pleasures of reading Orwell's essays is their clarity and apparent simplicity. I am always impressed with his nerve, too. There is his idea. There is the rationale. Take it or leave it. Orwell also says in his essay 'Why I Write' that he likes scraps of useless information. Having read his domestic diaries where he counts eggs and records the weight of potatoes harvested and the making of jams, I believe him. Sometimes, even for Orwell, this desire to collect information is in conflict with clean window panes of prose. Like Orwell, I am attracted to details although I wonder if there is any piece of information you could say with certainty was never going to be useful. There must be a boundary somewhere between collecting information and hoarding, but I am not sure I know where it is.

questions, hypothetical, but urgent: If I were to meet Charles Brasch; if he and I were together somewhere, he near the end of his life and me at 64, unsure how near the end of my life that is; if I were to take heart and step up to meet him; if I were to push on, past that famous reserve, I would be grateful to hear Brasch talk on any subject. If he spoke about his youth, or his writing, or the world in 1973, that would be great. If he happened to be aware of events in the world right now, and spoke of those matters, I would welcome his opinions.

If it were possible, without discourtesy, I would like to ask him what he found out about moving and staying in one place. I would ask him about the style of *Indirections*, whether it pleased him, and what he thought of the edited-down, published version. I would ask him if he ever wished he had spent his life in Italy.

I would ask if, from his perspective, New Zealand still looks fairly barbarous. I would ask him for his views on the Kāpiti Expressway and all the other Roads of National Significance. The role played by road transport in environmental degradation was not as explicit in his lifetime. Despite this, I think he would have been against the Kāpiti Expressway's grandiosity and its imposition on and destruction of parts of the local environment. I think he would have been in favour of a network of transport for freight and people which looked ahead 50 years, instead of being based on a single idea current in 2009. I would ask him what we should do now that cyclones and floods and fires are not a threat but an everyday event. I would ask if he thought there was such a thing as New Zealand literature these days and if it mattered that there was or wasn't. I would ask what steps he would take now if he were wanting to support literature here.

I would make tea for him and serve it in my best blue and white Japanese bone china cups.

The Rabbi's Son, a version of the story told by Rabbi Nachman (1772–1810), great-grandson of the Baal Shem Tov: Once there was a rabbi who only had one son. That son did what his father wished. Upstairs in his room the son studied and prayed but inside he felt there was something missing. He didn't know what the missing thing was so he asked his father to take him to see a tsaddik so that he could find out. His father said no because the tsaddik was not as learned as the son and the tsaddik's family was not as respected as the rabbi's family. The son went back to his studies but still felt a great yearning for something else. This time he asked his friends what he should do. They advised him to go to see the tsaddik, but again his father said no.

This went on for years. Finally, after the son had pleaded and pleaded the father harnessed his carriage and they set off. As they rode along the father set this test. 'If everything goes smoothly, the visit is from heaven. If not, then the visit is not from heaven and we return home.' At a small bridge one of the horses slipped and the rabbi and his son nearly drowned, so the rabbi decided they should return home. The son returned to his studies but again he recognised that something was missing in himself even though he did not know what it was. Once more he asked his father to take him to the tsaddik. His father agreed but set the same test. This time an axle broke so they returned home. Once more the son tried to return to his studies and once more he found he could not continue. This time he said to his father that because axles can break and horses can slip for any reason, they should not set the same test. This time they should only come home if something very unusual and serious happened. The rabbi agreed.

Come nightfall they stopped at an inn where they met a merchant (the Evil One, as we later find out) who struck up a conversation with the rabbi. At first the rabbi did not reveal the purpose of their journey, but the more they talked, the more he said until finally he revealed the name of the tsaddik they were travelling to meet. 'Him? But he is worthless!' said the merchant. 'I have been with him when he committed a sin!' With that the rabbi and his son returned home. Soon afterward, the son died.

There is more; the rabbi finally understands why his son did the things he did, but it is all too late. He has lost his obedient, gentle son and nothing can change that.

If you were a Dunedin barrister with a stubborn son who would not follow the path you had chosen for him, and if you prided yourself on being a rational man, not weighed down by superstition from Eastern Europe, you probably would not consult the stories of Rabbi Nachman for guidance. But what if you did? Wouldn't the sadness, first of the son and then the father, have melted your heart?

raw mean ugliness: Brasch was repelled by the 'raw mean ugliness'[110] of the buildings of the Presbyterian boys' primary school he attended for a few years, and 'the ugliness of some of the relationships' he met there. Writing about this many many years later Brasch sounds angry at the 'horrible malign influence' that buildings with no 'proportion, dignity or self-respect' have had on generations of boys. Such buildings, he says, are 'a public evil',[111] even worse than bad films and plays, because their influence is 'silent and unsuspected'. The word 'mean' comes up twice in two paragraphs about this school and once more in the description 'meanness of spirit'. The word 'raw' is also used twice, once in relation to the school buildings and once in relation to a cinder patch among clay banks, the place where the boys had to play. The description of his time at this school comes early in the memoir. This is the first time I have seen Brasch heated and virulent. Is all this emotion really about malign influence of bad buildings that made the school mean in spirit and him so unhappy? His years at this school were relatively soon after his mother's death, so maybe he was pervasively unhappy and the buildings are an analogue for that feeling? Perhaps he had experiences at that school of bullying, or worse, and these create the character of it in his memory? I wish Brasch had talked more about the relationships that were also raw and mean and ugly.

reasons for writing, general: Right from when he was young, Orwell says, he knew he had 'a facility with words' and a 'power of facing unpleasant facts'.[112] He uses both in his examination of his own and other people's motives for writing.

'Sheer egoism' is the first motive he explores. Writers all have this motive, he says, to a greater or lesser extent. The more serious the writer, the more egoism. In a typical Orwell moment, he widens the egoism critique to include all the high achievers in the rest of society, and, of course, himself. In the next sentence, he turns to matters of class and reminds us that most people do not have the choice to follow a personal and vain pursuit like writing serious books, but have to work unrelentingly until they die, just to keep a family alive. As I understand his argument, if you write what you want rather than what people will pay for, you have chosen to please yourself and are guilty of egoism. I can only agree.

The second motive is what Orwell calls 'aesthetic enthusiasm'. Although the term sounds sarcastic to my ear, Orwell's list of what ignites this way of thinking feels sympathetic. Aesthetic enthusiasm is all about 'perception of beauty in the external world', or 'in words and their right arrangement', pleasure in sounds or rhythm or in the 'firmness' of good prose. It is a desire to share an experience of value.

The third motive in Orwell's list is the urge to make a historical record. As a greedy consumer of historical records, I respect the desire to create a record and I regard the act of doing that as a worthwhile activity in and of itself. I don't think this motive interested Orwell much. He gives it two and a bit lines.

The final of Orwell's four motives is politics, where the writing is intended to stir things up and ignite change. As a young man, Orwell says, he was inclined to aesthetic enthusiasm, but exposure to poverty at a very personal level and his experiences in the Spanish Civil War changed him and his work. According to Orwell, a writer's subject matter is, in tumultuous times, 'determined by the age he lives in'. He sees his own experience as an example of that.

While the present might be determining a writer's content, Orwell says that the 'emotional attitude' of a person's writing is formed long before he ever begins to write. A writer's job, he says, is to find space between these two forces in which he can move forward without losing the connection with his early influences. If he does that, he will 'have killed his impulse to write'.

I am interested in Orwell's list of motives for writing, because I like hearing his sharp knife scraping along the bone as he dissects this subject, but I distrust the notion that any four motives, however powerful or well expressed, are sufficient to explain the whole universe of writing. For one thing, the framework lacks the influence of time on a writer's life and the influence of life stages on their creative focus and method. It is as if Orwell has constructed a stationary train.

When I asked people who had known Brasch what they thought his motives might have been for writing *Indirections*, their answers were much less abstract than Orwell's. One said he might have written it because he could not, at that time, write poetry. Brasch's own comment in the front of the memoir, that prose is the poor option chosen by people who cannot write poetry, would lend support to this idea. Another possibility is that Brasch might simply have been able to write this long piece of work because he was, by the late 1960s, free of his *Landfall* editing responsibilities. The second person said perhaps Brasch was seeking to keep control of the material about his private life by being the person who mined his journals and compiled the material into this memoir. I find their theories compelling in their tentativeness and multiplicity.

Despite this I cannot resist imagining a pie diagram to show Brasch's motives for writing *Indirections* according to the Orwellian list. Initially I allocate 'aesthetic enthusiasm' 100 per cent, because the pleasures and desires Orwell mentions fit so well with this book. But then I realise that I have not left any space for egoism, which must be significant because how else could you write hundreds and hundreds of pages about your own life and imagine that a reader might want to know so very much about your ideas and experiences? In a burst of puritan meanness of spirit, I allocate 'egoism' 100 per cent. I realise that without intending to do so, I have changed the mathematical rules. Now that the pieces of the pie no longer need to add up to 100 per cent, I continue unconstrained. I allocate 'making a historical record' 19 per cent because I know Brasch placed a lot of store by records and archives both public and private, and I allocate 'politics and changing the world' 1 per cent because there is no absolute zero. I might disagree with myself about that last allocation though. Knowing that Brasch was sympathetic and encouraging to young writers, I wonder if he considered that recording his life-and-death struggle with family expectations and with the brutality of parts of New Zealand culture might have benefit for others who find themselves similarly coerced.

relate: For most people the word 'relate' is a transitive verb but Brasch makes it intransitive. This leaves a hanging feeling, a pause in which what is related to what is never described.

> *To relate: that is one of the chief social – and spiritual – functions of the arts.*[113]

The arts, he says, deal fundamentally with 'human life as such'. Arts are 'the interpreters' of human life, 'they display its inexhaustible variety'.

Above all, they relate, bringing together things far apart and seemingly indifferent or hostile; through them men come to understand each other; for they speak a language of reconciliation.

rugger and cricket: Brasch 'hated rugger' because he was scared he would be hurt, and he was 'hopeless' at cricket. He enjoyed watching cricket, though, finding 'a deeply satisfying elegance and grace and sense of formal perfection which no other school activity offered'.[114]

sea, as earth's pulse:

In the sea you feel and hear and watch the earth's pulse; winds come out of space, ethereal breath, but ocean tides are the very breathing of earth itself.[115]

sexuality: While I was thinking about Brasch and writing about him I heard a family story from New Zealand of the 1930s. It starts with a man in a paddock, driving his tractor up and down, ploughing in neat lines. His wife comes from the house and signals to him that she wants him to stop. When the motor is quiet she tells him that their homosexual son has killed himself. 'Did he?' says the father and restarts the tractor. The person who told me the tractor story had remembered the harshness of it all these years.

Writing about any aspect of anyone else's identity is always presumptuous. Unintentionally perhaps, you will read the situation a certain way because that is what you understand and can see. When it comes to Brasch's Jewish identity, I have a sense that I understand some of the issues around it. This confidence is a risk I have accepted. Regarding Brasch's sexuality, I have neither confidence nor a sense that I must have a theory. I just listen to him. Every time I have written the word 'identity' in relation to his family, or about the grim business of suppressing your identity in order to be accepted or fighting to have a life that fits, or about Brasch's fears about returning to New Zealand and his doubts about his own place in New Zealand, I have been aware of a sort of doubling, a sense that all these considerations probably apply to Brasch's sexual identity as well as his cultural background.

But I don't feel I understand the nuances of his romantic and sexual life well enough to make it part of my content. Although there were moments when Brasch felt inclined to tell everything in his journal, and let it all be known a certain time after his death, his last decision in this area was to remove certain pages.

Since the 30-year embargo Brasch imposed on his personal papers was lifted it has become possible for readers of his journals to learn more about his romantic and sexual life. There are gaps, but more is in print than before the journals were published. Some people's eyes glitter when the subject of which men and which women Brasch 'slept' with comes up. Sometimes I find gossip enjoyable, but not about this. I think one reason is that when these relationships happened, same-sex relationships were dangerous in lots of ways, and although the social and legal context in New Zealand has changed to some extent I still feel Brasch's caution. That this long shadow of fear affects me, three decades after the law that made sex between men a crime was changed in 1986, surprises me, but there it is. A long heavy anchor drags behind me when I approach the subject. When the words people use to describe Brasch's sexuality are words for categories, I turn away. I listen instead to Brasch:

> ... *love is in its beginning undifferentiated & may be equally for man or for woman ... only social pressures determine that it is fixed so firmly on one sex.*[116]

Brasch foretold in his poem 'Man Missing' that people like me would pick over his life.

> Someone else, I see,
> Will be having the last word about me,
> Friend, enemy, or lover
> Or gimlet-eyed professor.
> Each will think he is true
> To the man he thinks he knew
> Or knows, he thinks, from the book.
> [...]
> And each, no doubt, having caught me
> Will deal with me plainly, shortly

And as justly as he can
With such a slippery no-man.

Typically, he expected fairness from the scavengers. My form of just dealing is to recongise that Brasch chose his intimate circle very carefully and he did not choose me.

student revolt: Speaking on the topic of 'The University and the Community' in June 1969, at a time when student protests had been happening all over Europe and the United States, Brasch, who was 60 that year, made it clear that he was on the side of young people.

One of the duties of young people was to keep reminding their elders what the world was about, he said.

Coming fresh from homes and schools into the world they can see clearly what older eyes have grown half-blind to. They see injustice, hatred and violence everywhere: the stark contrast of riches and poverty; the lies told so blandly in high places; the gulf between what men profess and what they do.[117]

to come to life: In the winter of Brasch's first year at Oxford, his great-aunt Agnes, his great-uncle and great-aunt Isidore and Emily de Beer took Charles and his sister Lel to Italy. Brasch noticed everything.

... food above all – the excellent crusty bread, the various coffees, nero, cappuccino, al latte, the rich hot chocolate with cream (cioccolato con panna) that I regularly took at afternoon tea, and the delicious ices of all kinds that we sampled in so many cafes and tea rooms ...[118]

In general, *Indirections* is not much concerned with the pleasures of food or drink. This is the first mention of food as a source of personal pleasure.

I seemed to myself to come to life and to live more fully in Italy than elsewhere, to be alert and responsive to a degree I had not known before both inwardly and outwardly; particularly in seeing, my keenest sense.[119]

If there was a place where all your senses 'seemed to wake up from a long sleep' each time you crossed the border, wouldn't you want to spend your

life there? Dunedin has extraordinarily beautiful light and hills, and for
Brasch it was full of family associations, but after Italy Dunedin must have
seemed extremely dour.

a tree, if I can:

> *To be like a tree, a dream told me, to be like a tree, patient, constantly
> growing & from within itself, regularly, with coherence & meaning like a
> tree; not to be scattered, a fortuitous concourse of atoms without shape or
> direction or identity …*
>   *A tree: if I can: insh'allah*[120]

trees: In the space underneath and between trees, Brasch could see his
preoccupations differently. Trees made him aware of the past, too. But not
all trees were the same. An English beech grove, especially one on a hill,
made him think about the history that place had lived through. But the ash
trees in the Museum Reserve in Dunedin just made him think of the living
nature and beauty of the ash trees. The land under the trees in the Museum
Reserve must not have had a past that mattered to him.

Sometime during the winter of 2016 I became aware that my relationship
with trees had changed. The first thing I remember noticing is how much
effort trees make to thrust their branches up into the air. If you look at
branches waving in the wind, you can almost feel the effort of reaching
towards the sun. And then I noticed that there were often flowers at the
ends of these branches, and I realised that all this effort was to place the
flower up, as high as possible in the air, so that bees would see them and
come to pollinate them. Long waving branches and flowers are a matter of
life and death for trees.

Just outside the window of the room where I write there is a pūriri. The
pūriri is a serious tree. I do not feel it as aggressive but I am aware of it as
a being, taller than me and taller than my house. Its dark-green leaves are
thick and do not move or change much. In early spring its coral-red flowers
attract tūī. A little further away there are two sycamore trees whose leaves
flutter and turn themselves upside down in the softest breeze. The way the
leaves move with so little prompting makes me think this is a tree without

much substance. When I see the leaves turn over in the wind, all at the same time, from green tops to the grey undersides, I hear a metallic rattle in my head, as if the leaves were all made of cheap aluminium. I think slightly patronising thoughts about this tree before realising that sycamore seedpods float for miles in the wind and take root by the thousands.

I am in awe of the pōhutukawa by the gate. It is dark, like the pūriri, but whereas the pūriri is shaved on one side by the wind, the pōhutukawa branches are a perfect ball shape. In summer, when it flowers, the whole tree is, from a distance, dark red. Close up though, each red flower is made up of a hundred red stems, each with a dot of gold on the tip – all for the benefit of bees, I know, but sumptuous as velvet studded with gold. For two or three weeks, the pōhutukawa is the ambassador from the Medici court.

Prompted by Brasch's defence of the poplars at Logan Park, I gave more serious thought to poplars. I like poplars. They make me think of rolling downs and shelter belts and sheep gathered in their shade. When I showed Brasch's letter to the *Otago Daily Times* in defence of the poplars to a friend, she said that she had no sympathy for poplars because they are introduced trees. I was a little disconcerted by this conversation. According to the attitude-to-poplars test, my aesthetic mind is revealed as a colonist, dreaming of sheep farms on stolen land.

Throughout this project I have been possessed by the need to say the names of trees and birds from the Kāpiti area, and the names of people who lived here in the past, and the names of their houses and their villages. I could not explain, even to myself, this need to name an ancestor of Te Ātiawa whose village was right near the Expressway and the meeting house now located in the heart of Waikanae. But I understand it better now. First I realised that Pōhutukawa and Pūriri and Tūī are important beings here. Then I realised that the words 'pōhutukawa' and 'pūriri' and 'tūī' are sounds. When said slowly and carefully they are slow, musical honorifics. They are the language from here. Nearly five years after I began to think about Brasch and Kāpiti, I have understood that to say the name of a tree or a bird or a person from the past is to call up their mana. We are lucky if the trunk of what was once a huge tree is returned to us from deep down in the peat. We are lucky if there is an archive, a pile of poems, or stories of a life, because then we can talk about what happened. As a friend from Te Ātiawa explained to me, sometimes the name is all that is left to us.

The Prettiest Road in New Zealand
A glossary of my acquaintance with the Kāpiti Expressway

the Alliance: The Mackays to Peka Peka Expressway (M2PP) was built by a group consisting of Fletcher, Beca, Higgins, the NZ Transport Agency (NZTA) and Kāpiti Coast District Council, supported by Goodman Contractors, Incite and Boffa Miskell. This group referred to itself as 'the Alliance'.

alliancing: *Verb*, gerund: to be in an alliance-style contract. Usually associated with infrastructure construction projects.

'animal' earth: Like many people, I believe, in my own unexamined way, that the big question of our time is our relationship with the entity 'earth'. Some people, whose feet are more firmly on the earth than mine, have always thought the earth has intentions, desires and agency. 'This whole district is trying to return to being a swamp and humans are stopping it,' a plumber said to me recently, using his own ground-level local experience and visible trends to reach two conclusions. First that the earth hereabouts wants to be a swamp, like it used to be in pre-colonial times, and second, that it, the earth, is actively working towards that. It would be quite a small step, I think, for this man to decide to stop laying pipes to drain land and take water away, knowing that the earth in this place wants to keep its water close and still.

annoyed: *Adjective*: used by NZTA to describe the reaction of people to road noise. *Synonyms*: agitated, bored, bothered, displeased, disturbed, exasperated, fired up, galled, irked, peeved, perturbed, riled, troubled, vexed, worried, abraded, bedevilled, beleaguered, chafed, distressed, harassed, harried, maddened, miffed, needled, nettled, pestered, provoked, ruffled, ticked off, hit where one lives. I think 'annoyed' misses the dimension of desperation present in 'beleaguered' or 'maddened'.

archaeology: 'Small things telling big stories.' I did not make up this definition of archaeology. I found it in a list of 'expert talks' on a flyer for ExpressDay, the day in February 2017 when locals could walk over five kilometres of the Expressway before it was opened for traffic. If you wanted, you could talk to the archaeologist on that day. I very much wanted to do this. I wanted to know what objects she had found in the peat and in the sand dunes and what she had learned from them.

arguments, technical: In matters to do with roading, I am a complete novice. A surprisingly angry man pointed this out to me early on in this project, when I said I had not expected to find that white fabric is used in the building of roads. In my attempts to understand the road that arrived in my community, I have found myself in many technical fields, from public relations to ecology and from transport planning to realpolitik. Left to myself I probably would never have chosen to enter these fields, but when I looked at the road I saw that it was surrounded by and received encouragement from many disciplines. I apologise now, to the angry man and all other affected parties, for my many failures to understand technical arguments put forward by roading and its associated disciplines.

In the face of the sheer volume of technical information about the road, which I estimate to be 20 football fields, each 10 metres deep, I have been somewhat influenced by Peter Munz, a man who once entertained Charles Brasch at a bach in Raumati South. Reading Brasch's account of this visit, it seems that they had an interesting discussion but no lunch. In an article in *Landfall* in 1950 Munz said that the history books that interested him contained a mixture of truth, trends and interpretations. I am not too sure I would know truth if I saw it, but I have described some events surrounding the Kāpiti Expressway in detail, because truth might be in the detail. Sometimes I think the details I have collected add up to a trend, and sometimes I have attempted interpretations of these details. Sometimes a different kind of knowledge arrives, not from the discipline of moving from detail to trend to interpretation but from flute music, or the sound of a word, or seeing a tattoo. I am not sure which is more trustworthy.

artefact: During my visits to the Alliance headquarters in Ihakara Street, Paraparaumu, between 2014 and 2016, I saw a very large poster board showing 70 years of Kāpiti transport history. Episodes in this history, including a plan made in the 1940s for a high-speed route through Kāpiti on something like the current Expressway route, are marked on a diagonal line. This line rises in steps from 1840 in the bottom-left corner to the plan for the Expressway in the top-right corner. From a semiotic point of view, Kāpiti Expressway, at the top of the steps, represents the peak of transport development. Perhaps I am over-sensitive, but it always seems to me that the purpose of the board and all the steps it described was to make the Expressway appear both logical and inevitable. This artefact is now housed in the Waikanae Museum. In 50 years, if the idea of a museum as a repository for physical objects survives, there might be a card beside the poster board saying it was made in the early twenty-first century when petrol-driven engines were common.

ATP: *Noun*: abbreviation of 'audio tactile profiles'. A term used by NZTA's review panel on the noise problem to refer to road markings often called 'rumble strips'. *As in*: 'It is understood that the Transport Agency is currently removing all ATP on the left-hand edge lines of the M2PP. The panel recommends that the Transport Agency also investigate whether vehicles regularly traverse the right-hand (central) edge lines and if so that ATP should also be removed where it is within 200m of houses.'[1]

benefit–cost ratio: The ratio of how much return there is, in dollars, for each dollar spent, on anything, is its benefit–cost ratio. Labour's spokesperson on transport, Phil Twyford, said in 2012, 'A leaked report by engineering consultants Beca shows the half a billion dollar motorway project [M2PP Expressway] has a benefit–cost ratio (BCR) of 0.2, which falls a long way short of break even at 1.0'.[2] Local campaigner against the Expressway Viola Palmer quoted a ratio of 0.6.[3] I am not sure what to make of these ratios. I am not sure how costs are measured. Isn't the loss of habitats, for example, or a rise in the use of oil and greenhouse gas emissions and the consequent change in climate, a cost forever?

big: Sheer staggering size impresses people. In respect of the Kāpiti Expressway, there was lots of size to be impressed by: the volume of sand and peat moved, the number of workers, the 18 bridges, the Brutalist-style concrete pillars that hold up the bridges, the height of the diggers, the size of their buckets, the massive capacity of the trucks, the size of the cut, and the $630 million it was estimated to cost. I am slightly embarrassed to say that some of this impresses me too. Thanks to my father, who admired every sort of machinery and took me to the Museum of Transport and Technology in Auckland when I was young, I have a fondness for diggers and pipes and purposeful holes in the ground. The Expressway offered many opportunities to look down holes, and even an opportunity to climb up into a giant digger and pretend to drive it. While they were building the half-interchange at Poplar Avenue, near my home, I saw women driving giant machines. One woman whom I saw often for a few months drove trucks taller and longer than my house. Early on in the construction, when all this was still a novelty, I tweeted a few witty messages like 'BIG TRUCK at Kāpiti Road site of #M2PP'.[4]

biodiversity, local: Neil Walker, NZTA's acting Wellington highways manager, said in April 2015 that the 1.3 million locally sourced, primarily native plants covering 140 hectares of land, and the additional five square metres of wetlands added to replace every square metre of wetland lost, destroyed or removed by the Expressway would 'improve the local biodiversity and ecological connections on the Kapiti Coast, helping flora and fauna to thrive'.[5] If you make new wet areas which have not acted as wetland ecosystems before, would the 'ecological connections' in those places be as complex as if the original wetlands had been left undisturbed? My understanding is that a 'wetland', as opposed to a wet area, needs the right balance of water coming in, water going out, water quality, plant species and fauna species. And time.

BMM: *Noun*: abbreviation of 'building modification mitigation'. A term used by NZTA's review panel on the noise problem to mean things like the installation of ventilation in a house. *As in*: 'However, where there has been an increase in noise level by 3dB or more due to the project, the Transport Agency could consider investigation of BMM.'[6]

Ventilation is one form of BMM. Ventilation might be needed because a house meets the criterion for acceptable noise levels with its windows all shut, but the temperature in the house would then make it impossible for people to live there. BMM is the final step in noise mitigation. Before this comes all the forms of prevention of noise by road design and noise barriers. Since the Expressway was opened a few houses have experienced rises in noise levels greater than predicted and consented, and noise bunds or walls have either not been provided or not been helpful. BMM is an option in this kind of situation.

bridge expansion joints: Waikanae River bridge expansion joints were found by the Independent Review Panel to be different from those prescribed in the consent. I could summarise the problems with the bridge joints as follows: Wrong type. Choice fails to meet consent requirements. Poorly installed. Problem needs fixing. Alternatively, in the language of the review panel:

The M2PP has seven bridges with mechanical expansion joints and two bridges with modular type expansion joints. The modular type expansion joints are known to cause higher noise levels than some alternatives. No assessment appears to have been made of noise from the expansion joints. Standard treatment options available to reduce noise from these joints such as surface plates and cavity lining/enclosures were not installed. The joint selection was therefore contrary to a project requirement (MR A5.12C) 'That the expansion joints at Waikanae River Bridge shall be selected to minimise the road noise from the joint.'

Furthermore the bridge joints have been poorly installed creating significant discontinuities in the vehicle wheel paths … The panel considers that noise from some of the bridge expansion joints may be unreasonable and mitigation is needed … Given that residents have been sensitised to bridge joint noise, the panel considers that a significant improvement is now required to address the issue. The remedial measures, to smooth the wheel paths across the joints, require extensive works.[7]

built environment, quality of in Kāpiti: *Historical buildings of note*: Rangiātea Church (Ōtaki), St Luke's Church (Waikanae), Whakarongotai meeting house (Waikanae), St Peters Village Hall (Paekākāriki), the Paekākāriki Railway Station. All wooden. All still used and, as they say, loved by members of their communities. It is typical of Brasch that he would have taken the trouble to go to Rangiātea, the oldest Māori Anglican church in New Zealand, on his way through Kāpiti in 1950.

Contemporary buildings of note: One: The office of Kāpiti Coast District Council (Paraparaumu). The existing two-storey, 1970s council building began its life as a bank. By all accounts it did not begin its life as a significant building like those bank buildings in Dunedin that Brasch defended. Someone called it a 'rabbit warren'. In 2012–13 a third of the 40-year-old building was demolished and a new extension added. The project won the NZIA Wellington Commercial Architecture Award in 2013 and silver at the 2014 Master Builders New Zealand Commercial Project Awards.

Contemporary buildings of note (in a bad way): One: The Links apartments (Paraparaumu Beach). This 13-storey building, built in 1996, is adjacent to the golf course and surrounded by one- and two-storey residential and commercial buildings. Subsequently it was found not to have been weathertight. There are amazing views if you are inside the Links looking out. There are no other buildings of comparable height in Kāpiti.

Religious monuments of note: One: Statue of Our Lady of Lourdes (Paraparaumu). Fourteen metres high, made of white concrete, the statue stands on a knoll above what used to be St Patrick's Church. The statue was dedicated in October 1958. Dutch sculptor Martin Roestenberg built the two-metre-high head of the statue in his Taihape garage, then built the Virgin's body beneath the head, on site. Our Lady of Lourdes is big, made of rather coarse lumpy concrete and has a door that allows maintenance to be done inside. She is tied down with wire ropes. She is also surprisingly beautiful. From her place up on the hill, she radiates spiritual force.

About the rest of the built environment of Kāpiti, the less said the better.

bully, red-fin: Longfin eels, lamprey, banded kōkopu, giant kōkopu and red-finned bullies were all found in water along the Expressway route. Temporary diversions were made to take them away for a few months from streams that would be disturbed by construction. Then they were put back. It was explained to me that most of the original streams were farm streams and not good-quality environments. Sometimes the fish were put back into a situation that had changed because of the construction, and sometimes a new environment had been created for them that was thought to be better conditions than they had before. Apparently eels and bullies are territorial, so no one knew if putting them in new territory would cause them to fight to create new territories. It was assumed that if they had enough space they would sort themselves out eventually.

bund: *Noun*: structure built of earth, peat or rock, sometimes reinforced with plastic. *Synonyms*: noise bund, noise buffer, noise-protecting wall, embankment.

Early on, a nine-metre-high noise-protecting bund near Chilton Drive in Paraparaumu was made quickly out of the mountains of dug-out peat to help nearby residents cope with construction noise. Later it was rebuilt in its permanent form, with plastic reinforcing. One resident of Chilton Drive said that the wall made living in her house 'like living in the bottom of a gully'.[8] The machines have all gone now and the bund remains, to protect residents from traffic and road noise. It also protects them from a view of the island and some afternoon sun.

businesses, local: According to Simon Bridges, then Minister of Transport, speaking at the time of the opening of the Expressway in 2017, of the $630 million cost of the Expressway, more than $200 million 'went into the Kapiti economy through local businesses',[9] and more than 5000 people worked on the project.

cats, feral: Feral cats were not trapped and shot during the construction of the Expressway. Some people thought this happened, but it did not. 'The expressway construction area is a massive swath going through grass and trees where critters used to live', Kāpiti regional councillor Nigel Wilson explained.

> *There are concerns about the wildlife – where they are scarpering to when the machinery starts up.*[10]

The term 'wildlife' here refers to feral cats, rats, mice and rabbits. Rabbits were shot, at night. Rats and mice were trapped and poisoned. But feral cats could not be targeted because there were too many domestic cats and who could tell which were which?

certainty, the appearance of: When the 2012 Board of Inquiry was held to consider the application for consent to build the Expressway there was a one-month window to make submissions. I did not make a submission. If the Board of Inquiry was held this week, though, I would make a submission. *Now* I know what the Expressway looks like and how it acts. Now I know that boards of inquiry and the Environment Court are the last-chance saloon for grassroots input. I know too that citizens can influence and occasionally even stop a government-backed infrastructure project. But all this knowledge has come years too late to have any practical use. More than 700 people or groups did make submissions. It is easy to say that submissions opposing the Expressway were a waste of effort because they did not stop it being built. Jenny Rowan, the mayor of Kāpiti in 2012, thought the Expressway was always going to happen because it had government support, and maybe she is right. But maybe she isn't. It is impossible to say how much influence submissions have until the process is completed. Everything governments say sounds confident. They put a lot of effort into that. But behind the scenes of any project some people are not sure they can carry it off. That's another thing I learned.

choke points, present and future: A choke point is a place where traffic builds up because a section of road becomes narrower. The wider section of road allows more vehicles than will fit on the narrower section of road, so traffic slows and even stops while drivers wait their turn to take their vehicles onto the narrower part of the road. Most people in New Zealand are more familiar with this situation than they would like.

Before the Expressway, driving north from Wellington, there used to be choke points at Waikanae and at Paraparaumu. The Expressway has fixed that. Driving south from Raumati there is a new choke point where the new Expressway meets the old State Highway 1 at Mackays Junction. We are told that this will be fixed when the Transmission Gully road opens in 2020.

Driving south from Kāpiti to Wellington, at peak time especially, there has always been a choke point at about Tawa. Traffic flow might be better at Tawa after 2020 because the new Transmission Gully road will take some vehicles to the city by a different route. However, commentators are saying that the south end of the Transmission Gully road will put all the vehicles back together and create a new and massive choke point at the entry to Wellington. Others are saying that Wellington itself is a choke point because the city does not have enough space to store the cars of people who drive to the city for the day. It is probably not an over-simplification to say that building new roads to fix choke points creates new ones.

collaboration: *Noun*: the process of working together to achieve something. *Also*: working with an enemy who is in control of your country.

Kāpiti Coast District Council accepted an invitation from NZTA to join the Mackays to Peka Peka Expressway Alliance 'contingent upon the Transport Agency and other members of the Alliance agreeing to a number of council objectives'.

> *The objectives, which the Alliance Board subsequently adopted as its Guiding Objectives, were based on district-wide community consultation and tied strongly back to the council's strategy and policy on a number of levels. These objectives set the framework for the project while the Board of Inquiry approved consents for the project with over 300 conditions to address community and environmental concerns.*[11]

Purely from a structural point of view, can you truly collaborate with central government, which has the power to direct policy and make funding decisions to match? You might get a seat at the table, but don't they always hold the big cards?

communication, outwards: Information about the Expressway dripped, poured and gushed out of the Alliance. There were regular update columns in the local papers, representatives were interviewed regularly on local radio and there was the information booth at Coastlands Mall. There was an online newsletter and a Flickr collection of images. There were posters at all the bridge sites showing, in diagrammatic form, how each bridge would be built. Beside the Waikanae River there were posters showing what that completed bridge would look like. Sometimes there were posters about problems I hadn't thought of, like how the design of the bridge at Raumati Road would help prevent the area underneath it from being an invitation

to crime. I didn't notice the day that all this began but I remember realising
that there was battle for hearts and minds going on. As well as the overview
information, people in areas that were more significantly affected received
flyers with more detail about what was happening near them. Individuals
who would be very close to construction received face-to-face visits.

communicative processes: In the case of the Kāpiti Expressway, there
was a moment sometime in late 2014 when community opinion swung in
behind the Expressway. You could feel it. For the majority of people, the
road was happening and they were increasingly sensitive to its charms, as
outlined by the Alliance. People who had been noisy in their opposition
knew they had been beaten and, if they had no direct contact with the
Alliance and the road, they went on with their lives. If the road was right
beside them, they were busy dealing with it. But that energy was being
channelled through the Community Liaison Group and defused.

There was also a moment in 2017 when 20,000 people were persuaded
to spend part of a day walking on a section of the nearly completed and
totally inert Expressway. I don't know how many staff were required to
make these and other changes in attitude and behaviour. Nor do I know
exactly what steps led to these achievements, but clearly there are powerful
communicative processes and technologies available that can be harnessed
to particular goals. That is something else I learned. If this can be done
to get people to accept a road, or to walk on a road, it could be done to
increase the participation of the population in general elections or to help
people understand what is planned in their communities.

community: A lot of Expressway staff were from the Kāpiti community,
or became part of it, buying or renting houses here. One staff member in
a specialised field explained to me that it was great to be able to get work
close to home for the first time and that it was comforting to know that she
was helping her own community.

community board: Right beside the sea, in Paraparaumu Beach, there is a
beautiful wide concrete walkway. One autumn day the sky was bright blue
and the sea was a different bright blue so I wrapped my mother up, put her
in a wheelchair and set off for a walk along this walkway. First, we needed

to cross the road. I found a driveway to take the wheelchair from the footpath to the road, but as I wheeled my mother out past the parked cars to look left and right and left again, she was exposed to the traffic. I wasn't prepared for how dangerous this felt, and I was not the one sitting helpless in the chair. I pulled the wheelchair back and I was standing there, on the footpath, thinking about how to cross this road safely, when a man came along.

'There should be a pedestrian crossing here,' he said.

I agreed.

'I'm on the community board and I'm working really hard to get a crossing for here.'

Then, quick as a flash, he put his business card in my hand, walked out into the road, looked both ways and called back to me.

'All clear now.'

I took his word for it, pushed my mother onto the road, over the road and onto the smooth concrete walkway on the other side. The man wasn't there when it was time to re-cross the road at the end of the walk, and I missed his help.

Later, thinking about the community board and the man who gave me his business card and told me about his pedestrian crossing project, I decided there was something miraculous about this tiny version of democracy where one man's voice could make a difference.

Community Liaison Group (CLG) *see* **Neighbourhood Information Forums (NIFs)**

consent levels, of noise, vibration: The consent process prescribed maximum acceptable levels for noise and vibration from Expressway construction and for ongoing noise from the road. Let's assume that these levels were, at some time, the result of expert recommendations. Let's assume experts know about the effects on humans of noise and vibration. Let's assume that the recommendations were *not* simply based on what noise and vibration is considered 'normal' for the construction of a road or from a functioning Expressway. Let's assume that the experts gave their evidence to the Board of Inquiry and then went home.

It is one thing to write a report about noise or vibration, and quite another to experience it for days or weeks or years at a time. There are hundreds of stories recorded in the media and in people's memories about what it was like for people in Kāpiti during the construction. One woman, a university lecturer, said the vibration caused by the pile driving was so bad that walls and the ceiling of her house cracked. She could not concentrate on her work and ended up doing her marking in her car. And so forth.

Now that the road is open, there are stories about what it is like to live with the ongoing noise from traffic on the road. It was often the people who live close to the proposed Expressway who opposed construction and made submissions to the Board of Inquiry. They lost, and not just the case. In the case of the university lecturer, her home and quality of life were affected exactly as she had feared. And that was before the road opened.

consultation: It is an interesting feature of consultation that the body asking the questions always thinks its business is the most important thing happening at that time. In the case of the public consultation about the route for the Kāpiti Expressway, the window for input was 10 weeks. That sounds like a long time and certainly there were considerable efforts to put information in front of the community, in the form of pamphlets, website information and meeting opportunities. But all this was during the time in which most people have children home from school and lots of people have their summer holiday. NZTA must know this. Even I know that this time of year is famously used by politicians to 'bury' an issue on which they definitely *don't* want public input. It is scarcely original to question whether governments actually want democratic participation, but, if they did, they would not expect people to jump to attention and make responding the biggest priority in their lives.

correspondence, unsuccessful: Charles Brasch's body of well-reasoned, elegantly composed and occasionally sarcastic correspondence with the editor of the *Otago Daily Times* inspired me to think that perhaps I could take part in the democratic process by letter. I was pleased with this idea. I would set myself the task of writing within the range of registers that Brasch used. I would be reasonable and constructive. I would comment on Expressway-related issues I thought significant and test my ideas by exposing them to scrutiny. I did not expect to influence action by public figures significantly, but I thought perhaps as part of a conversation, or in a behind-the-scenes context that I wouldn't ever see, opinions matching mine might coalesce and gain influence.

Every part of this was more difficult than I imagined. I found the process of moving from a blunt sense of disquiet, or even a sharp sense of outrage, to an opinion I could describe was very difficult. I was never sure that I had understood the background of an issue, and when I tried to understand any of the issues related to the Expressway, I found the language dense and the statements by participants to be full of omissions, elisions and allusions. When I did arrive at an opinion, or even a question, I found the experience of putting my name to these opinions stressful. I had not realised until I came to write about the Expressway, and to write these letters, that I have been a noisy person in private and a silent person in public. I was terrified that someone would shout at me if I expressed an opinion. One day I decided to free things up by writing a letter that would never be sent. It was a relief to write a few letters which were neither clear nor civil. But then I decided the unsent letters were the equivalent of a tantrum after which I did not feel better.

My letter writing was not a success. I sent a total of three letters. My first letter – a gesture of support for 'Let's Get Wellington Moving' and the notion of a collaborative approach to transport planning – was to the editor of the *Dominion Post*. It was not published. My second letter, to the mayor of Kāpiti Coast District Council asking why the council was not offering more support to residents affected by motorway noise, received a polite answer in which the issue was effectively dismissed. My third letter, to the new Minister of Transport Phil Twyford, written on 7 March 2018, was also about residents affected by motorway noise. My letter asked him to require NZTA to make the noise improvements recommended in the 2017 review quickly. On 1 July 2018 Mr Twyford answered. He said two things. First, that rumble strips on one side of the lane had been scheduled to be removed in May 2018. There was no indication that his office had checked to see if the removal work had been done or was under way, and no acknowledgement of the effects on the residents of noise from the rumble strips during the 15 months since the Expressway opened. Mr Twyford's second point was that I might wish to communicate directly with NZTA's principal project manager, whose contact details were provided. I did not pursue this avenue.

My letters, sent and unsent, and my frustration at the responses, show that this form of communication requires more optimism, patience, analytical thinking, courage and confidence than I have. Charles Brasch knew what he thought, could express his thoughts clearly and had the confidence to do that, despite living in a small city in a small country. He didn't always win his point. In fact he hardly ever did. But that didn't seem to put him off.

Corridor, Northern: The 110 kilometres from Wellington airport to the north of Levin, described by NZTA as the Northern Corridor, was designated a Road of National Significance in March 2009. The Northern Corridor is a nest of roading projects involving different transport problems, different kinds of land and communities, different reactions from the public, different contractual models, and huge sums of money. The Mackays to Peka Peka Expressway (M2PP) was the first part to be completed, in 2017. Other roads in the Northern Corridor are the Transmission Gully motorway, to be opened in 2020, the Peka Peka to Ōtaki Expressway (PP2O), under construction, and Ōtaki to North of Levin project (O2NL), which NZTA describes as in the 'investigation' stage. All these sections of the Northern Corridor are described by NZTA as expressways or motorways.

The section of the Northern Corridor that extends from Ngauranga Gorge to Wellington airport (T2T), is described by NZTA as 'tunnel to tunnel inner-city transport improvements',[12] suggesting that the improvements may not all be in the form of roads. In 2018 this section of the Northern Corridor is 'on hold', waiting for recommendations from Let's Get

Wellington Moving, a collaborative group made up of the Wellington City Council, Greater Wellington Regional Council and NZTA.

design life, of pavement: The time between construction of a road and the need to substantially repair or replace the surface, measured in years, is called the pavement design life. The design life of an asphalt road surface is commonly 15 years. The M2PP Expressway was built to have a design life of 20 years but it was clear within a few months of opening that major repairs to the surface were needed. Water leaking through a seal between the base – or pavement – and the asphalt was to blame. At the time of writing, there was no publicly available estimate of the cost for these repairs. Extrapolating from the $2.3 million cost of the first five kilometres to be repaired, the cost for the remaining 49 kilometres said to need repairs might be something like $20 million. Because of the Alliance-style contract, NZTA, or in other words the taxpayer, bears a share of these extra costs. There are several questions I would like to ask. One is whether the haste with which the road was finished, in order to save costs, could have been a factor. Another is whether the whole idea of building a road over peatland is fundamentally unsound from an engineering point of view.

desire, straight line of: (1)Whenever I visited the Alliance headquarters I could feel Determination in the air. Sometimes government policy falters when it leaves the fifth floor of the Wellington building in which it hatches. Sometimes it changes its targets in the face of practical difficulties. But not the Expressway. This road was going to be built and it was going to be built on time or early.

(2)While the Expressway was being built, I became fixated on the fact that it was a straight line. It isn't really a straight line. From Poplar Avenue it curves west, away from the line of the old Highway 1, and then takes a line roughly parallel with the coast. But in my mind, and from an aeroplane, or even from the top of the Nikau Reserve at Paraparaumu, it seemed to cut a wide, straight path across the countryside.

digger drivers: I heard that Goodman's digger drivers working on the Expressway noticed tiny buried objects or bones of fish and pointed them out to the experts. I heard that the drivers could position the two-tonne buckets as if they were the size and weight of a teaspoon and make precise cuts around valued creatures or objects. What they did was 'delicate and beautiful', one person said.

earthquakes: The Kāpiti Expressway has been built to withstand a one-in-2500-year earthquake. The bridge over the Waikanae River has been designed to remain standing and the road is designed to be able to be operational again quickly after such an event. Before piles for the Waikanae River bridge were driven, stone columns were built down to a depth of several metres so that the piles could be driven into something more substantial than river sand and gravel. This process, called 'ground improvement', was to prevent liquefaction after a big earthquake. The river might have moved, there might be new dry land or the sea might have moved inland, but people will be able to move across the bridge. That might help them, who knows?

El Rancho: Waikanae Christian Holiday Park, known as El Rancho, sits on a 50-acre site between the Waikanae River and the coast. The land was bought in 1961 for $5000, with the intention of providing a place where everyone, but especially young people, could develop their Christian lives.

In 1995 Te Ātiawa ki Whakarongotai asked the Kāpiti Coast District Council to include El Rancho in its schedule of wāhi tapu, because Te Ātiawa and Raukawa fought the battle of Kūititanga near there in 1839 and because of other culturally significant remains, including an important tree. El Rancho argued hard in court against its site being included in the wāhi tapu because the value of the land could be adversely affected, but in 2015 their case was dismissed. In this case, cultural significance was held to be more significant than a risk to property values, but the fight took many years, cost lots of money and energy, and even after the court ruling, it wasn't over for the Takamore Trust, which pursued the case on behalf of Te Ātiawa. In 2016 council records show discussions between the Takamore Trust and El Rancho about their ongoing relationship and the implications of the wāhi tapu status.

empathise (*see also* **sorry**, **sympathy**): *Verb*: to understand and share the feelings of another. *As in*: The mayor of Kāpiti empathises with residents who are being adversely affected by vehicle noise associated with the new Expressway.

Expressway, Kāpiti, its many names: The term 'Kāpiti Expressway' is the overall name for the 18-kilometre four-lane expressway from Mackays Crossing, near Paekākāriki, to Peka Peka, plus the Peka Peka to Ōtaki Expressway. The Mackays to Peka Peka Expressway is the first section of the Kāpiti Expressway. The name 'Mackays to Peka Peka Expressway' was shortened by NZTA to M2PP. The name 'Peka Peka to Ōtaki Expressway' was shortened to PP2O.

Therefore: M2PP + PP2O = KE

These abbreviations, which I personally like, because they are efficient, precise and friendly sounding, were and are used by members of the Alliance and NZTA but were never adopted by locals.

I stick to local usage and use Kāpiti Expressway to refer to the Mackays to Peka Peka Expressway. I have decided, unilaterally, that 'Kāpiti Expressway' is a proper noun entitled to capital letters. When I use the term 'the Expressway', referring to the Kāpiti Expressway, I give the term 'Expressway' a capital E, as a nod to its size and significance.

When I moved to Kāpiti in 2007, there was a road/rail crossing called MacKays Crossing. In 2016 the New Zealand Geographic Board changed the spelling to 'Mackays Crossing', because early settlers in the area were from the Mackay family. Occasional documents still use the MacKays spelling. I have kept this spelling where it has been used in quotations, but I use the current official version of the name. Mackays Crossing has no apostrophe.

fans: *Noun*: aficionados, supporters.*Synonyms*: admirers, devotees, fanboys, fangirls, flatterers, followers, hangers-on, party faithful, worshippers, fans are people who support a person, a team or an object.

The Kāpiti Expressway has fans. See the following excerpt from a typical fan letter:

> *The Kapiti Expressway ... has been built in a manner that has improved the landscape and indigenous ecosystems by draining swampy ground, forming attractive lakes and streams, planting a great number of trees and shrubs and sheltering any adjacent homes from the effects of passing traffic. The local community have been kept up to date with all aspects of this welcome development with regular, well-presented updates on all aspects of the expressway ...* [13]

future, whispers from: (1) Al Gore says the future whispers while the present shouts. It is true that the present occupies a great deal of attention. This happens at every level: personal, local, national and international.

(2) In Kāpiti the mayor is saying, at low volume but increasingly frequently, that if rainfall increases due to climate change, as is predicted, the stormwater system will not cope. There is absolutely nothing sexy about stormwater pipes. We don't want to see them, or think about them. We just want them to be there, working. But if the mayor is right, planning needs to happen now for the expense of upgrading the stormwater system. If we don't, people's homes will flood more and more often and raw sewage will end up on the beaches. Low-lying, peaty parts of Kāpiti, near streams, are prone to flooding now. Good on the mayor, for saying this.

As I was writing this, a real estate agent knocked on the front door. While explaining to me that he expected the economy to be strong for a couple of years, then falter because of increased government spending, he told me with evident pride that he had recently bought a beachfront property in Paekākāriki which he intended to renovate. Right on the beach, he said.

gardening, in self-defence: Then-Kāpiti district councillor K. Gurunathan describes a woman he met while walking by the Waikanae River in October 2014:

> *She was at the driveway. Tiny in a large hat. Busy gardening. You must be a serious gardener to be working in the rain, I say. 'I do it in self-defence,' she replies. Raising a garden to block off the harshness of the heavy engineering taking place around her home. Not enough to ignore the jolt of a drop in the recently released valuation.*

She has only kind words for the contractors and project staff. 'They have a job to do and they are cordial and kind,' she adds but her narrative includes words with emotional depth charges. Marooned. Eye of the storm. Accept but can't embrace. And then, that telling observation about how the Greater Public Good waxes by cannibalising the rights of individuals.[14]

K. Gurunathan is the mayor now. From that position, the Greater Public Good may look less like individuals in distress and more like the Battle of Waterloo.

girls, and their desires: One of the women working on the Expressway told me that she had always wanted to drive a steamroller when she was a girl, but that in the '60s, when she was growing up, this was thought to be weird. I understood that. Right from the start it was obvious that women were part of the outdoor labour force on the Expressway. Most of the women I saw outdoors were stop/go operators, although there were some in driving jobs. One day I saw a small group of people, all wearing the trademark orange vests, talking and pointing at things at the Raumati Road site. Their clean boots and expensive casual trousers said 'authority'. It took me a few minutes to realise that one of the group was a woman. I could tell she was the boss by the way she pointed to things while the men kept their arms by their sides.

One slightly built woman working on the Expressway told me that she loved wearing her steelcaps (boots) because they make her feet look bigger. She knew other girls wanted their feet to look small and didn't want to get dirty, she said, but she didn't mind the dirt. She had a career. She was working 16 hours a day, 6 days a week, planning, ordering supplies and managing a budget. You've got to have good relationships with everyone, she said, because you never know when you will need a favour. She took lots of photographs so that she could enjoy the daily progress in her area.

Grace, Patricia: Patricia Grace, great-great-granddaughter of nineteenth-century chief and later MP Wiremu Parata Te Kākākura, refused to accede to compulsory acquisition under the Public Works Act of a piece of land described as Ngarara West A25B2A, for the Expressway. The land, near the Waikanae River, had been owned by Te Kākākura.

Grace took defensive action. She took a case to the Māori Land Court asking that the court grant her application to have this land recognised as a Māori reserve. Patricia Grace agreed to surrender the land, with no payment, to trustees, to be managed as a reserve. The court agreed.

Grace also took the case to the Environment Court. The Crown lawyer said using an alternative route for the Expressway would cost $16 million. Patricia Grace said that cost could have been avoided with proper consultation. As explained in a summary by law professor Jacinta Ruru, the court focused on Grace's relationship with the land, noting the following points:

- *The land is a remnant of land once owned by her ancestor Te Kakakura who is better known in New Zealand legal history by a shortened version of his name – Wi Parata. He gifted substantial parcels of land to encourage developments including for railway and a school and 'it would behove this generation to recognise that generosity and to not take land once owned by him, unless it is absolutely necessary to do so';*
- *Mrs Grace's land is a waahi tapu, it is her ancestral land or whenua tuku iho, inherited land, which brings with it inherited responsibilities;*
- *Mrs Grace feels strongly about retaining the land for future generations and has voluntarily surrendered ownership of it for no value as a Māori Reservation.*

The court concluded:

So it is not accurate, nor fair, to regard this piece of land as an asset which an owner may use so as to extract maximum value. It is more than that, and needs to be seen in that light. That is not to say that any Māori-owned land is to be regarded as immune from acquisition under the PWA – that is simply not the law.[15]

At the time, April 2014, construction of the Mackays to Peka Peka Expressway was under way at several locations, but NZTA did not own the necessary land for a section of the route north of the Waikanae River. It was embarrassing for NZTA and for the government, and, in project management terms, a potentially catastrophic moment for the Expressway.

However, in negotiation between iwi and the Alliance, an alternative route was found and the Expressway proceeded.

Patricia Grace said later that while she won her legal case, she felt the victory was a hollow one because the Public Works Act was still used to take Māori land, including from neighbours and whānau.

> *We couldn't stop the motorway or the expressway, but we could stop NZTA from taking our land, which meant they had to go around our land. The rest of the whānau, the other block owners, did the best they could to minimise that and they supported where we were coming from. I felt bad for them, it was like, because of me, some of their land was being taken. A lot of theirs had been taken already.*[16]

greenhouse gas emissions: This is a topic that makes my eyes glaze over as I struggle to understand what is happening and therefore what we should do. The first part is simple. Greenhouse gases trap heat in the atmosphere, which makes the earth warmer. New Zealand's greenhouse gas emissions have risen 24 per cent since 1990. 'The five emission sources which have contributed most to this increase are road transport (carbon dioxide), chemical industry and food processing (carbon dioxide), enteric fermentation (methane), agricultural soils (nitrous oxide) and industrial and household refrigeration and air-conditioning systems (fluorinated gases).'[17]

After that things become more complex.

Agricultural emission, especially methane from animals, is considered relatively difficult to improve. We already use power generation that is substantially sustainable, so it is not easy to make changes there either. However, out of the tiny fragment of the total situation that transport creates, we could change several elements. We could shape the contingencies to take some trucks off the road; we could give car drivers a nudge towards public transport and walking and cycling where that is practical; we could actively encourage electric vehicles and ban new petrol- and diesel-powered vehicles from a certain date; and we could use existing routes rather than develop roads on top of wetlands and arable land. A truck carrying toxic chemicals rolled on State Highway 1 near Pukerua Bay in October 2018, causing the road to be closed. Within the first few hours after the road closure, trucks heading south to Wellington formed a queue five kilometres long. It was a sobering illustration of how much freight moves around by road. Right beside the line of trucks was the main trunk railway. Occasionally I see a freight train on the line, but only one or two a day.

heaven: One summer day, before they started on the bridge, I found heaven beside the Waikanae River. I saw hills in the distance, kōwhai trees with feathery leaves and overhanging yellow flowers, tūī swooping from tree to tree, and then a path. I followed that path until it disappeared, then I followed a dragonfly into a garden of flax bushes taller than a man. When the dragonfly disappeared, I followed a single tūī from one flax flower to another until I arrived at a pool of water.

Beside the pool was a wooden seat. I sat there. I noticed that the shape of the hills, the gravel road and the pool made the diagonal lines recommended for perfect composition. That was a clue. I saw long green weeds waving in a current. When I looked up I saw the sky and felt the sun on my face. I saw that there were clouds, and knew they meant no harm. I heard a steady hum, too, a sound I can only describe as warm, as busy, as full of life. It crossed my mind that I wanted to stay there for a very long time. That's how I knew for sure that it was heaven.

Later that summer, I took a friend there and we sat on the wooden seat together. We spoke of our troubles. Our voices rose and fell, my voice harsh and hers soft, hers a complaint and mine a consolation, over and over, until each of us had said enough. Then we listened to the hum. Yes, she said, this is definitely heaven.

honesty: People like honesty, a woman told me back in 2014. Her street had diggers on the doorstep. She saw her job in the Neighbourhood Information Forum as pushing the Alliance to be more upfront and straight.

housing: Kāpiti has a housing shortage. It has unaffordable rents, poor-quality housing and very little social housing. House prices have risen sharply in the past few years. In these ways, it is much like the rest of New Zealand. But Kāpiti's housing is under pressure for specific local reasons as well as the factors that are affecting the whole country. Kāpiti has almost no high-density housing. There has been some movement of workers and families to Kāpiti because of the Expressway and the later roading projects, and there are fewer houses here than there used to be because NZTA bought 54 houses to make way for the Kāpiti Expressway and another 50 for the Peka Peka to Ōtaki Expressway. Rising prices for houses in Wellington itself have forced more people to consider Kāpiti as an option. The Expressway project has also caused a shift in perception about how viable it is to live in Kāpiti and commute to Wellington and that has led to more demand for houses here. In fact, travel times to and from Wellington by car in the peak times are not better, but we are told they will be, one day. Train use continues to rise.

imagine: Imagine if, in 2009, instead of being told a coded, air-tight message about growth, people in Kāpiti had been told that the government's vision was to ignore climate change for as long as possible, that the M2PP Expressway was part of that plan, and that the government intended to support diesel-powered road freight and the use of private cars despite their role in accelerating climate change.

Imagine if residents had been told that there would be a permanent and significant change in the local visual, ecological and noise environment, that a few people would be massively disadvantaged and the rest of us would ignore their situation, that individuals of any age and capacity could find themselves negotiating directly with NZTA over compulsory purchases and noise, that people in the way of the road would have to sell their properties to NZTA, and that NZTA can afford to wait nearly seven years for a dispute over valuation to end but for a family that is a third of a childhood and it might be better for mental and physical health to sell their property for a low price than end up next to the new road.

I think lots of people would still have voted for that package, as long as it wasn't them. But sometimes it was them.

irony, invasion and limitations of: About 2014, I found William McGonagall's 1880 poem 'The Tay Bridge Disaster'. It was thrilling to find a poem about a bridge where the bridge was itself and not a metaphor. The poem strikes an unusual and, for me, mesmerising tone.

> Beautiful Railway Bridge of the Sil'vry Tay!
> Alas! I am very sorry to say
> That ninety lives have been taken away
> On the last Sabbath day of 1879,
> Which will be remember'd for a very long time …[18]

Under the influence of McGonagall's poem, I wrote a poem addressed to the Expressway.

Oh Road! I said, revelling in a chance to use the vocative case, I have heard it said that a man's soul follows behind him guessing at his intentions. Thanks to an excellent communications strategy I know you move 12,000 cubic metres of dirt per day, you have 13 partially completed bridges and, by the time you are done, you will have moved 3½ million cubic metres of dirt. Informative signage notwithstanding, I still know nothing of your intentions.

Oh Expressway! Oh high road across the dunes! Save us from the long tail of cars stretching all the way from Waikanae back to Poplar Avenue on a Friday night. Cars might be ridiculous with their sloshing buckets of petrol right behind the back seat but Peak Oil and human rights abuses in Saudi Arabia notwithstanding we feel we have a right to orderly access North and South.

Oh high road across the dunes! The beginning and end of the Christmas Holidays try us most severely.

Oh hard road through the wetlands! Please save me (personally) from being stuck again for 20 minutes at the traffic lights at Kāpiti Road with someone who hates me in the next-door lane. Oh hard road through the wetlands! A lot can happen in 20 minutes …

Oh high road across the dunes! If only Paraparaumu could be relaunched as a whole Shop, Work and Play concept like the new Westgate mall in

Auckland. The first step would be to rebrand the town as Kāpiti Landing because that is so much easier to say than Paraparaumu. Oh high road across the dunes! Thank you for Bridge Number Three with its arches and pillars and concrete girders. Thank you for the Kāpiti Road Interchange ... [Etc.]

The vocative turned out to have irony hiding behind its skirt. From there irony ran inside the house, made itself at home and would not leave.

Even as I was writing these sentences, I knew irony was a dead end. Underneath irony was powerlessness, and I didn't want to stay there.

iwi, Alliance awareness of demands on:

We [the Alliance] were keen to engage and consult with local mana whenua, but recognise it was often difficult for them to respond fully within the demands of the construction programme. They were volunteers, with day-jobs ... Their capacity to engage with Crown infrastructure projects really needed to have been built up prior to final design and construction phases.[19]

Kāpiti Coast District Libraries, Waitangi Day lecture series: In 2017 I attended a talk given at the Ōtaki Library by Mary O'Keefe, the archaeologist retained by the M2PP Alliance. I counted 40 people there, evidence that the talk was of considerable local interest.

I heard that 238 archaeological sites were found along the Expressway route and that the archaeologist's job was to extract the scientific information from the sites before they were destroyed by the road-building process. The archaeologist described this as a mix of losses and gains. Gains because she found out more about the area than she had known before the road, and losses because there is no second chance.

Ms O'Keefe showed photographs of some of the objects she and her team found. Some were placed beside a ruler, to show their size. The ruler, stamped with the message 'Everything is connected', had been made for NZTA. At the end of the talk I asked Ms O'Keefe about the ruler and she said she had used it deliberately. She was surrounded by people and I did not get a chance to ask her what this message meant to her.

At the talk it was clear that there were at least two ways of thinking on everything. Water for example.

Water as highway: According to Ms O'Keefe, the concrete Expressway is the second expressway in Kāpiti. The first was made of water and allowed people to move around the area in canoes.

Water as defence: According to a woman I met at the talk, Māori people sited their villages in watery places because that put them beyond the reach of men on horses.

Kāpiti Landing, gravitational pull of: Paraparaumu, the town, did not begin with a town square or botanical gardens or anything charming like that. It grew as a ribbon of shops and service stations near the main trunk railway and along State Highway 1. Before the Expressway, Coastlands shopping mall, built in 1969, had gradually become the commercial centre of Paraparaumu. For a while the council offices and the library were there, in what is now a cake shop. Coastlands is ugly, even when compared with other malls, but it was the de facto town centre. Since the Expressway opened, traffic on the Expressway now bypasses both Coastlands and that long line of fast food outlets on what used to be Highway 1. There is talk of significant drop-offs in takings. Secondly, a new commercial area called Kāpiti Landing has grown up in Paraparaumu, adjacent to the Expressway interchange at Kāpiti Road. You can almost feel the energy radiating out from Kāpiti Landing, pulling the commercial centre west.

If Kāpiti Landing ever becomes the town centre for Paraparaumu, it will be a catastrophe. Not that I am unwilling to shop at Mitre 10, or New World, when the need arises. But I hate the thought that somewhere with the name Kāpiti Landing, which makes me think of some British naval officer stepping onto the beach and planting a flag, would become the town centre of Paraparaumu. I want Paraparaumu to imagine itself as more than expedient, with a centre that is more than a mall, a stop on Highway 1 or an Expressway interchange. I know I am not alone. The people who

decided to renovate the Kāpiti Coast District Council building and build
the Paraparaumu Library definitely saw something more than roads and
commodities.

land, given, taken: In 1884 Wiremu Parata Te Kākākura gifted a substantial
amount of land for the Wellington and Manawatu Railway, which later
became the main trunk line. The gift was conditional on all trains stopping
at Waikanae. Approximately 10 years after the gift of land for the railway,
the town of Parata (now called Waikanae) was declared to be a native
township under the Native Townships Act of 1895. This Act allowed
the governor of New Zealand to declare any parcel of Māori land, not
exceeding 550 acres (222.5ha), as a site for a native township. By degrees,
the Act shifted land from Māori ownership and occupation and made the
land available for houses for Pākehā families.

The Expressway is a new road, and the people working on it are new
people, but the process of taking Māori land is old.

language, bastard: Some people use the language of their culture to
speak of the relationship between us and the entity 'earth', but I don't
have a culture that gives me that. Some can speak of this relationship in
the language of beauty but, while I might borrow a few words, I am not
at home in that language either. I use a bastard language, where the past
and the present, confidence and doubt, logic and intuition live as equals.
Increasingly I judge words by their sound. Some sound like a heart beating.
Some sound like a high-pitched whine and others like a fighter plane low
overhead.

language, as a form of control: I'm not the first to say that the language
of government communication shuts people out or that government
language silences people. Nor am I the first to say that technical language
shuts out ordinary people. My own experiences trying to read the NZTA
pamphlets on road noise were a tiny version of this, but the problem
of impenetrable language affected everyone who tried to talk about the
Expressway. The early diagrams of possible routes for the expressway
were the hardest to understand and also, arguably, the most important
pieces of communication. I am naturally disposed to think that language

is a powerful and infinitely flexible tool and I am certain that simplicity and clarity is possible. So if the language in some situation isn't simple and clear, either there has been a failure to consider the audience or the intention is to be obscure. If government agencies like NZTA were serious about participation, they would test diagrams and forms and pamphlets to see if ordinary people could understand them. Perhaps they do this now, but if they do, it isn't working. They could change that.

listen, to the sea: The sea, 'the only real thing left'.[20]

losers: Someone told me that the people who have lost by the Kāpiti Expressway are a very small minority of the community. For some reason I cannot stop thinking about this group. The idea that some people bear the cost of the Expressway bothers me. The fact that the community at large 'moves on' so quickly, and the unpleasant situation still happening to a few becomes invisible, bothers me even more. It is not yet two years since the Expressway opened and in local papers and conversations it is as if the noise problem does not exist.

machinery of government, not faceless: The machinery of government in 'Sixteen Chapters of the Kāpiti Expressway Noise Story' and in 'Alliancing. It's a Thing.' is neither nameless nor faceless. The officials are real people and so are the residents of Kāpiti. Sometimes the parties were in conflict. Sometimes the agencies and organisations were obstructive or pursuing their own ends. Sometimes the officials were trying to make the structures work as well as possible for the community. I never understood people's intentions. I am not even sure that there were stable groups. Because of this doubt, I have shown the action as it occurred in case the intention is clearer to other people than it is to me. Each of the people I met was generous with their time and knowledge, even when they could see that our views were different. Each discussion showed me wider and wider contexts for these events. Everyone I met could write their own book about these events and I wish they would.

masters and servants: It is considered normal in the professions to train in a discipline and then to take a job where you sell your skills in that discipline to a company or to the government, or some other entity. When they hire you, they buy your technical knowledge and your knowledge of how your profession operates. They buy your credibility, too, your ability to represent your employer in public, and your knowledge of, and ability to comply with, professional ethics and standards. When I worked as a psychologist, I sold that package.

During the process of my research into the Kāpiti Expressway I met a number of professionals employed on the project. Every one of them was impressive. They bristled with sophisticated skills and spoke of their complex work on the Expressway and their good intentions towards the Kāpiti environment and community. I warmed to all of them and respected them, but I was not quite sure if I trusted them. I trusted them completely to build the road or to make the required number of wet areas for every one the road destroyed. I would have trusted them with money or the care of a child. I wondered though if I should believe in the optimistic and uncritical views of their work which they all represented so well.

As it turned out, since the road opened there have been a few developments that suggest I was wrong to trust them to build the road exactly according to plan. The surface leaked within a few months; some of the bridge joints were lower quality than the consent required and some were poorly installed; and 20,000 plants used for beautification of the roadside had to be removed because they were not the local native plants specified in the contract.[21] Maybe there are other revelations yet to come.

Neighbourhood Information Forums (NIFs): As a condition of consent, Neighbourhood Information Forums were set up in areas where residents lived closest to the Expressway. The forums were made up of residents, representatives from the community board, Kāpiti Coast District Council and the M2PP Alliance. The forums fed into the Community Liaison Group (CLG). Both the NIFs and the CLG were channels for residents to raise concerns with the Alliance.

The groups were not just about residents letting off steam and the Alliance hearing grievances. Serious attempts were made to address the concerns. Specific individual concerns were met by offering temporary solutions like a brief stay in a motel or input into the timing of a noisy bit of work, or the building of a temporary noise bund. The groups ran during construction and for 12 months after the Expressway was opened. After that, or if you lived in an area where there was no neighbourhood forum, residents who wished to raise issues concerning the Expressway needed to make direct contact with NZTA. Little Person–Big Agency is not usually a recipe for good outcomes for the little person and it has not been here.

New Zealand Transport Agency (NZTA): The opening paragraph of the chair's foreword to NZTA's 2017 Annual Report provides a round-up of key ideas in relation to NZTA and its activities.

> *The Government's focus is on making sure the transport system is safe, supports economic growth and productivity, and provides the best value for money. The NZ Transport Agency is responsible for delivering this system, which it achieves through the goals and priorities that underpin its strategic direction, as well as through the National Land Transport Programme that it develops every three years to shape investment in New Zealand's land transport system.*

noise abatement panels: When building roads, it is more effective to avoid noise problems than try to mitigate them later. For example, it is preferable to avoid building new roads in residential areas. Careful road design which doesn't put roads higher than houses is a noise-avoidance option, as is tunnelling. Low-noise road surfaces, design gradients and speed management are other avoidance options. I have taken these ideas from NZTA's *State Highway Noise Barrier Design Guide*, version 1.0 from August 2010, which contains guidelines for bunds and wall-type barriers.

In 2015, a friend showed me a photo he had taken, looking towards the place where the Expressway would cross Raumati Road. There would be a bridge, he said, five metres above Raumati Road, and noise abatement panels to protect the people living nearby from the noise of traffic on the Expressway. The Expressway bridge crosses Raumati Road on the top of a sandhill, with houses lower down on each side.

There are noise abatement panels on the west side of the Expressway, in exactly the place my friend had photographed. But there are no noise abatement panels on the east side of the Expressway. I have heard that noise abatement panels would not be effective because the Expressway is higher than the nearby houses and noise abatement panels only work when the houses are on the same level as the road. I have heard that the original diagrams given to residents showed noise abatement panels on the east side, but they were never built. I have also heard that the shape of the land was changed to make it flatter for the road, and that this exposed the people on the east side to more traffic noise than would have been the case if the hill had been unchanged. I am not sure which, if any, of these statements is true.

What is *not* disputed is that some of the people worst affected by Expressway noise live on the east side of the Expressway near Raumati Road bridge, where the Expressway is higher than their houses.

noise worries: In February 2017, the Alliance put out a flyer outlining transitional arrangements as the Expressway was handed over from the Alliance to NZTA. The flyer contained a series of FAQs, one of which concerned noise.

> Q: *I'm worried about noise when the Expressway opens. What will be done to manage noise levels once traffic starts using the road?*
>
> A: *The Expressway has been designed and constructed using a range of detailed noise and vibration mitigations, such as noise bunds. These noise-management tools will continue to be monitored and maintained to ensure they continue to be effective in reducing noise.*
>
> *A noise-monitoring plan will be in place for up to three years.*[22]

The noise-management tools have been monitored. Noise is within consented levels. What if those levels are too high for a sound sleep and a good quality of life? The answer to that question seems to be that you should move, put up your own noise barriers or get used to it.

NZS 6806: The noise standard chosen by NZTA for the Expressway (*see* 'Sixteen Chapters of the Kāpiti Expressway Noise Story').

optimism, extreme: The real estate agent who said the recent investment in infrastructure would cut travel time to Wellington from 40 minutes to half an hour. Maybe he or she means travel by helicopter?

Orwell, George: George Orwell's politics were shaped by the rise of totalitarian states and the necessity to oppose totalitarianism wherever he saw it. Orwell was rock-solid certain that there was no such thing as keeping out of politics, that all writing is political – even, and perhaps especially, when it avoids political topics. In his novels, his non-fiction and his essays, he tried to marry aesthetics with politics, but even his friends told him he sometimes went too far in the direction of giving factual information. *Homage to Catalonia* contains a whole chapter full of quotations from newspapers. Friends told him, he says, that this lowered the aesthetic tone and made the book into journalism. Orwell defends the inclusion of the chapter by saying that not many people knew the things in the newspapers, and those things made him angry. That anger made him write the book.

Ōtaki's contributions to the Expressway: Lines of trucks carry what used to be mountains, and was then river banks, from Ōtaki, to form the foundation of the Peka Peka to Ōtaki Expressway, because the bottom layers of the road need to be hard rock. As construction first of the Mackays to Peka Peka Expressway and then the next section has gone on, a great deal of hard rock has been required.

GBC Winstone already had consent to 'sustainably take'[23] 40,000 cubic metres of rock from the Ōtaki River each year, but in 2016 GBC Winstone applied for consent to take 90,000 cubic metres of gravel per year from Ashford Park. In their consent application they promised that after 10 years they would create ecological islands on the site. Consent was granted.

paradoxes, aesthetic: Even though the bridge at Poplar Avenue, near my home, has been there now for a couple of years I still can't quite take my eyes off the pillars that hold it up. It shocks me that concrete pillars can be curved, that they can be massive and intimidating and a little graceful, all at the same time, and that these concrete pillars, buried deep down into what was peatland, have a Māori design symbolising water etched into them. I think the design on their skin is to remind the pillars of what is underneath their feet; that they may feel tall and strong in the air, but their oldest and deepest relationship is with peat and water.

peat, compression of: A considerable part of the Kāpiti Expressway route had peat underneath it. Roads need reasonably solid ground under them, so the original plan was to dig some of the peat out and then put 'preload', or layers of rocks, on top to squeeze water out of the remaining peat. Once a certain amount of compression had occurred, the ground would be solid enough to build a road on. That was the theory.

peat, as a resource: It turned out that the peat was both deeper and more widespread than had been expected. The Alliance team made this into a public relations resource. They offered peat to the public as a fundraiser for a local charity, while making sure that locals understood its limitations.

> Please note peat is not topsoil and typically tends to be at the acid end of the scale. While it's good for acid loving plants, you'll need to mix it with other materials like sand, compost and/or artificial fertilisers to make it into a good general growing medium. The peat we are giving away is in its original state and is being donated as is where is.[24]

They also stockpiled the peat and used it in the construction of bunds.

peat, as a carbon sink: Maintaining peatland undisturbed is increasingly seen as a significant climate change mitigation strategy because when peat is disturbed it is no longer able to function as a carbon sink. When disturbed it releases carbon into the atmosphere. In the discussions of peat and the Expressway, I did not see any reference to the possible effects of digging out peat, leaving it in piles and then building new structures with it.

pie shops, and crane businesses: Local company Goodman Contractors doubled its workforce between 2013 and 2014, from 60 to 140. Goodman Contractors managing director Stan Goodman said that 90 per cent of the employees were local, from south of Levin to Upper Hutt.

It's great to be home. It's not just us benefitting. Others like crane businesses and pie shops are doing really well.[25]

pink: In the first few days after the Expressway opened, a pink hatchback drove up one of the off-ramps. A motorist leaving the Expressway was surprised, of course, but could only beep her horn and pull over to let the pink hatchback go by. The pink hatchback then proceeded along the Expressway on the wrong side of the road and exited by driving down an on-ramp. I do not have a pink hatchback, but I know from experience that once you are going the wrong way it is very hard to turn around and start going the right way.

PPF: *Noun*: abbreviation of 'protected premises and facilities', a term used by NZTA's review panel on the noise problem to mean 'houses'. *As in*: 'The noise exposures of PPFs are described in terms of the categories defined in NZS 6806.'[26]

pūkeko: There were always pūkeko near the corner of Poplar Avenue and State Highway 1. During the Expressway construction almost everything about that corner was changed, but if there was a little bit of water lying somewhere, even if it had the glint of oil on top, I would always see one or two pūkeko. Lately I have noticed that it is a long time since I saw a blue bird there.

Pūkeko are extremely territorial. A local café owner told me that when he first bought his café and was fitting it out, a pūkeko who lived in the section next door used to wander into the café. I gather that this was initially funny but Bruce, as they named him, became a nuisance to the builders. Perhaps there were hygiene problems, too, but for whatever reasons, the café owner decided Bruce needed to be rehoused. He and his wife put Bruce in a sack and drove him a couple of kilometres to the corner of Poplar Avenue and State Highway 1. Next morning Bruce was back, waiting for them outside the café. After that they took him to the Waikanae River, but he came back from there too. After that, judging by the shifty look on the café owner's face, I suspect that they murdered Bruce.

questions, meaningful and answerable: A man told me recently that science tries to find questions that are both meaningful and answerable. Lots of questions are answerable, he said, but they are trivial and obvious. The inability of science to move beyond description frustrates him. Why can't it use its relentless detail to understand whatever entity is to be investigated? The problem, as he sees it, is that we are too trapped in our human ways of thinking. This man told me it would be better for his career if he set to and *did* more science instead of spending his time thinking about his philosophy of science. But the trouble is that the philosophy interests him as much as, or more than, the doing.

I have a slightly similar problem. I am interested in writing. But I am at least as interested in a quality of association between daily life, reading and writing as I am in writing itself.

Railways of National Significance: Viola Palmer posed the question: Why Roads of National Significance and not Railways of National Significance, or Coastal Shipping of National Significance?[27]

rip-rap: *Noun*: big rocks to prevent erosion or scouring. Rip-rap is heaped around the piles of the Waikanae River bridge.

road, as narrative: A man who had 'a close look' at the Expressway in July 2016, eight months before its completion, was so impressed that he wrote a fan letter to the newspaper. First, he praised the road itself. 'Every conceivable exigency of nature has been provided for,' he said. Then he went on to consider the road as a narrative:

Conservation and preservation of things natural was a shining thread through the narrative. They are planting well over a million plants, trees and everything inbetween in every possible place.

They caught all the fish and marine life in the waterways and created new places to return to. Run-off water from the road with all its nasties is collected and kept separate from the good water. There is a good cycle track; sound shields, nicely designed, and banks with trees on to reduce traffic noise. As one who listened sympathetically to the many who didn't want this road slicing through our district, I say now that we've got a good thing.[28]

I am grateful to this man for the idea that the road is a story, as one might consider a novel or a painting to be.

road, disappearing: When newly appointed transport minister Simon Bridges visited the Expressway site in December 2014, he said he was 'looking forward to returning and seeing people on cycleways, the wetlands and plantings. I think it will be a strong piece of beautification for this region.'[29]

I could not tell whether 'it' is the Expressway or the three mitigations of the Expressway he mentions. Either way, it seemed as if the minister looked at the Expressway on that day and saw that beauty, rather than a road, had been created.

road, the prettiest in New Zealand: In the lead-up to the opening, project manager John Palm was clearly proud of the new Expressway:

It's often been commented by people who have driven through the site that 'this must be the prettiest road in New Zealand' and I really believe that it is. If you drive south towards Wellington and you see what the roads look like there, nothing is as pretty as what we've created here on the coast.

Everything fits in and there are certain sections of the road where you wouldn't even know you were going through the middle of Paraparaumu.[30]

road porn: Journalist Joel Maxwell, taken for a ride on the new road in September 2016, described what he saw as 'grade-A road porn'.[31] This description is overlaid on a half-page photograph showing six men working on the Waikanae River bridge section of the road, which at this stage, was pale-grey concrete. The road curves away into the distance, narrowing in a perfect illustration of perspective. On the bridge itself, one man carries a mallet, one a long electric cable, three others are in a group and one man points to a section of pre-cast concrete. On the bridge are tool benches, a skip, a portaloo and lots of sections of pipe and steel bars. The bridge, which consists of two parallel sections, has a dark shadowy cleft in the middle. If you looked down there you would see the river.

I looked at this photograph for a long time, considering whether the term 'road porn' was simply a macho metaphor for the enthusiasm with which some people saw the whole size of the project – the sort of idea you might have, perhaps, if you liked a bit of DIY yourself and then saw this giant-sized bit of making and fell into a trance of envy and admiration.

Then I looked at the photograph for a long time, thinking about what in this scene might be erotic. The land around the road in this photograph is low, rounded hills. Clumps of trees soften the outline of the land. The whole impression is that the land is soft. Concrete is growing, minute by minute, on this soft green surface. If there is eroticism here, it is about domination.

Roads of National Significance, benefits: These vary slightly according to who is talking and when. In 2015, on a visit to Kāpiti, then finance minister Bill English described the benefits this way:

> *The project has created 500 jobs during its construction, but the real benefits are in safer roads, faster travel times and economic growth from more connections within Kāpiti and into Wellington.*[32]

rumble strips: *Noun*: raised strips on a road which make a rapid thumping noise if a car drives over them. The noise alerts a driver that they are veering off the road and gives the driver time to get safely back into their lane. The Expressway was built with rumble strips on both sides of both lanes. The cost of these rumble strips was approximately $135,000. In late 2017 NZTA offered to remove rumble strips from the left-hand lanes in each direction of the Expressway in response to noise complaints by residents. Cost unknown.

Kāpiti mayor K. Gurunathan said he was sorry for everyone involved, but was concerned that removing the rumble strips could cost lives. NZTA was 'caught between a rock and a hard place' as it tried to keep motorists safe and remedy noise complaints, he said. 'It's a lose-lose situation.'[33]

silences: Government is about who says what they want, how those opinions enter the political system and how the system takes account of all those opinions. I'm interested in all of that. But I am even more interested in all the people who say nothing and all the situations in which people say nothing. What does the country miss out on? And are these silences deliberately created or just accepted as inevitable? Those are my questions.

sorry, for everyone involved: *Meme*: Frequent in utterances by local body politicians concerning Expressway noise problems for residents.

soul tree: A term from Lars von Trier's film *Nymphomaniac*. Lying under a birch tree listening to it rustle, beside the Waikanae River in 2013, I thought perhaps I had found mine.

style, a note on: It can be a bit tedious wading through detail about how roads are made. 'The Prettiest Road in New Zealand' does, unfortunately, contain significant quantities of this kind of detail. People have written beautifully about roads, but when they do that the roads always turn into metaphors and the people turn out to be on figurative journeys. The Kāpiti Expressway can be read as a metaphor, but it is also made of concrete, and extremely real. Although I did not want to, I eventually needed to confront that.

Of course I did write a few lyrical moments from places in the natural environment which would be most changed by the Expressway. I could not help myself, because I loved these places. For a short time I imagined that a collection of these moments of beauty would form an implicit contrast to and therefore a critique of the concrete road, but I soon realised that this was a pretty weak way to show what was happening. Increasingly I had specific questions, too, and lyrical moments beside the Waikanae River were never going to yield answers to those questions.

This is the background to my decision to write about the Expressway in what has been described as a hybrid mix of journalistic and personal commentary style. The hazards of this choice are described by Karl Wolfskehl, writing in 1942 about contemporary English-language prose:

Even the more reflective publications keep at too much of a distance, at a reporter level, which is a combination of shrugging one's shoulders and desiring to shock. In other words they're only for the needs of the day.[34]

It is true that I did think some of what I describe is quite shocking. But I did not intend to keep a distance. Quite the reverse.

sympathy: Late in 2015, perhaps a third of the way through the construction of the road, the Expressway bridge over Kāpiti Road was opened to the public for a walk-over. Councillor Gavin Welsh, writing about the event in his column in the local paper, began by expressing sympathy:

I realise the expressway has proved to be a fiercely contentious issue for some, so I'd like to extend my sympathy to those people who have been, and continue to be adversely affected.[35]

Mr Welsh expresses his sympathy to those affected, as you might express sympathy to a recently bereaved person. Bereaved people often look away or change the subject when sympathy is expressed, because the dead person is still dead.

After the sentence about sympathy, there is a paragraph about the open day exemplifying community support for and excitement about the Expressway, a paragraph about the effectiveness of the district's economic development strategy, a paragraph saying that a strong local economy will deliver jobs and 'ultimately prosperity' for the community, a paragraph saying that development has to be balanced with the desires of the people, and four paragraphs about the 'amazing people who are building the expressway', thanking them for their friendliness, planning and management of personal and environmental impacts.

time: It has taken me five years and thousands of hours of reading and talking to people to reach a beginner's-level understanding of the roles of the various participants in the Expressway project, the Board of Inquiry process and the character of the Mackays to Peka Peka Expressway itself. This is the amount of time and effort necessary to turn a literate but uninformed citizen into someone who could take part in the democratic process related to just one bit of one expressway. By the time I had reached this point, the road had been built.

tōtara: I read that large tōtara logs found submerged in the peat were handed over to iwi for carving. For several months several dark wet logs lay in a rough pile at the site of the bridge over Raumati Road, and then one day they were gone.

tradition, dynastic: When Nathan Guy, National Party MP for Ōtaki, cut the ribbon to open the Kāpiti Expressway (along with transport minister Simon Bridges) he was the fourth generation of his family to have been involved with infrastructure in this part of the country and the third to hold public office. Nathan Guy's great-grandfather, Joseph Nathan, was chair of the Wellington and Manawatu Railway Company, which built the original rail line from Wellington, through Waikanae, Ōtaki and Levin, to Palmerston North. This became part of the main trunk line. Nathan's grandfather, Duncan Guy, then Horowhenua county chairman, opened the Ōtaki River bridge in 1955. And Nathan's father, Malcolm Guy, opened the Shannon to Foxton bridge in 1992 as mayor of Horowhenua.

trapped: If your house was right next to the Expressway, but not close enough that NZTA classified it as necessary for construction and bought it, your house was probably unsaleable during the construction of the Expressway. One man in this situation said that having tried unsuccessfully to sell his house for $70,000 below valuation, he would 'have to wait until the motorway is complete and hope somebody buys it'.[36] Interestingly, this man was not opposed to the Expressway. 'We think it is a bloody good idea,' he said. 'We're just against us having to live 20m from it.'

trust: In February 2016 it was explained to me that if the local community makes fewer formal complaints and does not take cases to court, a large project, like a road, is more likely to be finished sooner. Given that the Kāpiti Expressway cost about $1 million in overheads per working day, finishing on time or earlier was an extremely attractive goal. At some point the word 'trust' came into the explanation. It was explained to me that providing very good information to the community about what will be happening, face to face, at an individual level, and not hiding anything, helps to build trust. My notes record this explanation as 'Trust = Speed', but do not record my shock that a word from the humanistic discourse, like 'trust', could be paired so straightforwardly with financial benefits.

voices, for the future: Jonathan Boston suggests four ways to bring the future into sharper focus so that government decisions are not always for yesterday and today:

1. Strengthen our existing public institutions that speak on behalf of the future. The Parliamentary Commissioner for the Environment is an example.
2. Invest more in foresight, horizon scanning, scenario analysis and technology assessment.
3. Require governments to report on the intergenerational implications of major decisions and on slow-burner problems with cumulative impacts; and to produce periodic reports on their plans to tackle major intergenerational issues.
4. Develop better methods of measuring wealth.

'There is little point in celebrating fiscal surpluses or declining public debt if our ecological and social deficits are growing and our capital stocks, in aggregate, are falling,'[37] Boston says.

Waikanae River Bridge (*see also* **big**):

Noted for being the largest structure on Kapiti's biggest ever roading project, the Waikanae River bridge reaches 180m and comprises five spans, and is the longest pre-cast concrete beam across a river channel in New Zealand.

As well as being designed to withstand 100 year floods and 1 in 2500 year earthquakes, the bridge was the first built on three metre diameter piles in New Zealand, with the grounds of Kapiti containing higher levels of peat than anticipated.

Made up of 55 hefty 1800 super-tee beams, the Waikanae River bridge is the largest of the project's 18 road traffic bridges and, according to senior structures engineer Craig Service, is 'a lot bigger than any of the *other bridges we do' ... Alone, the Waikanae River bridge was originally estimated to cost around $28–30 million, with the total project valued at $630 million.*[38]

Waikanae River Woman: A man driving a digger on the route of the Mackays to Peka Peka Expressway found the bones of a woman who lived sometime before about 1830. This man was reducing the height of a sand dune. As he took the side slope of the dune away with his bucket, bones were exposed. The digger driver recognised what he was seeing and stopped work.

The Mackays to Peka Peka project archaeologist was there when the find was made because it was standard practice for the archaeologist to monitor the digger excavating these sand dunes. An iwi representative was also on site when the find was made because it was standard practice for there to be an iwi representative present whenever the archaeologist was monitoring earthworks. Although the archaeologist was not specifically expecting to find bones right there, she did not consider this an unusual find.

After the digger had exposed the first bones, the archaeologist went to the top of the dune and took off the top layer of sand. She then carefully excavated the remaining bones and sieved the sand. She noted which bones had been found and exactly where and how they were positioned.

In archaeological language, the bones were from a woman who had been buried in a crouched position, with no grave goods, on the crest of a sand dune. Her height and the ends of her long bones showed that she was an adult. Her skull and jawbone showed that she was Māori. Her teeth were in moderately good condition, suggesting that she had varied sources of food and was not much reliant on eating ground fern root that contained particles of sand and wore away teeth. Except for some tiny foot bones, all of the woman's bones were found. Her burial in the dune showed no Christian influences.

Archaeological speculation: It is possible that the woman lived in Horowhenua, that she came down to this area to help with fishing and birding, then became ill and died.

Other speculation: Perhaps the woman found near the river was a warrior?

The archaeologist placed the woman's bones into clean new pillowcases and handed them to the iwi representative. She told me that iwi did not wish for DNA analysis or radiocarbon dating of the bones and the woman had been reburied. So Waikanae River Woman lies still now, under the earth again, complete except for the missing foot bones. Whoever she was, she is being looked after now. It would be interesting to me to know when she lived and how, but she has no obligation to teach strangers about her life and death.

weekend excursion, for engineers:

A walk to the bridge along the Waikanae River trail makes for an excellent excursion on a sunny weekend.[39]

what if? (1) In the lead-up to the 2014 general election, Labour's transport spokesman Phil Twyford said that Labour would look to modify the 'negative' impacts of those Roads of National Significance already under construction and find '"affordable, safe and environmentally friendly" alternatives for those that were yet to start'.[40] Mr Twyford said his party had 'always felt the expressway project had been gold-plated and over-engineered, and it was likely there would be ways its design could be altered to better suit the Kāpiti community'. Given all the consents obtained, the contracts signed, the properties purchased, the construction plans developed and the quantity of sand already shifted by 2014, I found it hard to imagine what modifications could possibly be made to the Kāpiti Expressway. I contacted Mr Twyford and asked for more details. When they were in government he would have access to information to make these decisions, he said. Mine was a serious question. Either Mr Twyford decided not to tell me what changes they would make, or he did not know. A couple of months after the article I have quoted, the election happened, National won, and Labour's views became academic for three more years.

(2) As I write this, the Ōtaki to north of Levin section of the Northern Corridor is going through the stage of consultations between residents and NZTA about the best route for the road. All the same kinds of controversies are happening in Ōtaki as happened in Kāpiti back in 2010–12. Present

indications are that NZTA favours a route east of Ōtaki and Levin, despite residents being overwhelmingly in support of a route west of the towns. Residents say that the western route would be through sand dunes, and therefore less wasteful of good land.

whispers, from the future: The point locals are making about NZTA taking fertile, food-producing land for the Ōtaki to north of Levin road is one of those whispers from the future.

workers, caring, respectful: There were many comments during the construction about the politeness of Expressway staff. In December 2014 then mayor Ross Church put this down to many staff being local or having moved to the area, and therefore having 'a vested interest in ensuring this new road works well for everyone in Kapiti and those travelling here'.[41] That might well be true but I think the management culture had something to do with this too (*see* 'The [Taniwha] of Poplar Avenue').

you may feel some slight discomfort:

We've cleared large sites to the north and south of Kāpiti Road and this month we'll start driving the steel piles that will support the expressway bridge and interchange. This involves driving 15m steel rods that will need to go 8m down. The rods are first vibrated into the ground and then driven in with a hydraulic hammer. If you're in the area you may feel some minor vibration (like a train or bus driving past) and the noise (which will not exceed consented limits) sounds like a hammer hitting steel.[42]

Notes

Abbreviations used
CB Charles Brasch
ODT Otago Daily Times

Brasch Comes Over the Hill

1. CB, *Charles Brasch Journals, 1945–1957*, selected by Peter Simpson (Otago University Press, 2017), 22 Nov. 1950, p. 291.
2. Ibid., p. 293.

'Alliancing'. It's a thing.

1. Steven Joyce, 'First Roads of National Significance identified', 20 March 2009: www.beehive.govt.nz/release/first-roads-national-significance-identified
2. James Bentley, 'Statement of evidence of Dr James Bentley (Alliance Project Manager – MacKays to Peka Peka Expressway) for the NZ Transport Agency', before a Board of Inquiry, 7 Sept. 2012: www.epa.govt.nz/assets/FileAPI/proposal/NSP000005/Evidence/Dr-Jim-Bentley-Alliance-Manager-Evidence.pdf, p. 4.
3. Jenny Rowan, personal communication, 30 August 2017.
4. Ibid.
5. Ibid.
6. Darren Utting, 'Teaming up from concept to construction – M2PP Alliance', submission form, GEM Awards, 15 July 2015.
7. Ibid.
8. David Haxton, 'Expressway buy-in brought results', *Kapiti News*, 21 Feb. 2017: www.nzherald.co.nz/kapiti-news/news/article.cfm?c_id=1503789&objectid=11804771
9. Pat Dougherty, 'The power of central and local government collaboration', *Stuff*, 21 Feb. 2017: www.stuff.co.nz/motoring/news/89595678/pat-dougherty-the-power-of-central-and-local-government-collaboration?rm=m
10. Viola Palmer, 'Where's Railways of National Significance?', *Dominion Post*, 24 Feb. 2017, p. A7.
11. Darren Utting, 'Teaming up from concept to construction – M2PP Alliance'.

The Fight Against Muddle and Sham

1. CB, letter to *ODT*, 15 Dec. 1962, p. 4.
2. CB, letter to *ODT*, 16 March 1968, p. 4.

3. CB, Margaret M. Dunningham, G.R. Manton, Mary Martin, W.P. Morrell and Phillip Smithells, letter to *ODT*, 26 Oct. 1950, p. 8.
4. CB, 'Notes', *Landfall*, vol. 1, no. 1, 1947, pp. 3–4.
5. CB, *Indirections: A memoir 1909–1947* (Oxford University Press, 1980), p. 131.
6. CB, letter to *ODT*, 2 May 1961, p. 4.
7. CB, letter to *ODT*, 10 May 1961, p. 4.
8. 'Selection of extracts from Dr Charles Brasch's lecture on art in the Hocken Library' Part One, *ODT*, 12 Oct. 1971, p. 4.
9. CB, *Charles Brasch Journals, 1945–57*, selected by Peter Simpson (Otago University Press, 2017), 2 Dec. 1946, p. 134.
10. CB, letter to *ODT*, 10 Nov. 1962, p. 17.
11. CB, letter to *ODT*, 13 March 1967, p. 4.
12. CB, letter to *ODT*, 12 March 1969, p. 4.
13. CB, letter to *ODT*, 10 Sept. 1969, p. 4.
14. J.G. Blackman and CB, letter to *ODT*, 6 May 1971, p. 19.
15. CB, letter to *ODT*, 24 Nov. 1972, p. 7.
16. 'Be Reasonable', letter to *ODT*, 24 Nov. 1972, p. 7.
17. CB, *Charles Brasch Journals, 1945–1957*, 25 Aug. 1948, p. 182.
18. Ibid., p. 116.

Sixteen Chapters of the Kāpiti Expressway Noise Story

1. NZ Transport Agency, 'Frequently asked questions' handout, from meeting 4 Oct. 2017, p. 1.
2. Chris Parker, personal communication, 24 Aug. 2017.
3. NZ Transport Agency, 'Traffic noise' handout, from meeting 4 Oct. 2017.
4. NZ Transport Agency, 'MacKays to Peka Peka Expressway noise – what's happening' handout, from meeting, 4 Oct. 2017.
5. Ibid.
6. Ibid.
7. Sarah Alper and Stephen Chiles, 'Jacobs Road Traffic Noise Review', 22 Nov. 2017: www.nzta.govt.nz/assets/projects/mackays-to-peka-peka/docs/noise/M2PP-road-traffic-noise-review.pdf, p. 13.

Liking the Local, a reading of Charles Brasch's poem 'The Clear'

1. The final poem in *Charles Brasch: Selected poems*, chosen by Alan Roddick (Otago University Press, 2015), p. 143.
2. CB, *The Land and the People, and Other Poems* (Caxton Press, 1939).
3. CB, 'Back from Death', (6) 'Titus Reading', *Charles Brasch: Selected poems*, p. 142.

The Lady Engine

1. CB, *Indirections: A memoir 1909–1947* (Oxford University Press, 1980), p. 24.
2. Ibid., p. 48.
3. Ibid.

4. Ibid, p. 10.
5. Helene and Charles Brasch, c. 1911, Brasch Papers MS 996-12/59, Hocken Collections.
6. CB, *Indirections*, p. 10.
7. Ibid., pp. 10–11.
8. CB, *Charles Brasch Journals, 1938–1945* (Otago University Press, 2013), 15 March 1940, p. 89.
9. CB, *Indirections*, p. 12.
10. Ibid., p. 3.
11. Ibid., p. 9.
12. Ibid., p. 8.
13. Ibid., p. 11.
14. Ibid.
15. Ibid.
16. CB, *Charles Brasch Journals 1938–1945*, 24 July 1940, p. 147.
17. CB, *Indirections*, p. 13.
18. Ibid.
19. Ibid., p. 15.
20. Ibid.
21. Ibid.
22. Ibid.
23. Ibid., p. 16.
24. Ibid.
25. Ibid., p. 17.
26. Ibid., p. 23.
27. CB, 'One Starless Night', *Not Far Off: Poems* (Caxton Press, 1969).
28. This poem borrows significantly from poems in CB's collection *Not Far Off*, Riemke Ensing's collection *O Lucky Man: Poems for Charles Brasch* (Otakou Press, 2009) and Ruth Dallas's poem 'Last Letter, for Charles Brasch, 1909–1973', in Ruth Dallas, *Collected Poems* (Otago University Press, 1987).
29. CB, *Charles Brasch Journals, 1945–57*, selected by Peter Simpson (Otago University Press, 2017), 9 July 1952, p. 366.

The Human Hand

1. H.D. Skinner, *In Memory of Willi Fels CMG 1858–1946* (Otago Museum, 1946), p. 7.
2. CB, 'In Memory of Willi Fels (1858–1946)', in Skinner, *In Memory of Willi Fels CMG 1858–1946*, p. 6.
3. Skinner, *In Memory of Willi Fels CMG*, p. 11.
4. Ibid.
5. Ibid., pp. 12–13.
6. H.D. Skinner, 'Excavations at Little Papanui, Otago Peninsula', *The Journal of the Polynesian Society*, vol. 69, 1960, p. 187.

7. Ibid., p. 188.
8. Ibid., p. 187.
9. Ibid., p. 188.
10. Ibid.
11. Ibid.
12. Charlotte Macdonald, Merimeri Penfold and Bridget Williams (eds), *The Book of New Zealand Women: Ko Kui Ma Te Kaupapa* (Bridget Williams Books, 1991), pp. 373–74.

One Starless Night
A glossary of my acquaintance with Charles Brasch

1. Reference 30169, Ngā Taonga Sound and Vision.
2. CB, *Indirections: A memoir 1909–1947* (Oxford University Press, 1980), p. 51.
3. Ibid., p. 41.
4. Ibid., p. 52.
5. Ibid., p. 55.
6. Ibid., p. 113.
7. Ibid., p. 110.
8. Joseph Brodsky, 'In a Room and a Half', *Less Than One: Selected essays* (Penguin Classics, 2011), p. 464–65.
9. 'Selection of extracts from Dr Charles Brasch's lecture on art and literature in the Hocken Library', Part Two, *ODT*, 14 Oct. 1971, p. 4.
10. George Eliot, *Middlemarch* (Penguin Classics, 2003), p. 548.
11. CB, *Indirections*, p. 310.
12. *ODT*, 26 March 1969, p. 5.
13. *ODT*, 29 April 1969, p. 3.
14. CB, *Indirections*, p. 141.
15. *ODT*, 12 June 1969, p. 5.
16. CB, *Charles Brasch Journals, 1938–1945* (Otago University Press, 2013), 3 Jan. 1941, p. 217.
17. James Bertram, *New Zealand Writers and Their Work – Charles Brasch* (Oxford University Press, 1976), p. 41.
18. CB, *Indirections*, p. 106.
19. Ibid., pp. 106–07.
20. Ibid., p. 11.
21. Ibid., p. 114.
22. Ibid., p. 21.
23. James Bertram, 'Editorial Note', *Indirections*, p. xii.
24. Vincent O'Sullivan, 'Anniversary, is it?', *The Movie May Be Slightly Different* (Victoria University Press, 2011), p. 130.
25. C.K. Stead, 'The Gift', *The Yellow Buoy: Poems 2007–2012* (Auckland University Press, 2013), p. 97.

26. CB, *Indirections*, p. 37.
27. Ibid., p. 44.
28. Ibid., p. 48.
29. Ibid.
30. Ibid., p. 43.
31. Ibid., p. 50.
32. Ibid.
33. Bertram, *New Zealand Writers and Their Work – Charles Brasch*, p. 48.
34. Ibid., p. 49.
35. CB, *Indirections*, p. 94.
36. CB, 'Notes', *Landfall*, vol. 1, no. 1, March 1947, p. 6.
37. Ibid., p. 5.
38. C.K. Stead, *South-West of Eden: A memoir 1932–1956* (Auckland University Press, 2010), p. 47.
39. Ibid.
40. CB, 'Notes', *Landfall*, vol. 1, no. 1, March 1947, pp. 5–6.
41. Janet Frame, *An Angel at My Table* (Hutchinson, 1984), p. 127.
42. CB, 'Notes', *Landfall*, vol. 1, no. 1, March 1947, p. 5.
43. CB, *Indirections*, p. 117.
44. Frank Sargeson, letter to Denis Glover, 10 Feb. 1943, *Letters of Frank Sargeson*, edited by Sarah Shieff (Vintage, 2012), p. 58.
45. CB, *Indirections*, p. 354.
46. Ibid., p. 355.
47. CB, *Charles Brasch Journals, 1938–1945*, 7 Feb. 1941, p. 237.
48. CB, *Indirections*, p. 369–70.
49. Frank Sargeson, 'Writing a Novel', *Conversation in a Train and Other Critical Writing by Frank Sargeson*, edited by Kevin Cunningham (Auckland University Press, 1983), p. 60.
50. Tina Makereti, 'The Story That Matters', *The Fuse Box* (Victoria University Press, 2017), p. 98.
51. Stead, *South-West of Eden*, pp. 195–96.
52. CB, *Charles Brasch Journals, 1938–1945*, 27 Dec. 1940, p. 208.
53. CB, *Indirections*, p. 18.
54. Ibid., p. 71.
55. CB, *Indirections*, p. 71.
56. Ibid., p. 151.
57. Ibid., p. 111.
58. Ibid., p. 165.
59. Ibid., p. 44.
60. Ibid., pp. 22–23.
61. Ibid., p. 3.
62. CB, *Collected Poems*, ed. Alan Roddick (Oxford University Press, 1984), p. 19.
63. *ODT*, 12 June 1969, p. 5.

64. CB, *Indirections*, pp. 137–38.
65. CB, *Not Far Off: Poems* (Caxton Press, 1969).
66. CB, *Indirections*, p. 103.
67. Ibid., p. 108.
68. CB, *Charles Brasch Journals, 1945–1957*, selected by Peter Simpson (Otago University Press, 2017), 15 Feb. 1953, p. 402.
69. Bertram, 'Editorial Note', *Indirections*, p. xi.
70. Ibid.
71. CB, *Indirections*, p. 424.
72. Bertram, 'Editorial Note', *Indirections*, p. xiii.
73. Bertram, *New Zealand Writers and Their Work – Charles Brasch*, p. 4.
74. Bertram, 'Editorial Note', *Indirections*, p. xii.
75. Steven Sedley, 'Reflecting on the world: Jewish writers', in *Jewish Lives in New Zealand*, edited by Leonard Bell and Diana Morrow (Godwit, 2012), p. 117.
76. Leonard Bell, *Strangers Arrive* (Auckland University Press, 2017), p. 232.
77. Ibid., p. 235.
78. Peter Simpson, *Bloomsbury South: The arts in Christchurch 1933–1953* (Auckland University Press, 2016), p. 197.
79. CB, *Indirections*, p. 332.
80. CB, *Charles Brasch Journals, 1938–1945*, 19 May 1940, p. 111.
81. CB, *Indirections*, p. 333.
82. CB, *Charles Brasch Journals, 1945–1957*, 9 Feb. 1947, p. 147.
83. Ibid., pp. 151–52.
84. Bertram, *New Zealand Writers and Their Work – Charles Brasch*, p. 38.
85. CB, *Indirections*, p. 125.
86. CB, letter to *ODT*, 10 Sept. 1969, p. 4.
87. CB, *Indirections*, p. 67.
88. CB, *Charles Brasch Journals, 1938–1945*, 5 Nov. 1945, p. 571.
89. Ibid.
90. CB, *Indirections*, p. 160.
91. Ibid.
92. Ibid., p. 62.
93. Ibid.
94. Ibid., p. 74.
95. Ibid., p. 43.
96. Alan Mulgan, 'Literature and Landscape in New Zealand', *NZ Geographical Society Reprint Series*, no. 2, April 1946, p. 16.
97. CB, *Indirections*, 4.
98. CB, 'Man Missing', *Not Far Off*, p. 41.
99. CB, letter to *ODT*, 1 Aug. 1960, p. 4.
100. Sargeson, letter to John Lehmann, 22 Jan. 1941, *Letters of Frank Sargeson*, p. 39.
101. CB, *Indirections*, p. 124.
102. Ibid., p. 150.

103. Ibid., p. 151.
104. Ibid., p. 79.
105. Ibid., p. 113.
106. George Orwell, quoted in CB, 'Notes', *Landfall*, vol. 1, no. 1, March 1947, p. 4.
107. George Orwell, 'Why I Write', *Why I Write* (Penguin, 2004), p. 5.
108. James McNeish, *Dance of the Peacocks* (Vintage, 2003), p. 293.
109. Ibid.
110. CB, *Indirections*, p. 56.
111. Ibid., p. 57.
112. Orwell, 'Why I Write', *Why I Write*, p. 1.
113. CB, 'Notes', *Landfall*, vol. 1, no. 1, March 1947, p. 3.
114. CB, *Indirections*, p. 75.
115. Ibid., p. 20.
116. CB, *Charles Brasch Journals, 1945–1957*, 3 Dec. 1952, p. 388.
117. 'University radio stations, parliamentary seats urged', *ODT*, 5 June 1969, p. 5.
118. CB, *Indirections*, pp. 155–56.
119. Ibid., p. 157.
120. CB, *Charles Brasch Journals, 1938–1945*, 25 March 1940, p. 91.

The Prettiest Road in New Zealand
A glossary of my acquaintance with the Kāpiti Expressway

1. Sarah Alper and Stephen Chiles, 'Jacobs Road Traffic Noise Review', 22 Nov. 2017: www.nzta.govt.nz/assets/projects/mackays-to-peka-peka/docs/noise/ M2PP-road-traffic-noise-review.pdf, p. 11.
2. 'Low benefit of Expressway gets calls to scrap it', *KC NEWS*, Nov. 2012: www. kcnews.co.nz/story.php?storyID=6382
3. Viola Palmer, 'A Kapiti resident's view of the expressway', *Stuff*, 24 Feb. 2017: www.stuff.co.nz/dominion-post/comment/89731894/viola-davis-a-kapiti-residents-view-of-the-expressway
4. Lynn Jenner (@lynnjennernz), Twitter, 7 March 2015.
5. 'Massive plant project for expressway', *Dominion Post*, 27 April 2015, p. A5.
6. Alper and Chiles, 'Jacobs Road Traffic Noise Review', p. 10.
7. Ibid., p. 11–12.
8. Joel Maxwell, 'Highway sound buffer being rebuilt', *Kapiti Observer*, 29 Jan. 2015, p. 3.
9. Joel Maxwell, 'To Levin and beyond', *Kapiti Observer*, 23 Feb. 2017, p. 10.
10. Kay Blundell, 'Roading project creates pest headache', *Dominion Post*, 4 Dec. 2014, p. A4.
11. Pat Dougherty, 'Expressway shows a way to collaboration', *Dominion Post*, 21 Feb. 2017, p. A7.
12. 'The Tunnel to Tunnel Inner-city Transport Improvements', NZ Transport Agency: www.nzta.govt.nz/projects/wellington-northern-corridor/the-tunnel-to-tunnel-inner-city-transport-improvements

13. Neil Woodbury, 'Expressway hailed', letter to the editor, *Dominion Post*, 27 Sept. 2016, p. A6.
14. K. Gurunathan, 'Vision's good but keep feet on ground', Notes from a Corner Dairy, *Kapiti News*, 29 Oct. 2014, p. 9.
15. Jacinta Ruru, 'Public works – proposed taking not fair, sound or reasonably necessary – Grace', *Māori Law Review*, September 2014: http://maorilawreview.co.nz/2014/09/public-works-proposed-taking-not-fair-sound-or-reasonably-necessary-grace/
16. Aaron Smale, 'Tangata whenua in this country have given enough', *RNZ*, 8 Feb. 2017: www.radionz.co.nz/news/national/324087/'tangata-whenua-in-this-country-have-given-enough'
17. Ministry for the Environment, 'New Zealand's Greenhouse Gas Inventory, 1990 to 2015', publication reference no. ME 1309, May 2017: www.mfe.govt.nz/publications/climate-change/new-zealands-greenhouse-gas-inventory-1990%E2%80%932015
18. Robert McGonagall, 'The Tay Bridge Disaster', Scottish Poetry Library: www.scottishpoetrylibrary.org.uk/poem/tay-bridge-disaster/
19. Darren Utting, personal communication, 18 February 2016.
20. Philip Temple, *MiStory* (Font Publishing, 2014), p. 46.
21. Farah Hancock, 'Unwanted organism sold as native plants', *Newsroom*, 25 October 2018: www.newsroom.co.nz/2018/10/24/289264/unwanted-organism-sold-as-native-plants
22. Mackays to Peka Peka Alliance, 'Who Looks After Things Once The Expressway Opens To Traffic?', February 2017.
23. Adam Poulopoulos, 'Winstone decision expected soon', *Kapiti Observer*, 24 March 2016, p. 10.
24. 'Public peat grab day', *Kapiti Observer*, 16 Oct. 2014, p. 7.
25. Kay Blundell, 'Expressway creating a highway to jobs', *Dominion Post*, 3 Sept. 2014, p. B5.
26. Alper and Chiles, 'Jacobs Road Traffic Noise Review', p. 2.
27. Viola Palmer, 'Where's Railways of National Significance?', *Dominion Post*, 24 Feb. 2017, p. A7.
28. Selwyn Boorman, 'Expressway great', letter to the editor, *Dominion Post*, 5 July 2016, p. A6.
29. Michael Forbes, 'Kapiti expressway takes shape', 6 Dec. 2014, *Stuff*: www.stuff.co.nz/motoring/news/63896102/Kapiti-expressway-takes-shape
30. David Haxton, 'The prettiest road in New Zealand', *Kapiti News Special Edition*, 15 Feb. 2017, p. 3.
31. Joel Maxwell, 'The almost-there expressway', *Dominion Post*, 24 Sept. 2016, p. C1.
32. 'Expressway in action', *Kapiti News*, 2 Dec. 2015, p. 2.
33. Virginia Fallon, 'Kapiti Expressway to lose its "grumble strips"', *Dominion Post*, 17 Nov. 2017, p. A1.

34. Karl Wolfskehl, letter to Edgar Salin, 11 June 1942, *Poetry and Exile: Letters from New Zealand 1938–1948*, edited and translated by Nelson Wattie (Cold Hub Press, 2017), p. 85.

35. Gavin Welsh, 'Expressway will drive our community forward', *Kapiti News*, 2 Dec. 2015, p. 8.

36. Adam Poulopoulos, 'Couple trapped in home next to expressway', *Kapiti Observer*, 1 Oct. 2015, p. 1.

37. Jonathan Boston, 'The long and the short of it', *Dominion Post*, 4 April 2017, p. A7.

38. Cloe Willetts, 'Waikanae River Bridge', *Kapiti News Special Edition*, 15 Feb. 2017, p. 4.

39. Iain Smith, 'Kapiti Expressway: New Waikanae bridge construction', *Flow*, issue 16, Sept. 2016, p. 12.

40. Michael Forbes, 'Labour may modify expressway and gully', *Dominion Post*, 26 August 2014, p. A4.

41. Michael Forbes, 'Express service', *Dominion Post*, 5 Dec. 2014, p. C2.

42. NZ Transport Agency, 'Express lane', *Kapiti News*, 8 Oct. 2014, p. 6.

Acknowledgements

I AM GRATEFUL for all the encouragement and support I received during this project. Thanks first, and most of all, to Tony Pine, whose practical and emotional support made the project possible. Arohanui Tony. This book is dedicated to you. Thanks to the Todd Foundation for the Todd New Writer's Bursary, awarded in 2016, which allowed me time to research and write. The Robert Lord Writers' Cottage Trust provided me with a roof over my head, a warm bed, a desk, an armchair and the internet – in other words everything a writer needs – twice during the project. Thanks to the trust and the individual members who greeted me and organised everything, and to Gay Buckingham for sharing her memories of CB's house and some sturdy work with a shovel. Many people gave me advice, told me stories or introduced me to other people who gave me advice or told me stories. My particular thanks to Donald Kerr, Rewa Morgan, Vincent O'Sullivan, Jocelyn Harris and Vanessa Manhire for their interest, ideas and encouragement along the way. Thanks to M2PP staff and locals who talked with me about the Expressway. Thanks to Donna Watson, Julia Hume, Jack Austen, Wendel Foerster and Susi Williams for their support. Thanks also to Lynn Davidson, who read several versions of 'One Starless Night'. Members of my writing group, Pip Adam, Sarah Jane Barnett, Sarah Bainbridge, Dave Fleming, Alison Glenny, Bill Nelson, Tina Makereti, Lorry Patchett, Rachel O'Neill and John Summers, gave feedback on early parts of *Peat* and Bill Nelson and Alison Glenny on a later version. Thanks to the team at Otago University Press and to Tordis Flath for early assistance with the manuscript. Anna Hodge, who edited *Peat*, has my enduring gratitude and admiration. The maps and cover of *Peat* were gifted to me by Charlotte McCrae. Arohanui Charlotte.

Many thanks go to the following publishers, rights holders, literary executors and others for their permission to use material, and help in organising that permission: Alan Roddick as Charles Brasch's literary executor, and Hocken Collections, Uare Taoka o Hākena, University of Otago, Te Whare Wānanga o Otāgo, for organising permission to quote from *Indirections* and Brasch's poems 'Bred in the Bone', 'In Memory of Willi Fels (1858–1946)', 'Lady Engine', 'Man Missing' and 'One Starless Night'; Otago University Press for permission to quote from Charles

Brasch's journals, *Charles Brasch Selected Poems* and *Landfall*; the Frank
Sargeson Trust for permission to publish excerpts from letters by Sargeson;
Auckland University Press and Karl Stead for permission to quote
from 'The Gift' and *South-West of Eden: A memoir 1932–1956*; Victoria
University Press and Vincent O'Sullivan for permission to quote from
'Anniversary, is it?'; VUP and Tina Makereti for permission to publish an
excerpt from 'The Story That Matters'; Otago Museum for permission to
publish an excerpt from *Willi Fels CMG (1858–1946)*; and Melinda Allen,
editor of the *Journal of the Polynesian Society*, for permission to quote from
H.D. Skinner's 1960 article.

An early version of 'The Information Booth' appeared in *Turbine | Kapohou
2014*. 'The [Taniwha] of Poplar Avenue' appeared in *Extraordinary
Anywhere* (VUP) in 2016 and in *Tell You What* (AUP) in 2017. 'Liking
the Local, a reading of Charles Brasch's poem "The Clear"' appeared in
Landfall 232, Spring 2016; the poem 'In which Travis and I follow Charles
Brasch around Dunedin' in *Turbine | Kapohou 2017*; 'On Joy and Other
Obligations' on the *NZ Poetry Shelf* website in October 2018; and 'The
Fight Against Muddle and Sham' in *Sport* 46, November 2018.

Lynn Jenner is a writer and teacher of writing. She lives on the Kāpiti coast north of Wellington. Her first book, *Dear Sweet Harry* (AUP 2010) won the NZSA Jessie Mackay Prize for Best First Book of Poetry. Her second book, *Lost and Gone Away* (AUP 2015), was shortlisted in the non-fiction category of the Ockham New Zealand Book Awards in 2016. Lynn has a PhD in creative writing from the International Institute of Modern Letters at Victoria University.

Index